Better with Nuts
Classroom Survival & Success for New & Developing Teachers

by Carolyn Olga McGown

Fifth Edition 2014

D1275180

Fifth edition published 2014.
Fourth edition 2011.
Third edition 2008.

ISBN 978-0-615-50894-8

Praise for Better With Nuts: Classroom Survival

After having read this book, a new teacher (and even a somewhat seasoned teacher) can stand in front of a classroom of 30 children with the confidence of knowing that this book has touched on nearly every situation that he/she may encounter. I wish this book had been available when I first started.
~ **Ann Roer**, ESL/TESOL Teacher (retired), NYC

Better With Nuts is a must-have for all new and experienced teachers. This amazingly clever, entertaining and insightful handbook offers teaching advice that I could never have survived without! These small, yet unbelievably important ideas . . . cover topics that are commonly forgotten in graduate textbooks. Carolyn's first-hand experience and answer for every situation . . . has been a perfect guide . . . from supply lists to classroom games, behavior charts and transitional procedures, . . . As every teacher quickly learns, classroom management is the key to success in the education world. Carolyn McGown's expertise has helped me to provide a classroom environment where every individual has the opportunity to succeed.
~ **Suzanna Seltzer**, Third-Grade Teacher, Bronx, NY

Better with Nuts is a terrific hands-on, easy to read resource for teachers. Chock-full of solid, useful strategies and no-nonsense advice, this book offers guidance and ready-to-use techniques for educators in search of ideas to improve the quality and learning environment in their classrooms and practical ideas that can be immediately implemented in any classroom. This book is a must-read for new teachers.
~ **Maria Mysliwy**, Teach for America Corps Member
The Urban Assembly/NYC DOE

The weeks and days leading up to your first year of teaching are filled with excitement and anxiety of the unknown. During this time, I found myself referring to Carolyn McGown's informative and practical guide. Now, as a third year teacher I find myself again referring to **Better With Nuts**. It is interesting to go back and read the same information and to see it in a different light and still gain so much insight from reading it. My copy now has pages

Praise for Better With Nuts: Classroom Survival

with folded corners and stars in the margins, especially in the chapter about the point chart. This book . . . it is a MUST for behavior management.
~ **Kaitlyn McElhenny**, Elementary Teacher, NYC

Better With Nuts *is the perfect resource for new teachers. I use this book whenever I have a question. Carolyn McGown has literally thought of everything you need to know!*
~ **Rachel Schuckman**, Special Education, NYC

Better with Nuts *is the kind of practical, user-friendly guide that new classroom practitioners long for. Drawing on years of experience as a teacher and teacher educator, Ms. McGown gives emerging childhood educators the tool kit they need to create well-managed spaces where children can learn and grow. A must-read for preservice and recently hired teachers.*
~ **Wayne Reed**, PhD
Program Head, Childhood Education
Brooklyn College

A thoughtful administrator, charged with ensuring quality classroom experiences for a wide range of learners, will be eternally grateful for this nugget of common sense for their new and nearly new teachers.
~ **Kathy Gilmore**, Assistant Superintendent (retired)
Curriculum & Instruction
Roosevelt & Mount Vernon (retired), NY

Carolyn's book is a common-sense survivor's guide to your first year of teaching and beyond. You learned all the theory in school. Carolyn helps you translate that theory into practice in a way that will enhance your student's learning, creative a positive environment in your classroom, and allow you to get up every morning and do your very best for the children.
~ **Frank Headley**, Principal, Queens, NY

Table of
Contents

Table of Contents

Table of Contents

Table of Contents

Introduction

Introduction

Who is this book for? Who are you?

You are a <u>new teacher</u>, about to face your first group of students. You have taken some courses on teaching, and you have tons of ideas you are excited to try. You are filled with excitement as well as anxiety. *New teachers want a book that answers their many practical questions about classrooms, children, and teaching.*

You are a <u>second- or third-year teacher</u>, and your first years didn't go well. You know that teaching is the career for you – you had great connections with the kids and a number of "aha" moments, but you feel that you did not quite "get a handle" on the kids or your classroom. *Second-year teachers wish for a book that offers clear suggestions and easy-to-implement strategies with lots of advice about classroom management*

You are an <u>experienced teacher</u> who has been asked to help new teachers at your school in the upcoming school-year. You have had a variety of experiences, and you are looking forward to supporting new teachers as they discover the joys of teaching, but you are uncertain how to help them. You know how to teach children, but how do you go about supporting and advising new teachers. *Experienced teachers want materials to support their own teaching and to share with new colleagues.*

You are a school <u>principal or director</u>. You know how important classroom management is, and you very much want to ensure a successful and smooth year, especially for your new faculty. You have been disappointed with the materials available. **Principals** *want an accessible and practical book to distribute to staff, especially to new teachers.*

You are a <u>professor</u> in a teacher education program. You use a number of different books with your candidates, but the majority of texts are heavy to theory and pedagogy, rather than practice. *Professors want to assign a useful, practical, accessible text that addresses the many practical questions and concerns that teacher candidates and new teachers have.*

Introduction

You are a district or school <u>coach or mentor</u>. You have been unable to find a single text that discusses the practical logistics of teaching to your satisfaction.

Coaches and mentors need an engaging, fun-to-read, easy-to-process book that covers common problems and challenges that new teachers face.

You are a <u>parent</u>, and you want to understand more about what goes on in your children's school and classrooms. You want to know what kinds of questions to ask teachers and other school personnel. Since you do not have a background in education and pedagogy, many of the books you have found are not accessible.

Parents want an accessible and user-friendly book about schools, teachers, teaching, and learning.

Wherever you are in your teaching, parenting, coaching, or school leadership career, this book is for you. Better With Nuts: Classroom Survival & Success for New & Developing Teachers is for anyone who wants to understand and support effective and enjoyable teaching and learning.

Introduction

What's with the title?

This book carries an unusual title (*Better with Nuts*), and many have asked about it. While I cannot recall exactly how the title came to me, a few moments with a dictionary provides some definitions that are surprisingly relevant for teaching (and thereby "justify" my title):

· *Balmy, crazy*: Do you have to be nuts to be a teacher? I don't want to go that far, but an admiration for chaos, an appreciation of noise, and an affection for the unpredictability of children – certainly a *kind* of craziness – helps.
· *Effrontery, nerve*: Rare is the teacher who starts off with all the confidence s/he needs. What gets the good teacher through, and makes him/her successful, is a hefty portion of confidence – of committed (and often false) bravado – in other words, a teacher needs to have "nuts."
· *Difficult problem*: Lots of people teach, and lots of people do it acceptably, but only those who have the drive, commitment, compassion, as well as patience and tenacity, will "crack this nut."
· *Small metal block used for tightening or holding something*: A teacher is essential in establishing and holding together a learning community. A teacher is central to the operations of an effective classroom, and teachers are the "nuts and bolts" of a school.
· *Enthusiastic, keen*: Perhaps more than anything, a teacher needs genuine enthusiasm for the job. Good teachers are unwaveringly "nuts" about teaching and learning.
· *The usually hard-shelled dry seed or fruit of some plants (like hazelnuts, pistachios, peanuts)*: Teachers must have a "hard shell." As many have said before me, "Leave your ego at the door." Some things will go well, and some things will go poorly. But the bad minutes or periods or days will end, and you will have a fresh start the next day. Kids have a short memory, and they give you endless tries and re-tries. A kid that yelled in defiance one period may come hugging you half an hour later. If you allow the failures to get to you, you will have little chance of success and a very short (and miserable) career.

Introduction

How to Use this Book

Use this book as you would a recipe in a cookbook.

Read it carefully, identify the materials, think through the steps, and then give it a try. After the "dish" has been served, come back to the "recipe," record notes about the experience and add ideas for improvement the next time. A cookbook analogy may seem surprising at first, but there are uncanny and meaningful similarities between cooking and teaching:

- A lot of people cook, and a lot of people teach, but not all cook and teach well.
- There are basic skills required for both cooking and teaching, and one cannot be successful in the classroom or in the kitchen without mastering these skills.
- Many cooks and teachers have recorded their strategies for success, and these can be found in libraries, on the internet, and in this book.
- Teachers and cooks need to be willing to take chances.
- This includes being willing to fail.
- Laughing at mistakes, dusting oneself off, and being able to move on is necessary for anyone who wishes to succeed in the kitchen or in the classroom.
- Flexibility and improvisation are necessary in the minds, and in the practice, of both cooks and teachers.

When someone wants to learn to cook, s/he gets a cookbook or a recipe, usually one that someone recommended or that the new cook has heard is good and easy to use. The first time the new cook prepares a new dish, s/he follows the recipe exactly. The new cook does this in hopes of avoiding failure – a very sensible decision. It takes much of the fear out of the experiment, and it increases the chances that the cook will be successful from the start. If the cook follows the recipe exactly, it will turn out – not perfectly in all cases – but acceptably and edible. The initial success gives the new cook *confidence*.

Depending on the cook's personality and perception of success, s/he may follow the recipe as it is written several more times. The cook's confidence will grow and eventually, s/he will make adjustments: "Double the garlic," "Honey instead," "Omit cardamom," or "Better with nuts!" This is when the recipe becomes the cook's own. This is when an aspiring cook starts to be a chef.

Introduction

Approach this book the same way: like a new cook with a new cookbook. Read all the "recipes"; walk through the processes in your head; make notes in the pages; underline bits; fold over corners; cross things out; make changes.

Better with Nuts: Classroom Survival will be most helpful if it is dynamic; it should reflect your interests, your classroom successes, your failures, and your growing ability and confidence, much like a favorite well-worn cookbook. A year from now, this book should be thoroughly dog-eared, with notes throughout, and spattered with "cooking spills." There should be bits of paper and multi-colored sticky-notes hanging out. It should have your equivalent of "better with nuts" marked throughout.

Where to Start?
1) Read through the book once, making notes along the way.
2) After you have read through the entire book, put it aside for a while. The ideas need time to "simmer."
3) Depending on your timeline, you will go back to the book after a week, a few weeks, or perhaps a month. Re-read the book, with special focus on the sections that resonated with you – the "recipes" you were most interested in thinking about or trying. During this second or third reading, make sure to fold over pages, affix sticky-notes, and write in the margin.
4) Before the school-year begins, read through the book once more, pausing to review your own notes and comments.
5) Keep the book out and easily accessible during the all-important first days and weeks. Review the most relevant sections and add to the text regularly.
6) Start collecting "answers" to the questions in Appendix I.
7) Refer to the book throughout the school-year. Continue to make notes; this will help you reflect on the successes and failures in the classroom and to make good teaching decisions; it will also serve you well as you prepare for the next year.

And then . . .
8) After the end of the school-year, take some time to review the book. Make notes of things that worked well, things that didn't, changes you'd like to make, and new things you'd like to try.
9) Then put the book away and **enjoy your summer**

Disclaimer

Introduction

Those of you who have been in my teacher classes have already heard this: "I am not the end-all or be-all in teaching."

I enjoy teaching, I love working with children and students of all ages, and I have had successes in the classroom. I have also had the fortune to work in several schools, with many kinds of learners, and many different personalities "down the hall" and in the office. These experiences have informed every word in this text. But I am not the last word in education.

This book introduces things I did in my classroom that worked. It also reflects the thinking I have done about why some things work and others do not. It reflects the generous input from good teachers I have worked with and spoken with over the past decade and a half. But this does not mean that the strategies and approaches outlined in this book are the only things that work.

There are countless "recipes" for success, and I encourage you to research and try out as many as you can. I also encourage you to visit classrooms of other master "chefs"; speak to veteran teachers; read other "cookbooks." There are many effective strategies, approaches, and perspectives to teaching. Keep your minds open.

And don't forget: Laugh often and have FUN!

1

Schools & Schedules, Some Basic Information

Chapter 1: Schools & Schedules

Types of Teaching Positions

There are several different types of teaching positions. In most elementary and middle schools, there are two *main* types of teaching positions: (1) those who work with the same group of students all day and (2) those who work with different groups of students during the day. The first group generally teaches a range of subjects to one group of students throughout the day. The second group generally teaches a single subject (or related subjects) to different groups of students. These two groups can be labeled: (a) "classroom teachers" and (2) "out-of-classroom teachers." The specific terms used in this book may not be used in all schools, but the situations they describe exist in all schools.

Classroom Teachers

A "classroom teacher" is the teacher for one class of students. This position is sometimes called "homeroom teacher" or "self-contained classroom teacher." A classroom teacher has the same students with him/her all day and delivers instruction to the whole class in all or most subject areas. When people think of elementary school teaching, this is the kind of teacher they typically envision ("I loved my third grade teacher"). Because of the amount of contact, and the age of the students, a classroom teacher often develops a close relationship with his/her students. The classroom teacher is the one that parents recognize and think of as the teacher of their children (despite the significant role of other teachers in the school); the classroom teacher is the one parents see as responsible for their children's learning. This is also the person whom the administration generally holds accountable for student achievement, including test scores.

Note: In many junior high schools, middle schools, and high schools, the "homeroom teacher" has a different definition. This teacher is *administratively* responsible for one class of students. S/he takes the official attendance and is the conduit for official notes and school information. The homeroom teacher may or may not teach his/her homeroom class during the day.

Out-of-Classroom Teachers

Out-of-classroom teachers generally deliver instruction in one subject area or in related subject areas. They may work with all the classes in a school (typically the art teacher, PE teacher, etc), or they may work with certain grades only (the 5th and 6th grade social studies teacher, the kindergarten and 1st grade literacy teacher). These teachers often have expertise in their subject area. Though the classroom teacher often forms the closest bond with groups of students, the favorite teacher of many students is an out-of-classroom teacher.

In most school systems and schools, teachers are guaranteed one period for preparation each day – the "prep" – to be used for grading papers, planning lessons, collaborating with other teachers, tutoring students, contacting parents, etc. The out-of-classroom teacher generally provides this prep period for the classroom teacher by teaching the classroom teacher's students for one period. For this reason, an out-of-classroom teacher may be referred to as a "prep teacher." Out-of-classroom teachers are, however, much more than just answers to scheduling issues.

Out-of-Classroom teachers may be referred by a number of labels; these will vary by school.
• A specials teacher delivers instruction in (traditionally) non-academic subjects; examples are the art teacher or physical education (gym) teacher or music teacher.
• A cluster teacher teaches his/her subject to a "cluster," of grades; an example is the 4th/5th grade Social Studies teacher or the Early Childhood (K-2) math teacher.

Some out-of-classroom teachers have their own rooms, and classes of students go to these rooms for instruction (often art, music, gym, etc). Other out-of-classroom teachers travel room-to-room each day, carrying their materials with them. This is especially common in crowded and/or under-resourced schools. Some out-of-classroom teachers work with a few classes of students; others work with many different classes. In some large schools, an out-of-classroom teacher can see as many as 700 children in a week.

There are, of course, countless differences in the roles and responsibilities of classroom and out-of-classroom teachers (though there are far more similarities in their positions – they are all teachers, after-all!). Because of the emphasis on standardized test scores, and because the bulk of the test preparation falls on the classroom teacher, out-of-classroom teachers often have more leeway with curriculum and may be less closely monitored by the administration. They may have more freedom in terms of class-work, homework, and they may not be held to the same degree of standards compliance. At the same time, during periods of high test emphasis (often the month or two before a city/state test), the out-of-classroom teachers may be requested to aid with test preparation, at the expense of their own subject or program. Many out-of-classroom teachers do not get to know students as well as classroom teachers do and they rarely meet parents.

Another category of out-of-classroom teachers are "push-in" and "pull-out" teachers. These teachers are not usually prep teachers, because they do not "cover" a full class at one time (ie, they do not allow the classroom teacher to have a free preparation period). Push-in and pull-out teachers generally work with small groups of students in specified subject areas. A teacher who is a push-in works in the classroom with the main teacher, helping specific children with material. An example is a reading push-in; this teacher supports a small group of struggling readers during the regular reading lesson. Some special needs children will have push-in teachers assigned to work with them throughout the day. Pull-out teachers take small groups of children outside of their regular classroom to work with them. An example is the ESL (English as a Second Language) teacher; s/he works with groups of children during the day who need focused help in mastering English.

Which is better?
There are out-of-classroom teachers who would never want their own classroom and classroom teachers who would never want anything but their own class. Each type of teaching position presents its own challenges, but both can be equally rewarding. Some teachers enjoy both types and flip-flop during the years of their teaching careers. I have done both and I enjoyed both equally, though for different reasons. Most new teachers do not consider out-of-classroom teaching positions as they prepare for their first year. It is often with consternation and disappointment that they find they will have an out-of-classroom position. New teachers rarely have much sway in the type of position they receive their first year or years; being flexible and positive serves them well. There is so much to learn, and so much enjoyment to be had, in all teaching positions.

In this book, I will refer to all self-contained classroom teachers and homeroom teachers as "classroom teachers," and all prep, cluster, or push in/out teachers as "out-of-classroom teachers."

Chapter 1: Schools & Schedules

Schedules & Periods

What is a typical day of teaching?

Most school-days are approximately 6½ hours long, beginning as early as 7:00am and ending as late as 4:00pm. Increasingly, schools have "extended day" hours that may be optional or mandatory for students and teachers. Many charter schools, for example, often have longer days that the local public or private schools. High schools tend to start earlier than elementary schools and junior high schools. In communities where a majority of students use school buses, the start-times for the different schools may be staggered so that the same busses can be used to transport elementary, junior high, and high school students. This means that parents may have complicated morning schedules, as they must coordinate the leave-times for children in different schools.

Teachers typically have one lunch period and one preparation ("prep") period every day, each approximately 45 minutes long, though the length of the school-day periods varies by school, ranging from 40 min to one hour. The expectation is that the teacher is "off" during lunch but does school-related work during the prep. To think of it another way, "the lunch period belongs to the teacher and the prep period belongs to the school." Depending on the school, the prep period can be taken away occasionally for grade meetings, class coverages (see below), special events, etc. While these events may be the exception, teachers should know that they can lose prep periods at the last minute. A teacher should never plan to do something during a prep that *has* to be done that day.

Prep periods can be the first or last period of the day or any period in between. There are benefits to prep periods wherever they fall:
- First period prep periods let you ease into the day.
- Last period prep periods let you "turn off" earlier and get a jump-start on the next day's planning and grading.
- Preps in the middle of the day give you a "break."

I have always felt it was best to have a sprinkling of all kinds of prep periods, to lend variety to the week. For the most part, teachers have no say in when their preps are scheduled.

Some schools arrange the faculty prep periods so that teachers in the same grade or subject area have preps at the same times; these may be called "grade preps" or "common preps." This is to facilitate collaborative planning and grade meetings.. If you work in a school with common preps, you should speak to a veteran teacher to find out exactly what is expected of teachers on their prep periods, and what freedom they have to use the time for non-shared activities.

Teachers rarely lose their lunch periods, as most teacher contracts are fairly strict in this regard. New teachers, frantic to "do it all," however, often work right through lunch, rather than taking the time for themselves. This is a mistake. As the months pass, many new teachers complain of being exhausted – more exhausted than they had ever imagined. This exhaustion is mental as well as physical. There is not much a teacher can do to lessen the mental or emotional exhaustion, but a teacher can lessen the physical exhaustion – simply by saying "no" occasionally. From the very first day of school, do your best to stop, relax, and eat lunch during your lunch period. If possible, leave the school building, even if just to walk around the block. It is surprising how recuperative a few breaths of fresh air can be.

Coverages
A "coverage" is a period in which one teacher "covers" the teaching schedule of another. Coverages can happen for a variety of reasons – inclement weather, faculty absences, school emergency, etc. Some schools do not hire substitute teachers as practice – sometimes for budgetary reasons, sometimes because a school does not want teachers unfamiliar with the students/school mission/etc. Some schools cannot attract sufficient substitute teachers and so may be under-staffed when faculty are absent. Some middle and high schools encourage their regular faculty to, in effect, work as substitute teachers when other faculty are absent (there is usually additional compensation for this). Whatever the reason, when there are absences without enough substitutes, other teachers will be asked to cover classes. In these cases, teachers will be asked to work through their prep (or their lunch) to cover a class. There will not always be adequate notice.

New teachers should speak to veterans about the practice of coverages at the school. There may be a policy about the rotation of these coverages as well as guidelines about compensation. It is important to find out what these policies are early the school-year.

Chapter 1: Schools & Schedules

Plan-Book

A teacher's plan-book is much more than a place to record schedules, lesson plans, class trips, and homework assignments. Used properly, the plan-book serves as a record of everything that happens in a classroom. Looking at a teacher's plan-book for any given day or week can reveal lessons, assignments, topics of discussion, breaks in schedule, fire drills, discipline measures taken, etc.

Keeping the plan-book filled with all these useful tid-bits is not difficult or involved, though it may seem that way now. You simply need to make it habit to make brief notes in the plan-book. Since your plan-book will be open and out all of the time (the only way it is useful!), it is fairly simple to make brief notes during the day. Before you leave at the end of the day, expound on those scribbles ("Tomas" becomes "Wrote note to Tomas' mother in HW notebook," "Adj/adv" becomes "Class is still having a hard time distinguishing adjectives/adverbs"; etc.). In addition, make sure to note any special behavior concerns, who won the spelling bee, and what parent stopped in to speak with you.

Planning
This book is not about detailed lesson planning, lesson design and long-term instructional goals. This is because strategies for lesson-planning, design, and goals are fairly well-covered in other books and in most teacher training programs. Great lesson plans and tips on planning can be found in many teacher's guides and on countless websites. Furthermore, different schools, with different curricula, often have specified ways in which they wish their teachers to plan and to create lessons. My recommendations about planning pertain to the logistics of managing your time:
1) Generate an outline of the topics and lessons you intend to cover each week for each subject.
2) Plug them into the boxes in the plan-book, so you can get a sense of each day. This will help you think about lesson flow and transitions.
3) Plan each day's homework, keeping in mind what was covered that day and how much homework is being assigned in other subjects. Keep in mind, too, what you want to have reinforced by the homework, for the next day's lessons.
4) Record general topics/skills in the boxes of the plan-book, so that you can quickly see the last time you covered plural nouns or double-digit subtraction, for example.

5) Mark your own "homework" in the plan-book as well – what things you need to complete after-school on any given day.

2

Physical Classroom

Chapter 2: Physical Classroom

About this Chapter

This chapter addresses the physical environment of a classroom – what a classroom looks like, how it is decorated, and what items are displayed. Setting up and maintaining an attractive, inviting classroom is an essential part of effective teaching. Courses in teacher training programs often overlook the physical aspect of classrooms. Very few books on teaching cover the appearance of the classroom. This is an unfortunate oversight. A classroom where kids feel good and want to be is one where the most learning is likely to happen.

Kids crave structure, and they tend to feel most comfortable and perform best in a structured, attractive environment. They like to see their names and their work displayed; these make children feel that they belong, that someone values their work, and that the class is "theirs." Signs and charts that are bright and clear grab kids' attention. Shelves that are clean with items arranged sensibly invite kids to explore and question. An orderly, attractive room is a place where kids *and* teachers want to be.

For teachers who work in under-resourced communities, the orderliness and appearance of the physical classroom is often even more important. Children in poorer neighborhoods may not have orderly homes. They might live with many family members in smaller apartments or homes, and they might not have space that is their "own." In such communities, there are also more likely to be students who are in foster care or who live in shelters. Children in situations like these are likely to require structure even more than the average child. These children may not be able to succeed without it. It is a teacher's job to make the classroom warm and inviting, much like a second home.

Chapter 2: Physical Classroom

Shopping List

"What do I need to buy?"

Teachers rarely receive all the supplies they need. This is true for teachers in wealthy suburbs, under-resourced urban communities, or any of the school districts in-between. Many new teachers I have worked with have been appalled at not having a clock on the wall, not receiving a single ream of paper, not being given a stapler or waste basket. Others have been satisfied – or even delighted – with the supplies provided by the administration or the school's parent association.

Teachers need enough school supplies to get through the first few weeks of school. The first month of school is exhausting for teachers, and it is best not to have to make any additional stops at crowded, chaotic teacher and office supply stores. Some kids will bring supplies, some won't. Some will bring inappropriate supplies (like college-ruled notebooks for or fountain pens 1st grade). The teachers helps ensure a smooth start to the year if s/he makes sure her classroom is outfitted with essential supplies.

Many new teachers have asked me about the parents: "Don't the parents buy supplies for their children?" The response from parents will differ widely. There are parents who send their children to school the first day fully-outfitted. I some schools, supplies are purchased ahead of time and are ready at the school prior to the first day. There are parents who do not have the money to buy supplies. Others do not have the time to shop or who wait until the second or third week of school to do so. There are also parents who feel the school should provide all required supplies. You will address these issues later, but for now, plan to prepare the physical aspect of your classroom as well as possible.

The "standard" items teachers will receive from the school will vary by school and by district. Teachers entering schools in under-resourced communities often receive fewer basic teaching supplies than their counterparts in more affluent communities. Arguably, they should receive more, as the parents of their students are likely to have fewer resources. But that's not the way it is. While this is reprehensible, there is no point dwelling on it. The reality is that, in a few weeks (or days!), you're going to face a group of eager students, and it is your responsibility to be prepared.

Chapter 2: Physical Classroom

Teachers spend a lot of money before their first year; there is no way around this. Some school systems compensate teachers for a certain amount of out-of-pocket expenditures. Some school systems offer no such compensation. No matter what, new teachers spend a lot of their own money to prepare their classrooms. The items on this list will cost roughly $350. Teachers will continue to spend money throughout the year for their students and classrooms. Typically, teachers spend significantly less in successive years.

Make sure to save all receipts in case your school or district reimburses teacher expenditures. A senior teacher or a representative from the teacher's union should be able to provide information on this. In addition, tax preparers, may be able to suggest ways to track and record expenses for your taxes (these expenses can be considered "non-reimbursed work expenses").

The following is my "shopping list." It contains the top-priority items, the things that I feel are absolutely necessary to run an elementary school classroom. This list is not mandated anywhere; it is just based on my experiences. I went through this list every August and made sure I had everything before the first day.

<u>Chart Key</u>
Classroom teachers and many out-of-classroom teachers (see Chapter 1 for an overview of types of teaching positions) with their own rooms need all these items.
OUT: Out-of-classroom teachers/Teachers without their own rooms need only the items indicated in the far-right column.
* Starred items are things I always purchased but that are not strictly required.
*Italics:*Items in italics are things that you may find in your classroom and/or be given by the "supply lady" at the beginning of the year.

A full explanation/description of the items follows the shopping list.

Teacher Shopping List

ITEM	DESCRIPTION	QTY	OUT
Binder Clips	Medium, 1¼ inch	2 dozen	Y
Binder Clips	Large, 2 or 2+ inches	6	Y

Chapter 2: Physical Classroom

ITEM	DESCRIPTION	QTY	OUT
Books, hard-bound	Appropriate for age and/or subject	Any	
Boxes, Storage	Shoebox size, clear, plastic	6	
Broom & Dust Pan	Medium-sized, good-quality	1 each	
Bucket	Sturdy, plastic	1	
Calendar	See below	1	
Chains	1 inch link, 1 yd in length	2	
Chalk	White	1 box	Y
Chart Paper	Un-ruled, white	1 pack	Y
Charts/Poster Board	White poster board	10	
Charts/Poster Board	Grid poster-board, assorted colors, with spaces for 36+ students	3	
Construction Paper	Assorted Colors, medium (approx 11x17 in)	100 sheets	
Contact Paper		1 roll	
Crayons	Crayon "nubs" - find a can of them somewhere	--	
Door Shapes	Stars, apples, etc.	36+	
Glue	White, large, 16+ oz	1 bottle	
Glitter	Assorted color(s)	1 jar	
Hand-Soap	Regular pump hand-soap, large-size, plastic	2	
Highlighter	Your favorite color(s)	2	
Hole-punch		1	
Adhesive Hooks	Peel-back	12	
Index Cards	3x5	1 pack	Y
Index Cards	5x7	1 pack	
Lighter	Regular corner-store cheap model	1	
Locks	Combination	2	
Loose-leaf Paper	see Paper, Loose-leaf		

Chapter 2: Physical Classroom

ITEM	DESCRIPTION	QTY	OUT
Markers, Large	Permanent felt, large, black	2	Y
Markers, Fine	Permanent felt, fine point, dark colors	4	Y
Markers ("Magic")	Non-permanent felt, assorted bright	1 box	
Magnets	Any – strong, small	1 doz	
Magnet Clips	Strong magnets with solid clip mechanism	2-3	
Medications	For the teacher: throat drops, pain killers, cold medicine (day formula), etc.	Vary	
Neck Chains	Hardware-store key chains lengths, 1 yd each	5	
Notebooks*	Marble, composition style, black, sewn binding	32+	
Oak-tag	Bright colors, 8½ x11 inch	1 pack	
Paper, Loose-leaf	Loose-leaf (wide-ruled for 2nd -5th, extra wide for K & 1^{st,} college ruled for 6th+)	1 ream	Y
Paper, Newsprint	Large, newspaper-sized	1 pack	
Paper, Plain	See Printer Paper, below	1 ream	Y
Paper Clips	Non-skid (ridged), small (1¼ or 1½ inch)	1 box	Y
Paper Towels		1 roll	
Pencils	GOOD quality, yellow, #2	6 doz	
Pencil Sharpener	Electric, heavy-duty	1	
Pens, Student Use	Ball-point black or blue	3 doz	
Pens, Teacher Use	Your favorite	5	
Pens, Grading	Felt-tip, fine, non-permanent, any color(s)	4	Y
Plan-book	Teacher's Plan-book	1	Y
Poster Board/ Charts	White poster board	10	
Poster Board/ Charts	Grid poster-board, assorted colors, with spaces for 36+ students	3	
Printer Paper	White, cheapest brand, 8½ x11	1 ream	Y
Push-pins	NOT thumb-tacks	1 pack	

Chapter 2: Physical Classroom

ITEM	DESCRIPTION	QTY	OUT
Radio or Speaker*	w/CD player and I-Pod port	1	
Ribbon Awards*	Like the ones used for athletic competitions	100+	
Scissors	Heavy-duty	1	
Sentence Strips	Assorted colors	1 pack	
Sponges	Large (for chalkboards)	2	
Spray cleaner	Counter-top spray	1	
Stapler	Heavy-duty	1	
Staple Remover	Not the jaw-kind, the flicking kind	1	
Staples		1 box	
Stickers	Assorted, small simple (cheap!)	6 packs	Y
Stickers - Stars	Assorted small star-shapes, metallic colors	1 pack	Y
Sticky-Notes	Assorted sizes, assorted colors	3 packs	Y
Storage Boxes	Shoebox size, clear, plastic	6	
Tags, Price	Stiff, medium-size labels, with string (like those used in antique shops)	12+	
Tape. Masking	Masking, 1-in wide	2 rolls	Y
Tape, Clear	Clear Plastic ("scotch"), ½ wide	2 rolls	
Tape Dispenser	For clear plastic tape	1	
Thank-you Cards	Inexpensive, generic	20+	Y
Throat Drops	Extra-strength, favorite flavor(s)	I bag	Y
Wall clock	Easy-to-read, inexpensive	1	

Binder Clips
You will use these to bind student assignments, to organize worksheets, etc. Invaluable!

Books
Every classroom needs a good classroom library. New teachers inherit the books that come with the room; this collection will probably be adequate

to start the school-year. You will want to add to the classroom library, but this can be very expensive. There are many sources for inexpensive (often used) books for the creative teacher:

- Parents & relatives: many people may have a box of old children's books in the attic that no-one is using.
- Garage sales are good sources of inexpensive, used children's books.
- Public Libraries sell old books cheaply; many will give them free-of-charge to public school teachers. Books that the libraries will no longer keep are generally in surprisingly good shape.
- Salvation Army and Goodwill thrift shops sell books cheaply.
- Many bookstores sell used books and/or give discounts to teachers.

Boxes, Storage
See "Storage Containers" below.

Broom, Bucket, & Sponges
These are necessary for maintaining the classroom. The school is likely to provide these items.

Calendar
All teachers must have a calendar in their rooms. This is for practical, as well as educational, purposes. If you are teaching grades K-1 or 2, you need one of the large chart-type of calendars with moveable numbers and icons. For grades 3 or 4 and up, a regular wall calendar is adequate.

Chains & Locks
There will be some things teachers want to lock up within the classroom. Some cabinets have working locks; others do not. You can slip a chain through the handles of a closet or cabinet and lock it with a sturdy lock.

Chalk
Schools typically provide chalk (it is very cheap, in any event). If your school has white erase boards, you will need to replace the markers periodically.

Charts
Teachers need to make several charts within the first few days of school and throughout the school-year. Having different types of chart-paper and poster board on hand will save last-minute shopping stops.

There are different types of charts; some schools will mandate what kinds of things must be hung on the walls. Do not wait for someone to tell you what you're expected to have on the wall. On the first day you have to report to school, speak to another teacher in the same grade. Introduce yourself and ask what charts are considered top priority at the school. Prepare those charts (See Classroom Decoration).

The grid-charts are used for certain record-keeping and assignment monitoring (homework charts, book reports, etc.). This will depend on your curriculum, your interests, and what the school emphasizes. You will probably not prepare these charts in the first few weeks of school (as children may shift around).

Construction Paper
A must-have in every elementary classroom! Do not buy the discount variety. The colors are not "true," and they tend to fade quickly. They also do not fold or tear well (a necessity for many arts-n-craft projects).

Contact Paper
Contact paper is expensive stuff. It is clear plastic sheets that are sticky on one side, like giant sheets of scotch tape. Contact Paper may be used to reinforce signs, papers, etc. Using contact paper is like laminating. If used judiciously, one roll can last a full year.

If your school has a working laminating machine, you may not need contact paper (though a small packet is always useful).

Crayons
Students will eventually bring in individual boxes of crayons and bottles of glue (see "Supply List" in Appendix II). Teachers need some of each, however, to get through the first few days (or weeks) of school. Do not *buy* crayons. Someone you know has an empty cookie tin filled with crayon nubs. These will suffice until the kids start bringing in the supplies you stipulate. At the end of the year, you'll collect the nubs from the current class to start off the next year.

Door Shapes
One of the most important initial decorations for a classroom is the outside of the door. Each student's name should be clearly displayed. Many teachers pick a theme for this; they purchase little red apples, write a child's name on each one, and cut out letters across the top "We're a GREAT bunch!" Little stars might inspire, "We're reaching for the STARS!"

Chapter 2: Physical Classroom

Glitter
Very little makes a group of children (even big children) happier than glitter. It is necessary for many art projects throughout the school-year. Unbeknownst to non-teachers, there is good-quality and bad-quality glitter. Bad-quality glitter is not consistently sized, has jagged edges, and doesn't stick evenly to glue lines. Buy glitter that is in evenly-small sized pieces. You do not need multiple colors; one large container of gold or silver is adequate.

Glue
Buy one large container of white all-purpose "school" glue; this can be used to fill up the students' bottles as they get used up during the year. In subsequent years, you will have the previous year's supply to get you through the first few weeks of the new school-year. No to colored or glitter glue.

Hand-Soap
Some schools may not consistently stock the children's bathrooms with hand-soap. For this reason, it's good to have a large plastic pump-container of hand-soap, one each for the boys and for the girls. When students go to the bathroom, they bring the soap with them. Increasingly, schools stock (or request from parents) supplies of hand-sanitizer. I happen to hate the stuff, but that is personal bias. It is helpful to have a bottle for times when the soap runs out, the pipes break, or etc.

Highlighter
Teachers use highlighters for a number of purposes in the classroom - marking tricky spelling words, circling nouns on a chart, highlighting incidents in your plan-book, etc.

Hooks, Adhesive
These are peel-back sticky plastic hooks used to hang tags with students' names on them for Student Jobs (see Routines & Procedures).

Index Cards
Index cards have a variety of purposes in the classroom – labels, name tags, collecting information on students, art projects, etc.

Lighter
Teachers need lighters for random things during the year (lighting birthday candle, melting the end of a frayed rope, etc.). Keep this hidden and locked.

Chapter 2: Physical Classroom

Locks
See "Chains and Locks" above.

Loose-leaf Paper
See "Paper" below.

Magnets
Most chalkboards, and many dry-erase ("white-boards"), are magnetic.
Magnets are great for hanging posters, maps, etc. on the chalkboard.
Hardware and craft stores have cheap ones that are small and strong.
You should purchase at least a few that are also clips (these are often
shaped like little people).

Markers
• Permanent Large: All new teachers need markers – for more reasons
  that I can list. The large ones, mostly for charts and bulletin boards,
  should be black or blue. In the permanent variety, the other colors don't
  really show up – they all just look dark. It's a waste to buy yellow or
  orange permanent markers.
• Permanent Medium or Fine: These are primarily for outlining on
  charts, making photocopy masters, and labeling things. There are a
  number of popular brands that make skinny, permanent markers. The
  dark colors are best.
• Colored Markers ("magic markers"): You need to buy one box of colored
  non-permanent markers. I used these for checking homework and
  journals, among other things.

Note: You will use permanent markers to label *everything* on this
shopping list. Otherwise borrowed books will never get returned and your
broom will wind up in someone else's classroom.

Medications
Teaching is not like other jobs. No-one can hold your calls when you have
a headache. Substitute teachers cannot always be called in when you
become ill. There will be times when you'll have to work when you're not
feeling well. It's important to have headache medication as well as day-
formula (non-drowsy) cold medication. Throat drops are a must.

Neck Chains
Teachers handle hall passes in different ways. I make neck chains, with a
small laminated (contact paper) pass at the bottom. Students wore these
while out of the classroom; I found the passes never got left somewhere or

Chapter 2: Physical Classroom

lost. You can purchase appropriate chains at any hardware store; they should measure one yard.

Notebooks

Some schools mandate a specific type of notebook for certain grades and or subjects. I recommend buying one class set of the stipulated notebook. It is much easier to impose order and consistency if all students have all required materials from the beginning. For example, if your school prefers that 4th grade students maintain four spiral notebooks for schoolwork subjects and homework, buy one set of spirals to distribute on the first day. That notebook will be used for all work until the parents are able to provide the rest of the notebooks and other materials. If your school does not stipulate a certain notebook, you may still want to enforce consistency in your classroom. Buying a class set of your preferred notebook helps to establish this. I recommend black-n-white marbled composition books with sewn binding.

Oak-tag

Oak-tag is stiff paper, similar to card stock (the same material used in those beige-colored hanging files in most offices, including doctors' offices). Oak-tag is what teachers use to make signs, stencils, hall-passes, name tags, etc. It comes in a variety of packaging - giant sheets, various colors, and rolls. My preference was the 8½ x 11 inch size, in assorted bright colors, which came in a packet of 50+ sheets.

Paper

- Loose-leaf Paper: Many schools will supply loose-leaf paper to teachers. If not, make sure to start the year with at least one ream of the appropriate-ruled lined paper. There is extra-wide ruling for small children (generally grades K-1), regular ruling for grades 2-4, and college-ruled paper for older students. Ask a veteran teacher what ruling is best for you age group.
- Newsprint is blank newspaper-type paper. It is usually a dull color – pale grey or pale yellow, and it comes in packs of large sheets (generally newspaper-sized). It is very inexpensive, and schools tend to provide it. I found newsprint very useful for a number of purposes in the classroom.
- Printer Paper: The plain white paper is for drawings and art projects, as well as graphs and other un-lined assignments. Start the year with one full ream.

Chapter 2: Physical Classroom

Paper Clips

Buy regular, non-skid one inch and 1½-2 inch paper clips. Fancy colors and fancy shapes don't work better (they often work less well) and they cost more.

Pencils

Pencils are a horror. No-one outside of teaching understands this. Pencils disappear. Pencils break. Pencils are jabbed into unsuspecting little arms. Pencils are fought over. Pencils are thrown – out windows, at substitute teachers, at non-substitute teachers, and across the cafeteria. Without systematic vigilance, teachers can go through a dozen pencils an hour. Kids also eat pencils, or so it seems. They will "borrow" pencils from the teacher, and from other students, and they will never return them. You must buy a good supply of pencils, and you must set up an effective pencil-routine (see Pencils).

I would never start a school year with fewer than 5 dozen pencils. Do not buy the cheap ones - the eraser part falls off, the wood crumbles in the sharpener, the lead (graphite) breaks, the erasers leave pink smudges, etc. Stick to the known pencil companies – Ticonderoga TM, Dixon TM, etc. Buy only yellow #2 pencils. Do not buy colored or decorated pencils; you want to avoid the "No, I had the red one" fights that are such a joy to referee. In addition, you should always have the #2's on hand for standardized testing and practice testing. The better pencil brands, however, can be surprisingly expensive, especially with the cheap ones so apparently and tantalizingly similar. Suck it up, and keep an eye out for deals.

Pencil Sharpener

Many classrooms will have pencil sharpeners. If this is the case, you will not have to purchase one. If your classroom does not have a pencil sharpener, purchase a high-quality electric one. You will need to monitor its use, because you want it to last (at least) one year. It is amazing the items intelligent children will stick into a pencil sharpener.

Pens

You will do more writing that you would have ever thought possible as a teacher. Buy pens that you really like; it's worth the splurge. In addition to your favorite pens, teachers also need felt-tips pens. These pens are for grading papers. It's easier to use a felt-tip than a ball-point for this, because you can write at any angle with a felt tip (on a train or bus

Chapter 2: Physical Classroom

commute, waiting in line, etc.). You cannot use permanent markers for grading papers, as the ink will leak through the page.

Students in grades 3 and up start using pens for final drafts of some assignments. Teachers working in these grades should have a class set of regular blue or black ball-point pens.

Plan-book
All teachers need a plan-book. Many teachers are very particular about the plan-books they use. I preferred the ones that had the days going down the page (vertically), but horizontal days are much more common. In addition, many plan-books have only seven periods in a day; my school had eight periods. These details may seem insignificant, but they end up mattering *so* much. I recommend speaking to several other teachers to get a sense of what they do in this regard. Then look at a number of different plan-books to find the one that you feel fits you best.

Poster Boards
See "Charts" above.

Printer Paper
See "Paper" above.

Push-pins
These are necessary for classroom displays and bulletin boards. Thumb tacks are cheaper but they are difficult to remove. Since you will want to have students help you with this sort of thing, you need to buy the pins that will be easier for them to handle. Buy push-pins that come in their own snap-close container.

Radio/CD Player/Speaker
Though perhaps not strictly necessary, I cannot imagine a classroom without music. A radio with a CD player plus I-phone speaker is perfect.

Ribbon Awards
Ribbon awards are the ribbons that we associate with sports competitions or field day events. I purchased ribbon awards every year, and I used them for the homework competition. Ribbon awards are available from trophy shops. I had them imprinted with: "Class 3-309 Homework Champions." You can also order blank ribbons and write on them with a permanent silver or gold ink marker (See Homework).

Chapter 2: Physical Classroom

Scissors
Good, sharp, strong scissors are essential in any classroom. It is likely
that the school will provide a pair. If this is not the case, do not skimp:
buy good scissors (they will last for years).

Sentence Strips
Sentence Strips are strips of oak-tag with a dotted center line printed on
them. They reinforce proper letter-sizing and penmanship. Teachers use
sentence strips for vocabulary words, name labels (on desks), and various
wall displays. They come in rolls and 2 foot long strips. I prefer the strips.

Sponges
See "Broom, Buckets, & Sponges" above.

Spray Cleaner
Buy a common all-surface cleaner to wash desks, wipe down walls, etc.

Stapler & Staples
You will probable get a stapler and a box of staples from the school. If
not, buy a heavy duty stapler, along with a box of staples. No cute plastic
staplers allowed!

Staples Remover
To non-teachers, there is one kind of staple remover; this is the jaw-like
contraption for removing staples from the corner of stapled documents.
This is not the kind of remover you need. The kind of staple remover you
need is for removing staples from bulletin boards. It is a handle with a
staple-grabber at the end, and you use it to pull-flick staples from walls
and bulletin boards. Ask at any teacher or office store.

Stickers
Stickers are used for countless purposes in a classroom - as incentives,
rewards, tó put on excellent papers, and to post on the Homework Chart.
Stickers come in many sizes, shapes, and textures. For day-to-day awards
(see "Point Chart"), buy simple, inexpensive stickers. A number of
companies make adorable stickers that in packets of several hundred for
just a few dollars.

Sticky-Notes
Self-adhesive sticky-notes only became popular in the 1980's – how did
we ever live without them? Buy several sizes, including small-sized notes
(1x2 in) and medium-sized ones (approx 2x3 in).

Chapter 2: Physical Classroom

Storage Containers
There are many ways to organize the supplies a teacher keeps in the classroom. Since children are often seated in clusters or work-tables, one option is to organize the supplies by tables. Children who sit at one table store their supplies together. Their crayons, glue, scissors, etc. are kept in a single storage container. The collection of containers is kept on a shelf at the back of the room. I used inexpensive, clear, plastic storage containers (shoe-box sized). These do not have to be air-tight; they're for crayons, not leftovers.

Tags, Price
The type of tags indicated here are the small (approx 1x1.5 in) commonly used in antique stores and second-hand stores to list the price of the item. In the classroom, these are used for student jobs. Each child's name is written on a tag and it is hung next to the job s/he has for that week/month/etc (see "Student Jobs").

Tape & Dispenser
The school may provide tape; if not, make sure to have at least two rolls of both clear plastic and masking tape to start off the year.

Thank-You Cards
Thank-you cards are invaluable for teachers. For all the frustrations and challenges new teachers face, there will be people who go out of their way to help you. Develop a habit of thanking these people – parents, other teachers, administrators, etc. The power of a Thank-You card can not be underestimated.

Throat Drops
New teachers strain their voices – both because they struggle with issues of management and because their larynxes are simply not used to projecting for hours on end. Sucking on good drops really helps. See "Medications," above.

Wall Clock
The school may provide a wall clock. If not, purchase a large one, un-fancy one with clear numbers.

Where to Shop
Teacher supply stores are wonderfully convenient; they are usually easy to get to and they have everything that a teacher needs. Unfortunately, items in many teacher supply stores can be more expensive than items in

office supply shops or discount family stores. Many office supply stores have a good collection of teacher supplies. In addition, most of the larger office supply chains have regional outlets with expanded teacher/school sections. Other teachers are your best source for local shopping advice.

I bought everything from my shopping list at a large office supply store and local shops except the following: (a) door and/or calendar shapes, (b) oak-tag, (c) plan-books, (d) ribbon awards, and (e) sentence strips.

There are exceptional teacher supply stores, with a wide variety of good and affordable prices. They tend to be some distance out of cities, often on highways outside of suburbs. The only way to find out about these stand-outs is by word-of-mouth. If there is one near you, it is worth it to plan a trip there; you can get everything in one stop.

We tend these days to buy so many things online. And we've all come to expect the occasional disappointment – when an item was not as we expected. This isn't much of a problem for a pair of summer sandals, but it is a problem a week before the school year starts. For your first year, I strongly recommend buying items in-person – so that you can see and feel them. With subsequent terms and years, when you know good brands and etc, purchase online!

Chapter 2: Physical Classroom

Classroom Decoration

Classroom decoration is about much more than appearance. A well-organized and well-decorated room tells students that the teacher is prepared and that s/he is looking forward to a productive, enjoyable year. It tells students that they are expected. To this end, a classroom should be homey and comforting; it must be a place where kids want to be. For kids whose home lives may not be ideal, this can be especially important.

In some schools, classroom decoration may be partially mandated as part of a prescribed curriculum. In these cases, teachers may not have freedom to display what they want (see Bulletin Boards). Most classroom teachers will, however, have considerable freedom as to how they decorate their rooms. On the first day that teachers report, before you begin any classroom decorating, make sure to speak to an experienced teacher on your grade to find out what, if any, are the requirements for classroom decoration.

For classroom cork-board displays, use push-pins, as they are easiest for kids to remove. On cork-board bulletin boards outside of the classroom, use staples, because push-pins will be stolen (they can also be removed and used as weapons). Masking tape is the cheapest, most effective way of hanging papers directly onto walls. Clear plastic tape is more expensive; more importantly, it can ruin the underlying paint job, and almost always rips the kids' work. Make masking tape loops and affix all the shapes and words to the door (see Tape Loops, in Odds & Ends).

Bulletin Boards/Displays Inside the Classroom
In addition to any prescribed wall displays or charts, I recommend having the following in all classrooms:
· Behavior Management System (see Point Chart)
· Birthday Chart
· Calendar
· Class Rules
· Classroom Gallery
· Cool Words
· Heading
· Homework Chart
· Library
· Math Clues – maybe, maybe not
· Quiz Displays (top grades)

Chapter 2: Physical Classroom

- Schedule (2) – Door and Inside
- Vocabulary/Spelling List
- Student Jobs

Behavior Management System ("Point Chart")

Every teacher has some sort of system, temporary or permanent, for classroom and behavior management. Mine is the "Point Chart." The system/chart you use should be transparent for students. If there are visual aspects, these should be visible to all students and anyone visiting your classroom (see Point Chart).

Birthday Chart

This is a large, colorful poster chart that lists the birthdays of everyone in the class. It is used for a variety of educational purposes throughout the year. The Birthday Chart does not get posted until the third or fourth week of school, because class-rosters may change throughout the first few weeks of school (see Day 1 & Week 1).

Calendar

- In the early grades, the calendar is part of the morning routine. For this reason, you need a prominent calendar display, including moveable numbers, weather icons, etc. Some teachers post the calendar (especially if wall space is a problem) on a moveable cork board. This can then be taken to the rug area or wherever the morning routine is done. The calendar can then be placed anywhere during the rest of the day (see Morning Routines K & 1).
- In the middle and upper grades, the calendar is for reference, but it is not usually a part of every day's routine. It can simply be a purchased wall calendar. This can be hung in any corner – but it should be visible from most areas of the room.

Class Rules

Most schools require that teachers post the class rules and the consequences for breaking them. These rules should be written on poster board. I recommend hanging them way up high to conserve lower and more-easily accessible walk space (see Day 1 & Week 1).

Classroom Gallery

The Classroom Gallery is a wall or bulletin board reserved for special projects, photographs of the students, etc. Having a "gallery" is not required, but I always had one, and the kids and parents (and visiting administrators) really liked it. On a back wall, I posted the words "Our

Gallery" (cut from neon oak-tag). This is free space – for posting odd things the kids bring in, notes or special pictures they make, and photographs of the children in class, on trips, etc. Since you won't have anything for the Gallery at the beginning of the year, write an explanation on chart paper or newsprint: "This is our place to post our favorite things and special projects . . . Look out for some neat stuff!"

Cool Words
In addition to the weekly vocabulary or spelling words, you and the students will encounter cool, new words. When a student asks about a new word, this becomes a "teachable moment." When such a word comes up, post it on the Cool Words wall. You do not need a full bulletin board, or even any backing. Rather, you can post the words directly onto the wall. The title can be: "Words we think are COOL." Print each new word on a sentence strip. You also need to come up with a definition and write that on an index card next to the word (I say "come up with" because the dictionary rarely gives a definition that is meaningful to kids; I'd start with the dictionary definition – and then discuss with the kids what to write as the definition in their own words). These words can then become "bonus" words in the weekly vocabulary quizzes, for use in essays, etc.

Heading
The "heading" is what students are expected to write at the top of their papers. This usually includes the child's name, date, class, etc. Some schools have uniform requirements for the heading; in other schools, individual teachers stipulate what is required for a heading. In either case, you will need to display the heading so that students can see it. Many teachers opt to write the proper heading on one part of the board and not erase it. I never liked losing valuable chalkboard space, so I wrote the heading on a chart (half a standard poster board) and taped it to the wall above the chalkboard.

My school did not mandate a certain proper heading form. My heading:

(top wide space empty)	
Class -309	Full Name
Subject	Full Date
(skip one space)	
Title of Assignment	

Chapter 2: Physical Classroom

I stipulated that students write their full names in grades 2 and up. For the lower grades, I allowed "Maria M." I also insisted that students write out the full month words.

Homework Chart
Different teachers will handle homework differently. In addition, schools may have different rules about how homework is assigned. I tracked all homework on a chart – the "Homework Chart." I hung this chart on the back of the classroom door, but kids did occasionally get conked in the head as someone entered the classroom, though there never were any sustained injuries (see Homework).

Library
Most classrooms have a library, some small, some large. It is very important to organize the library in a way that is attractive and makes sense to your students. You should have an attractive "Library" sign (construction paper or bright oak-tag cut-outs). In addition, you need to have small signs, designating the sections and genres of books. Early in the year, you must explain each of these to the kids, for two reasons: (1) so they can find the books they want, and (2) so they are more likely to put books back where they belong.

The library sections/genres will depend on the collection of books you have and the level of the students. Some schools may also stipulate the organization of the library. The trend currently is many elementary schools is to have books organized by levels, so that children can easily find books that are at their reading level. It is important that any teachers new to a school learn about any requirements for the organization of classroom books.

I organized my classroom library into "Fiction" & "Non-Fiction"; then sub-divided the books into the following (approximating a regular library, as well as the terms that people actually use when discussing books):
- Biography & Autobiography
- Chapter Books
- Drama
- Fairy Tales
- Folk Tales
- Geography
- History & Social Studies
- Picture Books
- Poetry & Rhyme

Chapter 2: Physical Classroom

- Reference Books
- Story Books
- Additional categories will be dictated by your preferences, grade, and the existing books.
- If you can find books on local history or about the town/neighborhood, these are good additions. Travel guides for your city/region make good library additions.

Math Clues

This is a section that I have thought about omitting from the current edition of this book. A math clues chart is a wall display, much like the "Cool Words" display. It contains a list of math "clues" – words and phrases common in mathematics word problems and on tests. The purpose of the math clues chart is to develop familiarity with the language of mathematics, thereby improving student performance, specifically on standardized tests.

The problem with such a chart is that it suggests an absolute word/term-to-operation relationship. It does not allow for the nuances of language – or of some of the most complicated word problems. If a weak reader looks only for the clues outlined, s/he will make some errors. A better strategy (this author feels) is to work deliberately to incorporate targeted reading strategies in mathematics.

That being said, many schools require teachers to post some kind of a math clues chart. You do what you must. As you cover a new term, concept or trick (i.e., "When you read 'more than' or 'less than,' you're going to have to subtract, and 'in all' requires addition"), add it to the Math Clues.

MATH CLUES

How do I know what to do in a math word problem?	
If I read:	Then I know to:
"less than"	Subtract
"in all"	Add
"share"	Divide

Quiz Displays

Some teachers give quizzes infrequently; others give them at least once weekly. I gave short quizzes fairly often. Since I liked to spotlight kids

Chapter 2: Physical Classroom

who do well, I always had several small bulletin boards of top scores. For many of my small quizzes, I used small paper (or loose-leaf cut in half length-wise), so these displays could be small. I changed the work at least every other week. I generally had quiz displays for the following subjects:
• Vocabulary/Spelling
• Math
• Science/Social Studies
• Miscellaneous

I posted only the top grades on the Quiz Displays. Generally, this meant all "A" and "B" grades, or approximately 40% of students' quizzes. There are teachers who disagree with posting only top grades; these teachers feel that it is unkind and/or non-supportive for the students whose papers are not posted. I found that, by having numerous Quiz Displays (as well as other displays), all kids regularly had work acknowledged and posted.

Schedule – Door and Inside
All teachers with their own rooms should post a weekly schedule inside their classroom and on the outside of the door.

Door Schedule: The purpose of the schedule hanging on the outside of the door is to let any visitor – another teacher, administrator, visiting official, parent, etc. – know where the class is at any given time. Some teachers create a small wheel with various school locations (cafeteria, library, computer room, etc.) listed on the edge and an arrow in the middle that can be moved to indicate where the class is at different times. These things look sharp, but they do not work as well as one hopes: it is easy to forget to move the arrow, the arrow can fall off, etc. I recommend making a small chart of the weekly schedule (on a 5x7 inch index card with construction paper backing). Include subjects, lunch, etc. and all activities and room numbers. When your class is somewhere unexpected, and not on the calendar (like in the auditorium, practicing for a play), post a sticky-note on the schedule: "Class 3-309 is in the auditorium practicing for our play." If your class' schedule changes entirely, which happens at least once during the year, it's quite easy to make a new chart.

Inside Classroom: The purpose of the inside-classroom schedule is to let the students know what the schedule is each day. Since it is for the students, it should be large and colorful. This schedule must include: all subjects, periods, start & end-times, room numbers, and teacher names. Draw the calendar on a piece of poster board with a small key (green is math, blue is reading, orange is lunch, etc.). I recommend not making this chart until the third or fourth week of school, because schedules may not be fixed until then. My students really liked the class schedule; they liked being able to check for themselves what was happening, when they had different subjects, etc. Checking the schedule makes kids more resourceful and encourages them to think for themselves. It also reduces a lot of silly, repetitive questions. Even though most kindergarteners and 1st graders may not be able to "read" a complicated schedule, they can be taught to recognize the colors and the patterns.

Student Jobs

Most teachers have a set of classroom tasks that they assign to students. These should be posted, so they are clearly visible to you, the students, and any visitor.

At the top of the Student Jobs display, post the words "Student Jobs" in bright cut-out letters of oak-tag or construction paper. On a small (3x5) index card, write the name of each job, and frame it with a quarter-sheet of construction paper. Affix those to the wall, and below them, stick the peel-back adhesive hooks, leaving enough space between to accommodate the hanging name-tags. Write each kid's name on one of the name tags. At the bottom of this display, post a small chart (8½ x 11 sheet of graph paper on a backing of construction paper) with the names of all students and all the jobs. Once a kid has a certain job, mark it (so that kid doesn't get the same job until all children have had a chance). By the time the middle of the year comes along, you will not remember who has done what, and you want all kids to have a chance at each job (see Student Jobs).

Vocabulary/Spelling List

The vocabulary or spelling words for the week should always be clearly visible, for reference and reinforcement. Write the week's words on a half-sheet of newsprint or chart paper. Tape it to the wall where all kids can see the words from their seats. Above the list, with bright construction paper, create a title: "Class 3-309's Weekly Words." Each week, you replace the newsprint with a new half-sheet. I always saved the newsprint lists; they're great for cumulative activities later in the year (see Vocabulary/Spelling Words).

Door-Decorating (for Classroom Teachers)

The single-most important way to prepare the room for kids is to get their names on the door. This tells them that the teacher knows who they are and wants them there. You want to engender in the students a sense that the classroom is "theirs," that this is a place they belong, and it is a place for them to feel secure and comfortable.

For the classroom door, you need a class set of pieces of paper or oak-tag in some kind of shape. You can cut them out from construction paper yourself, but this is time-consuming. Your first year in the classroom, you've got way too much preparation to do to take the time to cut and trim 32 little yellow construction-paper buses.

Many teacher supply stores have shapes for various purposes: buses, apples, schoolhouses, etc. These are cute, but items from teacher stores are (generally) over-priced. Instead, I went to a large office supply store. In the section for shop-owners, there were packages of neon circle-stars, on which merchants could write price specials. These stars are approximately 3.5 inches in diameter and come in packages of 40+. Write the first name of every student on a shape (with last initials where there are duplicate first names). Then cut words out from bright colored paper (or neon oak-tag), something like "Class 3-309 reaches for the stars" or "Class 3-309 is off to a BRIGHT start." If you decide to use teacher-store pre-cut shapes, you might cut out the words: (for apples) "Class 3-309 is a great bunch!" or (for buses) "Class 3-309 is zooming to a great year."

"Everyone tells me my roster is going to change!"
Rosters can change in many schools throughout the first few weeks of school. This is especially true in areas where there is a lot of mobility (like densely-populated urban areas); it is less true in established and wealthier suburbs, though there are often some shifts. There are kids whose names appear on your roster but who will not show up and there are kids whose names are not on your roster who will be in your class. Some veteran teachers may tell you not to prepare name lists or items because of the uncertainty regarding final class rosters. These teachers will tell you that you should not waste your time and money on names until you know for sure who your students are. In all cases except the door, I agree. I do not make homework charts, book-report folders, or laminated anything. About the door, however, I feel differently and strongly: kids need to feel you expect and welcome them, and the cost of a dozen neon stars is not great.

Since your class roster *may* during the first month of school, you should expect to make changes to the door decoration. This means you will need extra door shapes. Add apples as the administration adds students. When a child is moved to another class, give him his apple as you wish him luck with the new teacher. When you re-decorate your door in October, save the stars or buses. I usually put them up, later in the year, around the chalkboard or as trim on a bulletin board. The kids always loved seeing their "welcome" stars again.

<u>For Out-of-Classroom Teachers (with their own rooms)</u>
Many of these suggestions for displays are applicable for the out-of-classroom teacher as well as the classroom teacher. Some, of course, are not. Out-of-classroom teachers are less likely to have the need for displays for subjects other than their own. In addition, an out-of-classroom teacher sees many children and may not be able to display work from all students. Out-of-classroom teachers with their own rooms should have at least the following displays:
- Grade/Class Display: Create a display for each grade or class that you see – list of names, schedule, topics being worked on, etc. These class displays will be limited by available wall-space.
- Behavior management system (see Point Chart)
- Superstars: Exemplary samples of student or class work and projects
- Words/Terms: A display of words and their definitions, specific to the specific subject(s) or from materials covered

<u>Door Decoration for Out-of-Classroom Teachers (with their own rooms)</u>
Out-of-Classroom teachers typically see many students and cannot list every one on their door. These teachers can list the *classes* that they see. You may use the same kind of shapes as recommended above – or you can use shapes that have to do with your subject (pencils for a writing teacher, paintbrushes or pallets for an art teacher, leaves for a science teacher, half notes or instruments for a music teacher, etc). Write the name of each class on the shapes. As a matter of preference, I avoid using the teachers' names; I prefer the official class names ("Class 3-410" rather than "Ms. D's Class"). Come up with a similarly clever line to accompany the shapes. A writing teacher might display:
- Writing Rocks!
- Move over, Shakespeare!
- Writing is the Key!

Inside the room, make a chart or bulletin board of all the classes that you see. Across the top, label it: "Ms. McGown's (your name) Musical Masters." Then have a class list of each class below. Back each one with a sheet of different colored construction paper. Even though the classes may change and shift (this happens a lot the first few weeks of school); and even if your schedule changes (as to which classes you see), the initial impression for the kids is one of welcome and preparation. That makes them feel good and safe. As a bonus, this kind of decoration is cheap and easy and changing the lists is quick.

Using a Ladder
Many classrooms, especially those in older buildings, have very high ceilings. This means there may be a lot of wall space that is rarely used. There are a few items which can be hung very high because they generally do not change during the year. Some of these items are:
• Class Rules
• Heading
• Birthday Chart
• Schedule
• Class Law (not until the second month of school); see "Routines and Procedures."

Each school has at least one ladder, and it will be in high-demand at the beginning of the year. The custodian staff is responsible for the ladder, and you will need to speak to the main custodian (or the custodian for your grade/floor) to arrange use. The ladder generally cannot be left in the room during school hours because of the danger of a child climbing and falling off. My recommendation is to wait a couple of weeks until things slack off a bit. In that time, you will decide what you want to hang where and which items you would like high up and out of the way. Arrange with the custodian to use the ladder; remember to place a Thank-You card in his/her box.

Chapter 2: Physical Classroom

Furniture

Each classroom should be outfitted with appropriate furniture before the first day of school, but this is not always the case. Classes and teachers may have been re-assigned over the summer such that an early childhood room is scheduled to have 5th graders and a third grade classroom from last year will have kindergarteners this year. There may have been a shift in population or enrollment so that a school that had five 4th grade classes last year will only have two, but the number of 1st grade classes has grown from three to five. Floors may have been re-finished, such that all furniture was moved to the cafeteria or the auditorium. These shifts often happen over the summer, when there is little or no staff available for returning moved furniture.

The desks and tables that a teacher finds in the classroom at the beginning of the term may not be appropriate for the expected students. For the upper grades or in a middle school, this is not so important, as most of the furniture in those settings is adult-sized. For the lower grades and in elementary school settings, however, the difference in furniture size is pretty dramatic. 2nd and 3rd grade students cannot sit in chairs designed for kindergarteners, and kindergarteners cannot work comfortably at desks designed for 4th grade students.

Some teachers come to school before the first day for the express purpose of securing the proper furniture for their classrooms. I recommend this. The important thing to know is that the correct-size furniture does exist in the school; it's just a matter of finding it. The custodian usually knows what furniture is in what classroom. Of course, if the chairs and desks for your students are on the fourth floor and your classroom is in the first, and there is no elevator, there's going to be a lot of huffing and puffing before the problem is solved. Many teachers bring older children or friends to help with this. This is a situation you are likely to encounter in subsequent years; treat your helpers well!

<u>Uniform Desks</u>
It is much easier to have students work in groups or pairs if the desks are the same size. You may not be able to find desks all the same size. If this is the case, group desks of the same size together. This allows students at one table or group to spread projects out. It also encourages group work and conferencing. Spare odd-sized desks should be used for one-desk stations – Time-Out, near the library, etc (see Routines & Procedures).

3

Administration & Faculty

Chapter 3: Administration & Faculty

About this Chapter

This chapter covers two non-teaching aspects of a teacher's life – school dynamics and administrative responsibilities. Because these things are non-pedagogical (ie, they are not about teaching and learning), many enthusiastic new teachers discount their significance. In addition, few teacher preparation programs address the issue of school or administrator dynamics. This is unfortunate; getting along with school employees, meeting administrative responsibilities, and working well with the team, is essential to the success of a new teacher. Most teachers who quit in the first year cite "administrative problems" as the primary reason they leave. It does not take much to start on the right foot and avoid many new teacher pitfalls.

This section also covers some of the administrative responsibilities that can take up so much of a teacher's time, especially a new teacher. These are things that, initially, may seem unimportant but are vital when it comes to writing report cards, meeting with parents, referring a child for special education, or making a case that a child should be in a higher class or eligible for special services. There are also the little details which ensure a classroom runs smoothly. In the beginning, new teachers are overwhelmed with so many things, and it seems so easy (even necessary) to postpone some of the paperwork and record-keeping. This is another mistake not to make! The effort and the extra time necessary to make sure all files and records are in proper order from the first day are well spent.

Chapter 3: Administration & Faculty

The Principal & Assistant Principal(s)

The administrators set the tone for the school. If the administration maintains high standards for students and faculty and establishes a sense of community, camaraderie, and professional accountability, the teachers feel respected and empowered. Teachers in schools run this way are more likely to enjoy coming to work, to feel effective, and to have a positive relationship with the administration. They are more likely to remain and build a professional career at that school. Unfortunately, some administrators run the school in less effective ways, often relying on orders, threats, and intimidation. In such schools, decisions are made by two or three individuals, generally none of whom are classroom teachers. This management style frustrates teachers as it ignores and dismisses their professional experience. It also dis-empowers them, as it does not give them a role in school direction and decisions. There tends to be high turnover in such schools.

The fact is that new teachers are often surprised by the environment they find themselves in. A new teacher, interviewing for his/her first position will do all that s/he can to find out about the school, the administrative style of the principal or assistant principals, teacher retention rates, the culture of the faculty, and the attitude toward and the support for new teachers. But this research will not be fail-safe: the person who interviews new teachers has a specific job, and that is to staff vacancies in the school. S/he may not share information that paints a negative picture of the school, staff, or faculty. It is in the best interest of the interviewing teacher to be every careful, and very thorough, in all interview situations. The interviewing teacher should visit the school, speak to other teachers, and try to get a "sense" of the school and the teacher attitudes. The interviewing teacher should also seek out new teachers in the building, as they will be good resources to determine the kind of outreach and support that is offered to new teachers.

Whatever the school situation, the new teacher is going to have to find a way to survive and thrive at the school, and to help his/her students to do the same. Maintaining positive relationships with the administration and with the faculty will be essential in doing this.

In some schools, the principal knows every teacher, and speaks to each one daily. In other schools, the principal is somewhat isolated, focusing on management and administrative issues, rather than with instructional issues and the teaching faculty. In still other schools, there is no direct link between the teachers and the administrator. In these schools, teachers answer to an AP or supervisor and rarely interact with the principal. The second and third of these scenarios are frustrating to teachers, but they are quite common. New teachers must keep in mind that, no matter how the principal addresses them, nor how s/he delegates power and authority, the principal *is* the ultimate boss and supervisor of every teacher in the school. Teachers must treat the principal with respect. Greet the principal every day, every time you see him/her, using Mr. or Ms. (do not use first names, unless specifically instructed by the principal, *regardless* of what other staff members do). Not all principals respond in kind; do not take this as a personal insult.

Assistant Principals and Supervisors
Teachers generally work most closely with the immediate supervisor, who may be an AP or a staff developer. The relationships between a teacher and supervisor can be either the most rewarding and helpful or the most contentious and counter-productive. The supervisor is the person responsible for observing teachers, offering feedback on their performance to them and to the principal, and submitting final evaluations. This person is also usually supposed to offer professional guidance and development opportunities. Where these relationships work, they really work. Where they don't, they can be very difficult. As stated previously, the best things a new teacher can do is to be professional and pleasant. If the AP or supervisor turns out to be unpleasant or un-supportive, there is little the teacher can do. Smile, say thank you, and walk away.

Other Teachers

One of the biggest challenges for new teachers, after classroom management, is navigating the dynamics of the school – consisting of the faculty, support staff, and administration. A teacher's successes and failures will be greatly affected by other teachers in the school. The greatest support comes, generally not from designated staff developers, but from the successful old-timer down the hall. The shoulder the new teacher cries on will usually belong not to the supervisor but to an understanding teacher who's "been there." New teachers often feel isolated, and it is the other new teachers in the building who become the lifeline for the inexperienced teacher. When new teachers are asked what made them stick it out their difficult first year, most cite the informal support system of other teachers.

Make no decisions about other teachers, staff members, or administrators in the beginning of the year. Just as many teachers feel they "shouldn't smile until Christmas," many administrators and faculty members start the year more formally, maintaining a distance between themselves and others. It may take several weeks, or even months, for certain faculty members to relax with one another. This can go both ways. The friend you thought you had in the office may turn out to be artificial and unfriendly, and the meanie you expected to hate all year has offered more practical help and support than you could have imagined. The person who is most welcoming can be the staff malcontent, whose association is not going to do you any good in the long run. Just like the kids, it takes adults a while to show their true colors. Wait this time out before making any sure alliances. As in any new situation, keep your mouth shut and smile – at everyone – until you get a sense of the "lay of the land."

<u>The Teachers' Lounge</u>
As in any work situation, there will be politics, clashing personalities, and "history" among different members of the faculty and staff. In addition, every work environment has a coterie of gossips who complain, undermine good effort, and malign colleagues. Schools are no different. Much of this unproductive and divisive chatter happens in the teacher's lounge. It is hard to avoid the teachers' lounge entirely – the microwave is usually in there, as is the coffee machine, and sometimes teachers' magazine and books. In addition, the lounge may be the only place where a teacher can eat lunch or grade papers. But be careful! If you find yourself in the lounge when the conversation has taken a negative,

gossipy turn, or if you hear that an absent staff member is being discussed, or a child is being spoken about inappropriately, excuse yourself. The person being discussed will learn you were in the lounge at the time and the assumption will be that you participated. It is in the best interest of the new teacher to steer clear of these conversations. As a general rule, the teachers' lounge is where people congregate to gossip; whenever possible, avoid it.

Chapter 3: Administration & Faculty

Testing

The culture of education, to a large extent, has become a culture of testing. The emphasis in many schools and districts has shifted to test scores rather than performance or achievement. Testing is what the media covers. The emphasis is specifically on standardized tests, and children as young as six and seven may have to sit for one hour exams (or longer!) at several points during the year. Depending on the city, state, and grade, students sometimes face four or five two-hour exams in a single year. Schools and administrators are judged by the scores their students earn on standardized tests. In addition, coveted spots in magnet schools, gifted programs, etc are doled out to the highest scoring students. This creates a great deal of anxiety throughout the school community, including students and parents, which translates into an inconceivable degree of pressure on teachers to work to ensure that students score as well as possible.

The emphasis becomes not whether kids learn the curriculum but on how well they do on the tests. The test scores, unfortunately, do not necessarily indicate real learning; they indicate the degree to which students have learned to decipher questions, eliminate answers, and make good guesses – ie, how well they take tests. Teachers, new and old, feel frustrated by the focus on test scores rather than on the intellectual growth of the students. They feel pressured to "teach to the test."

The fact is that there is little a teacher can do to change the testing policy of the school, district, city, or state. Furthermore, there *are* rewards for high scores; students who score well are more likely to have access to special programs and scholarships. In some cases, there is funding or, or alternative rewards, available to schools that raise their students' scores or maintain high scores. A teacher who de-emphasizes testing and test preparation strategies is making a statement at the *expense* of the students, and possibly the expense of the school. If the students are in a low-performing school or district, this can be especially devastating. Your classroom is not where you should make a political statement; it is where you need to do as much and as possible to benefit your students. If testing is a focus at your school, you must respect and support it.

In the weeks and months leading up to testing periods, there is an incredible amount of stress placed on teachers to increase student scores. Much of the ordinary curriculum, textbooks, supplemental materials, and usual activities are put aside, for several weeks, or several months, as various test-preparation booklets and exercises are implemented. This is often a difficult time in schools to begin with – the weather has gotten nicer, everyone has been cooped up inside for months, spring is beckoning, and there's an element of cabin fever to all classrooms. Rather than being able to "loosen up," teachers must insist that students focus on testing. To make matters even worse, test preparation materials are often un-engaging and dry. Surviving the first season of test prep is one of the biggest challenges for new teachers.

Strategies for Coping with the Testing Season
There is an element of "grin and bear it" about the testing season. Many teachers view test preparation as something to be survived: It cannot be changed, so why fight it? While this may be true, it is also defeatist. Some districts prioritize testing such that the tested grades spend two or three months on test preparation activities. That is more than a quarter of the school-year. It is a disservice to the students to only "grin and bear" this period. Additionally, kids will pick up on the attitude the teacher has about testing and test preparation, and they may adopt the same attitude. It is their lives that can be affected by the test scores; it is only fair to "do the right thing."

The way a class responds to testing, in addition to how they ultimately score, can be greatly affected by how well the teacher prepares them. These are some of my recommendations:
• Review old tests as early in the year as possible. Adopt questioning strategies of the tests – at least some of the time – that mirror the style of the tests.
• Do not wait until the administration decides it is time to begin test preparation. Ask a senior teacher for test prep material. Include practice sessions every week.
• Give many quizzes and tests during the year. For some, use bubble-in sheets (many schools have left-over standardized test forms). Make sure to practice formal test-taking procedures (see Routines & Procedures).
• Do not complain about tests or test preparation. Do not tell the kids that you hate tests or that some people just "do poorly" on tests. Under no circumstances, say that you always did poorly on tests.
• Present tests as positively as you can and insist that everyone has the ability to test well.
• For the day of testing, emphasize enough sleep, proper breakfast, and an early arrival.

Chapter 3: Administration & Faculty

Testing & Out-of-Classroom Teachers

Testing pressure is primarily felt by classroom teachers, as they are the ones who are held most accountable for student scores. Out-of-classroom teachers should, however, expect to be involved with test preparation activities. In some cases, they will be asked to put their own program or curriculum aside in favor of practicing test strategies for one or two months. This is most likely for out-of-classroom teachers who teach the tested subject areas or related subjects (math teachers, creative writing teachers, etc.). New out-of-classroom teachers should speak to experienced out-of-classroom teachers to learn when and how testing is likely to them and their programs.

Tracking

Tracking refers to the practice of placing students into classes according to their academic performance, often determined by scores on standardized tests. The theory behind this is that test scores reflect ability and aptitude. By grouping similarly-abled students together, the teacher can concentrate on one level of instruction. This means that higher-level students are not held back by slower classmates, and lower-performing students can get more specialized instruction. Schools that track students have "top" classes, "middle" classes, and "bottom" classes. Other common tracking terms are "Gifted," "Resource" (for both high-level and low-level students), and "TAG" (gifted and talented). Tracking is most prevalent in school districts which emphasize standardized test scores. This is because tracking students allows the school to structure test preparation with the most emphasis on the classes that are most likely to raise the school's overall scores.

Tracking sounds like the "heterogeneous" and "homogeneous" grouping that teachers often use in their classrooms, where heterogeneous groups are mixed-level groups and homogeneous groups are same-level groups. It is not the same thing. Individual teachers group children for specific learning goals throughout the teaching day. But these groupings – pairs, triads, teams – change. Kids get to work with all different kids during the day – with those of higher abilities, lower abilities, and those of similar abilities. A kid is not "trapped" into one group because of his/her ability.

The reality of tracking in a school is that the "bottom" classes often get ignored. The lowest-performing students are not expected to perform well on the tests, so little effort may be spent on them. Bottom classes typically receive the newest or weakest teachers. In addition, scores alone rarely determine a child's placement. Behavior factors into class placement. A bright child who is disruptive is not going to get a place in one of the top classes, because s/he may impede the progress of the other students (and potentially impact the overall test scores of that class). This means that many behavior "problems" may be grouped together, often in a "bottom" class. Having all the behavior "problems" in one class helps to ensure that these students cannot bother the other students who may score well. It also makes for a very difficult year for that teacher, especially so if that teacher is new (which is often the case).

As a policy, tracking is in disfavor. Few school districts will admit to tracking students. Many school districts, however, do track students even if they do not do it openly. This means that it is very likely you may work in a school that tracks students. Furthermore, as a new teacher, it is likely that you will receive a "bottom" class (I did and nearly every teacher I know did when s/he was new).

Regardless of the levels of the students in the class, do not discuss these labels with the students. Treat all students as bright, capable, and able to learn. If you have the bottom class, treat them as if they are a "top" class. Speak to them intelligently; convey your confidence in them and their abilities; hold them to high expectations for themselves and their peers. If you receive a middle or top class, do not allow them to think they are better than the students in any other class. Keep in mind that other teachers will undermine your efforts, praising a top class and criticizing (and putting down) a bottom one.

Chapter 3: Administration & Faculty

Anecdotals

In teacher/school speak, an "anecdotal" is a written account describing incidences of exceptional student behavior, positive or negative. Anecdotals are generally kept on students who consistently exhibit negative behaviors. These negative behaviors may include a spectrum of school issues – poor performance, low participation, incidences of violence, social isolation, etc. Anecdotals usually form part of an administrative evaluation or review. Written records are necessary to get special services for a child (counseling, physical therapy, special education, etc.), and anecdotals may form an important part of such a review. Written records are also invaluable during parent-teacher conferences, when a teacher must "prove" that a child is not doing well or behaving poorly. Such records are also required for discipline measures, including suspensions or expulsions.

Schools rarely mandate what form an anecdotal must take. What is important is that teachers keep written records of all extraordinary events within the classroom and/or involving the students. All such written records should be dated with the time indicated. This is to create a paper trail – to protect the teacher as well as to provide information on the development of a student.

The easiest option is to maintain a notebook in which you record all outstanding events, from day one. The notebook will then serve as a chronological record of all episodes in your classroom. If one child proves to need more careful supervision and possible intervention, you can start another notebook just for him/her. Make sure to keep these notebooks secure.

Anecdotals should include measurable, observable behaviors. Writing "Tom was disruptive during math class" is virtually meaningless; a much better record is "Tommy sat in the corner singing during the math lesson," or "Tommy kept slamming other students' books shut during math." Since an interim intervention may involve a visit from the school social worker or guidance counselor, it is best if that person knows the kind of behaviors that are causing so much trouble within your classroom.

The following are sample anecdotals for a single third-grade student:

- 10/26 1:40 Student is jumping and pushing other children on stairwell; when I ask him to stop, he says another child started it.
- 10/26 1:45 Student won't take out homework notebook to copy homework. I ask him to do so, and he responds "You can't make me; you're not my mother." I tell him that I'm his teacher and he must copy his homework.
- 10/26 1:50 Student yells at other child "Stop staring at me"; student then moves his desk away from the group.
- 10/27 9:30 Student refuses to take out homework notebook for me to check it. I tell him that he'll never be able to win a homework race if he doesn't do the homework. He runs into the closet where he remains for 15 minutes.
- 10/27 9:45 Student will not come to the rug area for a read-aloud.
- 10/27 10:05 When I hand out puzzles for classwork, Student rips up paper.

Anecdotals must be recorded almost immediately after the event. This is for the purpose of accuracy (fairness). No matter how good our memory, small details will slip away quickly. If nothing else, make a quick notation in the plan-book at the moment of the event, and expand on it later in the day.

4

Classroom Management

Chapter 4: Classroom Management

About this Chapter

Classroom management refers to all the systems, routines, philosophies, and procedures that make a teacher effective. It refers to all the elements that make a classroom run well. Good classroom management improves attitudes, builds community, generates enthusiasm and loyalty, and it significantly increases learning. Classroom Management is also one of the few things under the full control of the teacher.

It is the *responsibility* of the teacher to manage his or her classroom. It is the expectation of parents and the rights of students to have a classroom that is a safe, inviting, well-organized place, where different kids can be heard and their opinions respected, and where engaged teaching and learning take place. Creating such a learning environment is not an easy task; it takes true commitment, vigilance, and compassion. Classroom management is, however, part of the *job* of being a teacher. A teacher who does not manage a classroom well is not doing the job for which s/he was hired. In addition, such a teacher will be frustrated with teaching almost from the start. Students in that room, regardless of intelligence, aptitude or prior achievement, will fail to complete assignments, refuse to cooperate or help one another, forget notes and papers, run through the halls, quibble with neighbors, and exhibit a thousand other irritating and counter-productive behaviors. And the fact is, students in poorly-managed classrooms, have been *given permission for these behaviors by their teacher.*

Another way of saying this is: "Teachers get the classrooms they deserve."

Classroom Management is not a skill that is separate from instruction. Classroom Management is not something a teacher "does" once, or occasionally, or for a short while, and then stops. A good teacher weaves classroom management techniques and practices into all lessons, assignments, activities, and games. Effective classroom management is on-going; it is part of *everything* a good teacher does. This whole book is about Classroom Management, even though this is the only chapter that gets the title.

Despite the importance of effective classroom management, few teacher training programs devote much time to teaching the skills and techniques of effective management. There seems to be a feeling that classroom management is not worthy of attention, that it is too practical, too "nuts

Chapter 4: Classroom Management

and bolts." Many teacher educators seem to criticize any emphasis on the mundane practicalities of teaching, as if this somehow detracts from the "art" of teaching. What this means, in practice, is that new teachers are routinely sent into classrooms unprepared to deal with the many challenges that await. These new teachers have few "tools," spotty information about management strategies, and rarely a clear idea of what classroom management means and requires – what classroom management "looks like." New teachers, therefore, often have very little chance of being successful.

An effective classroom management strategy will have the following four characteristics:

Effective classroom management must reflect <u>teacher confidence</u>: The teacher must believe that s/he can manage the classroom and control behavior. S/he must believe that the elements of the management systems are important and that the management systems will work. Teachers must act confidently even when they are new and, quite probably, not confident. Kids can sense "hesitancy" a mile away, and they tend to push and test the overly-hesitant and under-confident teachers. Whatever classroom management systems a teacher chooses, s/he must study them, internalize them, and stand by them.

Effective classroom management must involve <u>student buy-in</u>: Students must believe that the classroom management systems implemented are good. It is the teacher's job to ensure this; the teacher must explain why s/he is covering certain rules, consequences, and rewards. The teacher must discuss how the management systems will contribute to a comfortable environment where students will learn and have fun. S/he must invite questions and response from the students about the rules and systems. The teacher must actively work to ensure that students accept and "buy in" to the classroom systems.

Effective classroom management must be <u>positive</u> (not negative or punitive): Positive reinforcement trumps negative reinforcement every time. Kids should be doing the "right thing," either because it is the right thing to do or to earn privileges, rather than to avoid punishment. Negative reinforcement and "punishment" are seductive, because they get response immediately. Their effects, however, are rarely lasting. Positive reinforcement is a part of all good classrooms.

Chapter 4: Classroom Management

Effective classroom management must be <u>consistent and predictable</u>: Any system a teacher uses must be consistent and predictable; every student should know exactly what will happen, given specific circumstances or behaviors, and they should know the same thing will happen, regardless of the specifics of time or individual. Teachers must use their classroom management systems every minute of every period of every day (at least in the beginning of the year). They must make sure to reference the systems, the rules, the rationales, and the accompanying rewards regularly. Students should know what behaviors are desirable (and why) and how they will be encouraged and rewarded.

Any good system takes some time to work well. Few systems work well from the very start. Many new teachers make the mistake of "giving up" on a system if it does not work the first day or week. These same teachers will try system after system, implementing each for only a few days or a week, and then tossing it out. A good system needs time and practice before it becomes habit – for both the teacher *and* the students. It is like a good diet; you don't lose all 15 pounds the first week. Instead, you lose weight slowly and healthfully over time, providing you follow a sensible regime. Both diets and classroom management systems work over time. An intelligent, deliberate approach may not work the first time, the second, the third, or even the fourth, but if consistently implemented, it will work the fifth.

No two days of teaching – or in life – are the same. Likewise, no effective management system is going to work the same way everyday either. Continuing the diet analogy, there are times when you are eating healthfully and working out, but you stop losing weight, and this is discouraging. Rather than giving up, you have to continue doing what you *know* makes sense and works (despite being frustrated *now*), and you will start losing weight again. In the classroom, when a system stops working, or stops working well, the correct move is not to toss it out, but rather, to wait it out. Keep on doing what you have been doing, and what you know to be good practice. The order and the consistency of a good strategy will triumph.

A new teacher's expectations are often unrealistic. 32 children are never absolutely silent. A group of children will never all be doing exactly the correct thing at exactly the same moment. A new teacher may think that a classroom management system is not working because the class is not silent or "perfect." No class is ever perfect; no-one is ever perfect (What is perfect, anyway?). Stand back and look at the group: there may be a relatively high level of noise in the room, but the class may be focused. A few kids may be talking and laughing, but they may also happen to be cooperating on a group project or helping a neighbor find the correct page of the text. New teachers are often unable to "see the forest for the trees"; they get caught up in the noise or motion level and fail to notice that the kids are engaged and performing well. Teachers need to recognize "productive noise." They also must understand that teaching is not a quiet job. New teachers are categorically unable to gauge their performance and effectiveness. It takes time for new teachers to realize good things are happening, and that they are happening, in large part, because of the classroom management system.

Classroom management presents countless challenges to new teachers. Since they are unlikely to have taken a course in classroom management, or had it emphasized during their teacher preparation courses, new teachers are likely to be ill-prepared to handle many of the logistics of teaching. This book and chapter will not address the entirely of this problem; the strategies outlined will, however, give teachers great starting points to managing a classroom effectively.

Chapter 4: Classroom Management

"Don't Smile Until Christmas!"

All new teachers are given this advice – "Don't smile until Christmas!" No-one understands what this warning means, so few heed it. What *does* "Don't smile until Christmas" mean? Are you really not supposed to smile until Christmas? At all? How can you not smile for four months? What about when you're reading aloud from a favorite book and you come to a funny part? What if a kid tells a really good joke? And, how do you get through a day without a single smile? Is that reasonable? Can anyone *do* that?

"Don't smile until Christmas" isn't really about smiling at all; it's about attitude. "Don't smile until Christmas" is about being consistent and firm from the very first day of school. Mentors and teacher educators give the advice, "Don't smile until Christmas" to help prevent new teachers from making the error of being too lenient. New teachers, worried that they will not be accepted or liked, often hesitate to be strong and authoritative. They equate being nice or nurturing with not being strict. This is unfortunate, because nice and strict *do* go together in effective teachers. Rather than liking the teacher for his/her laxity, students lose respect and take advantage of "soft" teachers. Since teachers cannot start the year over, they should err on the side of firmness. A teacher can always back off on certain rules and consequences, but it is very difficult to implement new procedures and classroom norms once the year has started and bad habits have been established.

When questioned about favorite teachers, kids and adults almost always offer that the favorite teacher was also very strict. Some will offer that they recall being afraid of or intimidated by this teacher at the start of the year or term. Think back to your own school years: Who was a favorite teacher? Try to recall your first impressions of him or her. Did s/he seem intimidating? Were you (perhaps just a little) afraid? Was that teacher a push-over? As time went on, you found the teacher consistently strict; was this a bad thing? What was the relationship for you between affection and respect for that teacher?

It is worthwhile taking a moment to think about the teachers who *were* pushovers. They may have been, or seemed, really nice, right from the start. ;They probably were not very strict. Most likely, they did not seem intimidating either. How did the relationship of affection and respect play out for you with that teacher?

Chapter 4: Classroom Management

<u>Smile Every Morning</u>

Smile at your students *every* morning when you first see them. Yours may be the first smile they have seen that day. For some kids, it may be one of few. No matter what is going on in your life, no matter how tired or ill you may feel, no matter how difficult the class was yesterday, the students should all see a warm, welcoming smile on your face every morning. Your smile needs to tell the students that you're glad to see them and that they are wanted. If you are really tired, think like an actor, get into character (*"It's show-time!"*), and go smile at your kids.

Chapter 4: Classroom Management

Honeymoon Period

Most teachers speak of a "honeymoon period" at the start of a school-year. This period does exist. The honeymoon period in a classroom is not unlike the honeymoon period in any new relationship. During a honeymoon period, everyone is on his/her best behavior. New couples bring flowers to one another and never leave the cap off the toothpaste. During this time also, the individuals involved are getting to know one another. They are observing one another; they are also "testing" one another, determining (subconsciously) what the limits are. In classrooms, the same thing is happening. Both the teacher and the students are observing one another, getting to know one another, and determining limits.

During the honeymoon period, students tend to behave better than they will as the year progresses. This is not only true of students; it is true of everyone (think of how you conduct yourself in the first few weeks on a job compared to your behavior after a year). This "artificially" good behavior can be a surprise to new teachers. They often respond after the first week or so with: "Gosh, my kids are pretty good," or, "My behavior management system is really effective" or worse, "I guess I don't really have to worry about classroom management." Though this may be true, it is more likely that you are in the honeymoon period. New teachers should expect, sometime between the fourth and sixth week of school, students to start testing limits and pushing buttons (both of the teacher and of other students). It is about this time, as well, that teachers, especially new teachers, tend to start feeling the exhaustion of the first month of school.

When this first happens, the reflex reaction, especially for new teachers, is to get angry. They will assume that the classroom management methods do not work; they assume that the kids hate them; and they think they are failing. While all of this could be true (though unlikely), it is far more likely that the honeymoon period has ended. *It is worth noting that mid-October (roughly six weeks into the new year in many American schools), about when the honeymoon period ends, is when many new teachers quit.*

> ➤ This is due to a combination of the "shock" of the end of the honeymoon period and the exhaustion of the first month of teaching.

Chapter 4: Classroom Management

In the face of all these doubts, many new teachers panic. If they don't quit (and most do not), they throw out well-thought-out systems and race to change to "better" ones, going through one system after another without careful thought or planning. It is important *not* to do this; instead, try to take a breath, re-focus, and maintain routines. Do not get harsher or more strict; rather, stick with the established routines, remain as calm as possible, be consistent, and let the minor infractions slide. This is difficult, because in the period after the honeymoon, you will be tested in ways you never imagined. Successful teachers are those who stick to their systems, concentrate on not getting frazzled, and remain focused.

Chapter 4: Classroom Management

Student Investment

Students need to be invested in their education and in their classrooms. Kids must believe that you have their best interests at heart and that everything you do is about them and their education. This includes the various management strategies and routines that are part of a well-functioning classroom. Kids respond better to meaningful discipline – rules and routines they understand – than they do to rules prescribed or dictated with no explanation.

Teachers must explain exactly what they expect the students to do and how they expect the students to behave ("When we line up, everyone should be facing forward, with their hands at their sides"). Teachers also need to discuss the rationale behind these requests and expectations ("When we are quiet in the halls, we get where we want more quickly and we do not disturb other classes"). Give the kids words to describe good practices and their behavior and let them add comments or ask questions ("Maria is very *generous* with her supplies"). Encourage students to take part in the monitoring and praising of one another's behavior. Develop certain words or phrases for specific situations that the kids may repeat ("Leave spaces for size places"). Kids enjoy choral participation, even the older ones, and it helps them to remember the words or phrases and the actions they represent. As the year goes on, the kids will reinforce these behaviors with one another. This makes the teacher's job much easier, and the kids will develop "ownership" of behaviors and routines within the classroom.

Generating Class Rules

On the first day or two of school, most classroom teachers plan an activity during which they generate "with" their students a list of rules for their classroom. Is this a genuine activity? We teachers know exactly what rules we want in our classrooms; and we know what rules we will post (if we choose to post rules). Yet we schedule valuable time for this activity, regardless of its worthiness. We do this because we think we should. We think this activity will build student ownership of the rules. Hogwash! The rules generated are nearly identical with the rules in every other classroom, and they are the same as the prior year. We know this and the kids know it. The artifice of this activity has always irritated me, in addition to the loss of valuable teaching time.

Chapter 4: Classroom Management

Far better: Plan a discussion with the students about your (4-5) classroom rules. Discuss with the kids why these rules are important. Facilitate a discussion about how these rules help the classroom function and how we feel when we are in a comfortable and orderly place. Invite the students to describe what it "looks like" when a person is following the rules and when a person is not. Post the rules or don't; this is your preference and the practice within the school.

Chapter 4: Classroom Management

The Point Chart

There are many good systems for managing behavior in a classroom. The Point Chart is my favorite, because it is easy. It does not require any supplies and it does not interfere with the flow of a lesson or of the school-day. I used the Point Chart during the years I was a teacher for different ages, subjects, and populations – as a classroom teacher, an out-of-classroom teacher, as an ESL teacher, as a push-in teacher, for 1st through 7th grades, for "top" and "bottom" classes, and for regular and special education students. I found it reliably easy to implement and well-received by learners of all ages.

New teachers are often told that they need to find a management system that agrees with their teaching personality and style. Unfortunately, new teachers have not been in a classroom yet, so they do not know what their teaching style is, and they have not yet developed a "teacher personality." That takes time. I have never understood what veteran teachers think new teachers ought to do, in terms of classroom and behavior management, while waiting for their teacher personality to emerge. I recommend using the Point Chart, as a good starting point because it works.

<u>To Start</u>
Draw a grid on the chalkboard, with as many columns as there are clusters or tables of students.

1	2	3	4	5

The Point Chart is designed for classrooms where kids are seated together in groups or tables. Group seating is standard in most elementary and middle or junior high schools these days. This is because such seating fosters cooperative/group learning. Many new teachers find group seating arrangements (as opposed to more traditional rows) difficult to manage. This *seems* true, initially, because of the greater chance of chatting and socializing. Group-seating, however, is ultimately

Chapter 4: Classroom Management

far easier to manage than individual desks or rows, once you get the hang of management by incorporating an effective system, such as the Point Chart.

The Point Chart is simply a chart on which the teacher records incidences of positive or targeted behavior. Positive behavior is all the good stuff you normally want from your students: completed assignments, attentiveness, participation in discussions, writing neatly, helping one another, etc. Targeted behaviors are specific things you ask of your students at specific times. Some behaviors are targeted for increase, like working together or lending a pencil; other behaviors are targeted for decrease, like interrupting or bothering a neighbor. Targeted behaviors generally have specific prompts: "Take out the Social Studies books and turn to page 67," or, "All desks should be cleared, hands folded on desks, and eyes on me," etc.

Using the Point Chart involves a lot of talking on the teacher's part, especially in the beginning. For the first few days, you will talk non-stop, regularly referencing the Point Chart. You will acknowledge every incidence of positive behavior as well as all targeted behaviors. Every targeted or positive behavior must be mentioned *explicitly*. It is easier for students to meet (or exceed) an expectation when that expectation is made clear. Though the students may be really bright and capable, you do not know what their classroom experiences have been like in the past. You do not know what was allowed, forbidden, overlooked, etc. If you explicitly tell the kids what you expect from them, they are more likely to perform to that expectation.

The teacher should draw the Point Chart on the chalkboard, or whiteboard, or easel, before the students enter the room on the first day of school. You will award points to any groups that exhibit positive and targeted behaviors. You will say things like:
• "Tables 2 and 4 walked in the room so quietly."
• "I love the way Table 2 and 3 got their notebooks out so quickly!"
• "Table 4 – you're all working so well together!"
• "Tables 1, 2, and 5 all tied in getting their math texts out."
• "Wow, everyone has their reading books open to the right page; every table gets a point!"

Each of the tables mentioned will get a point on the Point Chart. Mark the points as you praise the table; it is important to give immediate reinforcement (this is especially true in the beginning of the year and for younger students). Pause briefly after you mark points. This draws attention to the Point Chart, which is necessary in the beginning, as you are establishing its role in the classroom.

Never Take Away Points
The Point Chart uses positive reinforcement to eliminate negative behaviors. Rather than penalizing tables that exhibit negative behaviors, the other tables get rewarded for *not* exhibiting those behaviors.
• "Tables 2, 3, 4, 5 – I like the way you're remaining in your seats."
• "Table 4 is the quietest table in the room!"

The tables where the negative behavior is not exhibited get a point. If a student at one or more tables misbehaves, then the other tables get points. You never erase or take away points. This is very important; the Point Chart is a positive strategy, and it should be viewed positively by students. This will not happen if points are deducted. It does not sit right with students to have teachers take away points they have previously earned (why does talking now erase the fact that we un-packed quickly before?).

Teamwork
A main component of the Point Chart is teamwork. For a table to win points, the kids themselves are responsible for making sure that the other kids at their table are behaving and doing what is required. They get rewarded as a group, so they must work together to win. This is much more important than it sounds, because responsibility shifts from the teacher to the students. The teacher will spend a great deal of time setting this up in the beginning; ultimately, however, the teacher will spend very little time monitoring the misbehaviors in the classroom because the students will be monitoring one another. This shift allows the teacher to put his/her efforts where they are most needed – in teaching.

Teamwork is not intuitive for many kids, especially little ones. The teacher must explain, and model, good team behaviors. S/he must tell children how to encourage their classmates and how to cooperate and behave. One effective way to do this is to pretend to be a "good" kid and a "bad" kid. I would explain to the class that I was going to pretend to be a kid at a table where another kid started talking out of turn. "What could I do?" I would ask the class. I would pause and think for a moment. Then I'd burst out, "Shut up, Baby!" This would cause a round of excited (and focused) "Ooooooh's" because teachers do not say that kind of thing *and* because "shut up" is a forbidden phrase in school. I would ask the students if they thought my response was a good one. We would then talk about better options for responding to the talking child. I usually had several pairs of children role-play this scenario, using different responses to encourage good behavior among their peers. We would do this with a number of the more common table infractions (not turning to the correct page, not having materials out, poking or touching other kids, fiddling with things in one's desk, getting out of a seat, etc).

Point Chart Do's & Dont's

Do not give multiple points. One positive or targeted behavior gets one point. If you give double or triple points or the kids will always expect double or triple points. Giving multiple points does not increase the incidence of positive behaviors. And when the while class shines, give everyone a point. The kids love when you do this, and they never figure it out that every table getting a point is the same as no table getting a point. Don't enlighten them.

Never take points away. The kids have earned those points; even if they later misbehave (even two minutes later). Either give points to other tables for the bad behavior they are not exhibiting or walk away. It irritates kids to lose points they think of as "theirs." You do not want the Point Chart to be viewed as negative or as punishment (that *will* undermine its effectiveness).

Do not worry about giving too many points. It is not possible to give too many points. In the beginning of the year, each table may end up with more than 30 points per round (see below). The total number of points per round will decrease as the Point Chart "takes hold" and the kids respond to it. At different times during the year, however, when the class becomes less responsive or unruly (which happens periodically, often for a variety of reasons and circumstances), you will find yourself awarding more points, until the class calms down again. This is fine. The Point Chart is a tool; use it.

Tallying-Up

For the Point Chart to be effective, you must stop and tally the points regularly. The frequency of the tallying depends on the age of the students and the time of year. In the beginning of the year, you'll tally more frequently. For younger children, you will tally more frequently throughout much of the year. The following are some general guidelines:

Chapter 4: Classroom Management

Teachers using the Point Chart for 1st grade (and less mature 2nd grade classes) may find this age responds better to more frequent rewards. For these ages, I recommend tallying up three times everyday for at least the first month of school. You may then go down to two tallying rounds per day (one before lunch and one before afternoon dismissal).

Classroom teachers (for 2nd through 4th grades) should tally three times a day for the two weeks of the school year. Try to do this at "natural" breaks in the day, before lunch, before an out-of-classroom period, and upon dismissal. After the second week of school, tally-up twice per day, for an additional one or two week period. By the third or fourth week of school, tally up just once, at the end of the day. During the year, if you feel the children are getting looser and need more regular monitoring, start tallying twice per day for a week or two until they settle down.

Classroom Teachers with 5th grade and up start with tallying twice daily and go down to once per day within two weeks from the start of school.

Out-of-classroom teachers tally the Point Charts and give rewards at the end of every period.

Counting the points and acknowledging the winning table is positive reinforcement. This is not something that should be rushed or skipped. Kids, of all ages, look forward to counting the points and to "winning." Students should be encouraged to count-up the tally-points for their table. This reinforces math-concepts and keeps the class involved and focused on the Point Chart during tally time. Allow 2-3 minutes to tally the points and to acknowledging the winning table(s).

Rewards
"What do we get if we win?"
There is considerable debate on how and when to reward students, whether children should be rewarded at all in school, and on what kinds of things should make up classroom rewards. In this book, I am not engaging in this debate. I believe that a classroom management system that utilizes positive reinforcement and small rewards is a good thing. I understand and appreciate arguments against rewards systems, but a discussion of the pros and cons of rewards is beyond the scope of this book.

I believe token external rewards used well are beneficial to classroom communities. My reward of choice is stickers. I like stickers because they are intrinsically attractive to nearly all kids and because they are cheap. When buying stickers, I recommend choosing the cheapest, simplest stickers you can find. You will go through a zillion stickers during the year and you simply cannot afford fancy, glittery ones. In addition, fancy stickers do not achieve greater response than do the cheapest ones. The students *won't* behave any better because of the costlier reward. Furthermore, once kids are accustomed to fancier rewards, they will grow to expect them, and the children will never accept the smaller less-expensive stickers. If you find fancy stickers you cannot resist buying, do so and save them for special classroom occasions or gifts.

Where kids put their stickers is of some interest and worthy of discussion. Young children, you may find, like to put stickers on their noses. I discourage this (I am not sure why; I just do not like stickers on noses). Encourage students to "collect" stickers. I always suggested to my students that it would be cool to put all their stickers on a certain notebook. I would tell them that they would be able to keep track of the stickers this way, and they could compare their sticker collections with other students. This stops the stickers from being put on desks, the floor, and one another. The notebook collections also serve to reinforce the Point Chart, as kids will compare their stickers ("I have 2 of the pink penguins and 3 smiling bears!").

You can use stickers for the duration of the year. They do not lose their effectiveness, and they are easy to manage. For younger children (K through 3rd or 4th grades), there is no reason to change rewards. Some teachers of upper-grade students (4th or 5th grade and up), however, opt to use different rewards as the year progresses. One option is to have the tables save up points for a whole week. Members of the winning table can each take one item from your Goodie Can (see Odds & Ends). Some teachers invite the kids from the winning table to a weekly celebratory lunch in the classroom. They eat lunch in the classroom with the teacher rather than in the cafeteria. Kids can bring in music (teacher-approved), the teacher provides a special treat (chips or candy), and the group can play a board game together.

Dealing with the "Cool" Kids

Across the middle and upper grades (3rd and up) you will have a "cool" kid. This child will say that s/he does not care about the points or the stickers. This response can cause alarm for the new teacher. The key thing is not to flip out. For the most part, this child is simply testing the teacher. The following responses work well.

Ask the student if s/he has a younger sibling or cousin. Suggest that s/he take the sticker and give it to that little relative. Add, "Your mom will think you're really sweet for that." This allows the kid to accept the sticker and be cool. The student is probably not going to give the sticker away, but s/he has earned an "out" in front of the class. S/he retains her/ his coolness *and* gets the sticker. Everyone wins.

Say: "Oh, you don't want any stickers . . . okay . . . is there someone in this class who wants Kimberly's sticker when her table wins?" Every single kid will raise his/her hand, showing Kimberly that it is okay to want the stickers. Suggest that, when she wins, she should give the sticker to one of her classmates. Odds are she will not opt to give any stickers away.

When the student says s/he does not care about points or winning stickers, ignore the comment and walk away. In most cases, comments like these are just to test or push you, and the kid is looking for a response. The content of the comment is immaterial; the kid is just looking for a reaction. If the kid gets a reaction, s/he will make a similarly irritating comment at the next opportunity. If s/he does not get a response, s/he probably will not keep trying.

Regardless of what you use to counter this comment, do not argue with the student about the points or stickers, no matter what. If you feel you must discuss the issue, do it later, on a one-to-one basis (do not "take on" the child in front of classmates).

Special Education Note
The Point Chart is not consistent with certain theories about educating special-needs children, Special Education, and behavior modification. I have used the Point Chart successfully with these populations, and it works. If you are teaching special-needs children, however, I encourage you to speak to your administrators or supervisors and other Special Education teachers for advice on managing your classroom and appropriately modifying student behavior.

Chapter 4: Classroom Management

The Point Chart for Out-of-Classroom Teachers

Out-of-classroom teachers have a special challenge when it comes to management. This is because they do not have the same relationship with the students as a classroom or homeroom teacher does. They are not as likely to be able to reward the kids with special privileges because they do not have equal "access" to students. Nearly always, kids behave better for the classroom teacher than they do an out-of-classroom teacher. This is one of the reasons that some people do not like out-of-classroom teaching positions. It doesn't have to be this way, however, if you use the Point Chart.

Some people will say that a "visiting" teacher should use the same management system as does the classroom teacher. These people claim that a change in systems confuses students. I have never found this to be the case. Kids are surprisingly flexible; they know that different people in their lives have different requirements and rules; this does not bother them for a moment. Think about how effortlessly you transitioned from Mom's rules to Dad's rules to Grandma's rules. The management system one teacher uses can, therefore, be different from the system used by another teacher. It is important to remember that, when you are in a classroom, it is your classroom, even if you are not the primary teacher. I am not suggesting that an out-of-classroom teacher undermine anything the classroom teacher says or does, but the out-of-classroom teacher can have his/her own rules, rewards, and consequences.

Entering the Classroom
When an out-of-classroom teachers enter a classroom, there is usually some disorder. This is because the previous lesson has ended. The classroom teacher has probably had the kids put materials away. If the classroom teacher is effective, s/he has activities that keep the students focused and calm while waiting for the prep teacher (with a quick game of hangman, some out-loud drills, etc). Unfortunately, this is not always the case. Sometimes the classroom teacher is rushing off to lunch, to a meeting, or to his/her prep period, and the students have been allowed to get disorderly.

As you enter the room, do not even look at the students, especially if they are loud or unruly. Walk directly to the chalkboard and draw the Point Chart. If the class is especially rambunctious, take care to draw the chart S-L-O-W-L-Y. If this is the first time you are in that classroom, the kids

Chapter 4: Classroom Management

will probably settle because you are behaving differently than teachers usually do when faced with disorderly, screaming students (ie, you are not yelling, demanding order or related). If this is not your first time in that class, and you used the Point Chart with them previously, you will hear loud whispers behind you: "Oh, she's drawing the chart!" "Look, the point chart!" "Shhh! We want to win!"

Wait until the students are quiet. Do NOT turn around until the commotion behind you has lessened significantly. Just stand at the chalkboard, staring at the Point Chart, with your back to the class. When the energy and noise has settled to an acceptable level, turn around, slowly. In most cases, by the time you are facing them, they will be silent and expectant with their hands folded on their desks. Say "Wow! This class is wonderful! Every single table deserves a point!" Mark points for every table. They will probably smile and cheer. Give an initial clear instruction: "Please clear your desks of everything except one sharpened pencil. Reward the tables that were ready most quickly: "Tables 2 and 3 tied for being ready first; they each get a point." Move onto your lesson, awarding points as outlined in the section for classroom teachers.

Kindergarten & 1st Grade Out-of-Classroom Teachers

For prep teachers covering kindergarten and first grade classes, I recommend the following: Three to four minutes before the end of every session, send the children back to their assigned seats (it is fairly common to work with the little ones on the rug or in a story-corner). Then walk around and shake hands with each child. Thank each one individually for being such a good student. Address the children with a serious, but pleasant, tone of voice. Young children get a kick out of shaking hands "like big people." If a child has not behaved or has not participated sufficiently, shake his/her hand, but make your voice serious (not yelling) and say: "Today wasn't a good day for you. Please try to be better next time."

If you are satisfied with the behavior and community in your early grades class or classes without stickers or similar rewards, there is no reason to introduce them. If you do wish to use stickers as incentives/rewards, wait until late October or December to do so. At that time, at the beginning of the class, tell the students that you have stickers and explain that those kids who participate fully and behave well will each get one sticker. At the end of the period, when you would normally make the shake-hands round, you give out stickers instead. This can be tough, because the kids who do not get stickers will *cry*. Expect this and try not to let is upset you (it is a function of their age). Apologize to the children who do not receive stickers and assure them that you will bring stickers again. Do not bring stickers the next session. Instead, let two or three sessions pass before you bring stickers again. Stickers are most effective with small children when they are "special" events.

For 1st grade, your decision about classroom management systems will be based on your perception of the maturity of the class. First grade tends to be a cusp year, with some children being very babyish while others seem more mature. You will have to "average" the class; for immature first grade classes, you will use the kindergarten system described above. If the class is more mature (this often depends on the classroom teacher, his/her way of interacting with them, and prior school experience), you can use the Point Chart as it is outlined above, for classroom teachers. If you use the Point Chart and you feel it is not effective, or it is upsetting students, try it a second and third time before giving up. If you don't feel more positive after several attempts, then revert to the group-sticker system outlined for kindergarteners.

Chapter 4: Classroom Management

Classroom Management for Kindergarten & First Grades

Classroom teachers in kindergarten and first grade need a system of management as do teachers of any grade. The problem is that the level of maturity of these age groups often precludes using the Point Chart. The practices described so far are great for out-of-classroom teachers, regardless of grade, but these teachers only see the kids once or twice in a week. A classroom teacher needs something on-going and cumulative.

There are many options for tracking behavior and rewards. This is one: display a version of the Point Chart, on poster board:

	M	T	W	Th	F	M	T	W	Th	F
1										
2										
3										
4										
5										

At the end of each day, with the class, decide which tables deserve stickers. Ask the kids to tell you why their table does or does not deserve a sticker. Put stickers up for those tables. Ask those kids to stand and the other kids should applaud them. It is essential that the grouping of students at tables is fair, so that each table gets to be applauded equally over time.

There are teachers of young students who use the Point Chart and who do so positively and effectively. I often used the Point Chart with early grades students. I do not mean to suggest that it is not possible or appropriate. I simply want new teachers to anticipate some of the problems that may arise and another option that they have.

Chapter 4: Classroom Management

Good Kid Letters

Good Kid Letters form an effective and occasional part of a strong classroom management system. They are not essential, but they are so easy, and they produce long-term results. Good id Letters are simply letters that the teacher sends home to parents – letters that compliment a child's behavior or participation. Good Kid Letters are effective in three ways: (1) They emphasize things that really matter to the community and feel of a classroom, (2) They increase parental buy-in and involvement, and (3) They win over difficult and/or reluctant kids.

Parents do not expect to hear from teachers unless there is a problem at school. Most parents do not hear from the teacher until parent-teacher conferences unless their child is in trouble. Parents of children who have behavioral or academic issues rarely hear anything positive about their children. This may be especially true in crowded or under-resourced community schools, where teachers and administrators are (often) over-extended. Early, positive feedback will standout and can, therefore, be very effective. A Good Kid Letter is a significant departure from the normal teacher-parent communication. Because of this, parents and kids really respond to Good Kid Letters.

There are different types of Good Kid Letters. The version discussed in this section is about behavior and classroom attitude or participation. I focus on these issues, because they are the most important at the beginning of the year. In addition, issues of behavior and classroom attitude tend to be of primary concern for new teachers. Good Kid Letters may be sent home the fifth or sixth week of school (see Initial Contacts & Letters), after the Honeymoon Period, when students have begun to show their "true colors"; the Good Kid Letters should be sent to parents once the teacher has a sense of how the kids really behave.

Teachers can send Good Kid Letters out later than the fifth or sixth week of school, as well as periodically though the year. The first round of these letters, should not, however, be sent earlier than the fifth or sixth week of school.

Which Kids Get Good Kid Letters?
Teachers, especially new ones, often feel uneasy about praising and not praising students. Choosing which students should receive Good Kid Letters is tough for the new teacher. Teachers want to be positive and to

support the learning and development of all students. New teachers are likely to feel that praising only a few students is inconsistent with their philosophy. The teacher has to realize that the health, learning, and development of the *whole* class is the goal. This is not an easy achievement, and some of the steps a teacher must take may feel uncomfortable.

The children whose parents should receive Good Kid Letters are those whose behavior or attitude warrant recognition. These are students who may not be the strongest academically, but they are ones who have behaved relatively well and consistently since the beginning of the year. Keep in mind that these letters are part of the management system for the classroom; the purpose is to encourage positive behaviors. In a class of 32 students, about one-fourth (or seven-eight students) should receive Good Kid Letters.

A template Good Kid Letter is in Appendix II. The letter should be individualized, so that the name of the student and the parent are within the text of the letter. The Good Kid Letters should not look like a form letter, with the names of the student/parent just written in. The font for the Good Kid Letters should be a "friendly," inviting font. The purpose of this is to distinguish the letter from the many school letters that parents already receive.

The teacher should sign each Good Kid Letter with his/her full (never sign Mr., Mrs., or Ms.). The letter should be put it in a sealed envelope, addressed to "Christopher's parents." The letters should be distributed at the end of the day. When you give the letters out, say: "These are for your parents; please don't open them now." A bunch of kids will chime: "Oooh! You're in trouble!" Just say (calmly), "No, actually, these are *good* letters. They say nice things."

The next day, several of the kids will come into class crooning:
"Ms. McGown, that was really nice what you wrote in that letter."
"Oh, really?" (act calmly surprised)
"Yeah, my mom was so proud - she said that we could go to Coney Island this weekend."
"Wow! That's neat."

The other children who received letters will probably add similar comments. If they do not, invite them to share, *in detail*, what their parents said and did in response to the Good Kid Letters. You will find

Chapter 4: Classroom Management

that the parents were both pleased and surprised with the letters; many will have promised various things as rewards for their children. Make sure to have this conversation in class, with the other kids listening. You want the other kids to hear that the parents of the kids who got the letters are happy and PROUD.

Other students in the class may complain or whine:
"Man! Ms. McGown, I want one of those letters."
"Ms. McGown, You gonna send more of those?"
"Please, Ms. McGown, I promise to be good!"

The impulse for a teacher, after such enthusiastic response, is to promise another round of letters. Do not do this. Instead, tell the students that you might send some more letters, but that you do not know when. Do not commit to anything. Another round of Good Kid Letters should be sent no sooner than three weeks after the first round.

Sending Good Kid Letters accomplishes the following:
- The kids who received letters are going to be more likely to behave than to follow the lead of any disruptive kids in the class.
- The other kids are going to remember the possibility of receiving such a letter; this will increase positive behaviors.
- Parents who received these letters are going to be more receptive and helpful to your comments and requests.
- Parents talk; other parents *will* hear about these letters. Even parents who did not receive these letters will be pleased ("This teacher took time to send out nice things – not just something bad").

More Good Kid Letters
Teachers can send just one round of Good Kid Letters, and the letters will have been very effective. Teachers can also send letters periodically throughout the year, both to reinforce the initial affects of the letters and/ or to encourage/reward additional behaviors. I found it most effective to send letters approximately every seven-eight weeks. The emphasis of the letters was always behavior, attitude, and cooperation.

For the Out-of-Classroom Teacher
Good Kid Letters are a great tool for out-of-classroom teachers. In addition to the above results, sending out Good Kid Letters gives credibility to the out-of-classroom teacher (many children and parents view these teachers as secondary and less important). An early outreach, such as a Good Kid Letter, helps to shift the view students and teachers

have of out-of-classroom teachers. Since these teachers have several classes, they cannot easily send letters to students in every class. Instead, the out-of-classroom teacher should start with only one or two of the classes/groups.

A sample Good Kid Letter is in Appendix II.

5

Routines & Procedures

Chapter 5: Routines & Procedures

About this Chapter

In my work with new teachers, the first few days and weeks of every school-year, my phone and e-mail inbox are swamped with teachers calling for advice on lining kids up, taking attendance, dealing with pencils, assigning, collecting, and checking homework, etc. They want to know about the *details* of teaching, not the theory or philosophy or content of teaching. They do not ask about lesson-planning; they want to know about the logistics of running a classroom. New teachers cannot believe that no-one ever told them how to put kids on a line or how to take attendance efficiently. Even more significantly, new teachers cannot believe how important these routines and procedures are!

At the beginning of a school year, most teachers emphasize routines and procedures. *Experienced* teachers are not generally as concerned with lesson content or delivery the first month of school; rather, it is classroom behavior and management that take the majority of their time and energy at the start of the year. The emphasis, at the beginning of the year, is on the procedures and logistics that make a classroom run smoothly. A veteran teacher will prioritize procedures, routines, rules, etc; once these are established, s/he will then shift the emphasis to teaching, to implementing creative content-filled lessons, to delivering curriculum. This shift, for the experienced teacher, generally happens a few weeks after the start of the school-year. Effective veteran teachers will, however, maintain a focus on procedures and routines throughout the year. Many new teachers spend several *months* (if not the whole year) struggling with management and routines rather than teaching. This is a waste of everyone's time – students and teacher. Determining good routines and procedures and taking the time at the start of the year to establish them is essential to success in the classroom.

Effective management, with sensible routines and procedures is not complicated. Creating and establishing important classroom routines is a skill, and like most skills, it can be learned. Routines and procedures form a part of the overall classroom management system of the classroom. Unfortunately, there is no standard practice to help new teachers learn the tenets of effective management systems and of the required routines and procedures. In many schools and districts, there is little, if any, outreach to support new teachers as they work to establish themselves in the classroom. Most teacher preparation programs provide little information about management systems, routines, classroom procedures, etc. Instead, new teachers are left on their own, with the expectation that they will sink or swim. Many do "swim," but many also "sink." It doesn't have to be this way!

In this section, I will present essential classroom routines and procedures. I will also discuss why these strategies are important, what typically goes wrong for new teachers, and what I recommend to prevent the myriad classroom problems and to establish good practices.

Chapter 5: Routines & Procedures

Quiet-Attention

"Settle down."
"I'm not going to talk over all of you."
"Shhhh!"
"Come on, guys!"
"I'm *waiting*."

Without an attentive class, teachers cannot teach. For this reason, teachers work very hard to get their students to settle down and pay attention. Many teachers begin each lesson with one of the above pleas. Oftentimes, these pleas do not work. In many classrooms, an inordinate amount of time is spent trying to get students to be quiet and to pay attention. Some teachers lose half their instructional time in pursuit of silence and attention. Teachers need to establish an effective and quick method for getting the class to be quiet and pay attention, and they need to rehearse it with the students. Doing this should be a priority from the first day of school.

There are countless different times and reasons that you need the kids to get quiet – the beginning or end of a period, between lessons or activities, before leaving the classroom to go to lunch, etc. Kids tend to be fairly receptive at the beginning of a class or period; they know that they need to get some information from the teacher at the beginning of class. They may whine and complain, but they tend to listen (at least) for the first few minutes. This window is, however, often short. Depending on the class, the subject, and the time of year, this window can be very short indeed. Teachers should not waste instructional time, so it is very important to get the lesson started as quickly as possible.

A teacher establishes so much about his or her class and teaching expectations in the first few minutes. A teacher who is prepared, who expects to use time well, who believes that students will participate and complete the activity, who knows they will think and learn and enjoy themselves does not waste time. The students know, from the first day, that they will be engaged from the moment class starts. This is the habit, and the mindset, you want in your classroom!

It is essential that students are engaged from the second class starts. An easy and effective strategy is to have directions or an engaging quick activity on the board at the start of the lesson/period. This allows students to start something right away. Once students know there is important information for them on the chalkboard, checking the board will become habit. Reading directions, or checking for the starting or "hook" activity, shifts the focus from the teacher to the student. The students do not have to ask for directions; they can check the board upon entering the room and they know what they must do immediately. This helps avoid the chatting and socializing that can take over at the start of a class and it puts the focus on the completion of a task (see Do Now). The kids will naturally calm down as they follow the directions:

- Open the science texts to pg. 78 and take out yesterday's questions. Review the questions and your answers. Make changes if you wish.
- Open your journals to the next page, write the heading, and copy the following prompt: "If I were principal . . . . "
- Look around the room and write down all the items that are circle shapes.
- Quick Quiz – Papers are on your desks; begin work immediately. You have six minutes.
- Clear desks. Table Monitors get the art boxes. Paper passers give each student one sheet of drawing paper. Write your name and date at the top of the paper.

Each of the above tasks will take a few minutes. As the kids finish, they will turn to you for further instructions; that will be your "in"; the kids are calm and you can begin the lesson. Another option is to have a set routine that is followed every day – in the morning, after gym, after lunch, at the start of math, etc. This isn't so very different than having the class quietly check the chalkboard and follow directions; instead of developing the habit of checking the chalkboard, the class learns to follow a set of routines throughout the day.

Interrupting Students at Work
Once the lesson is underway, you may realize you forgot to give some instructions. It is difficult to be heard over 32 students. How do you get their attention? You need to establish a silent means of communication within the classroom. For getting the kids' attention, my favorite was flicking the overhead lights. You must be explicit when you introduce the flicking lights; you must explain exactly what you expect the kids to do in response. I introduced this the first week of school. I explained that they did not have to sit down, they did not have to return to their seats – all they had to do was freeze and put their eyes on me. At that moment, I would give them the next piece of information or clarification.

Chapter 5: Routines & Procedures

In the beginning, we would practice the flicking of lights frequently (see Point Chart): I would flick the lights, and I would check that all students had turned to me. I would award points to the tables that responded most quickly. On the day I had introduced the light-flicking, I practiced this several times. The kids enjoyed it and we reinforced good procedure. As the days passed, I would do it less frequently, but in different situations – during pair work, group work, when kids were unpacking or cleaning their desks, etc. It was important to always tie this into the Point Chart (see Classroom Management, the Point Chart).

Chapter 5: Routines & Procedures

Raising Hands

Students have to raise their hands to speak. Period.

The students know this. You know this. Everyone knows this. But you are going to have problems enforcing this rule. In addition, you will let children slide sometimes, as all new teachers do, generally in an effort to be open and responsive. A student is going to call out and you are going to answer him/her. This is a mistake, as it tells the students that it is not necessary to raise a hand and that it is acceptable to yell out to get your attention. Your actions speak much louder than your words; by acknowledging the child who spoke without raising a hand, you are communicating that calling out is *okay* and that *calling out works*. Whether it is the loud kid who is hard to ignore, the screaming kid embarking on a tantrum, the shy kid who rarely speaks, the sweet kid who behaves but forgot this time, you must insist that ALL students raise their hand for your attention and to speak.

This is very hard in the beginning. New teachers are overly concerned that the kids like them. Teachers sometimes over-compensate by being too nice and too receptive. There is time to be nice and there is time to show students that you like them and want to hear what they have to say. You have a whole year for that. But you only have a few weeks to lay the groundwork for solid routines and procedures in your classroom. From Day One, do not respond to any child who calls out. When a student calls out, try to ignore him/her. You can say, "Anyone who wishes to speak must raise their hand." Try not to look at the student who has called out, as that just gives him/her attention and acknowledgment.

Teachers need to establish guidelines about raising hands. These may not be part of the posted rules, but you must discuss and explain them in the beginning of the year, and periodically thereafter:
- Do not raise your hands when another person is speaking: When someone else is speaking, you are supposed to respect and listen to him/her. If you are waving your hand around, you are not listening to the person speaking.
- All eyes should be on the individual speaking (this increases focus, and it is polite).
- Raising hands is a silent undertaking: There should be no "Oooh-Oooh!" and "I know!" accompanying the raising of hands. Make sure *not* to call

on kids making sound effects. You may want to say, "I'm picking Kim because she raised her hand without making any noise."

- Off-topic questions cost points: Your comments and questions should be about the lesson/activity we are working on. If we are doing math, and everyone is supposed to be figuring the answer to a problem, and you raise your hand to ask to go to the bathroom, every other table will get *two* points on the Point Chart (See Point Chart).

But I Don't Think Kids Should Always Have To Raise Their Hands

You're vaguely bothered by the requirement of raising hands, and you like the idea of "organic discussion" – where conversation is fluid, and participants contribute naturally, without raising their hands. Encouraging and facilitating real dialogue in a classroom, where students are active participants, is important. It is an essential part of raising informed and competent individuals. I am, for these and many other reasons, a huge fan of genuine (noisy, somewhat disorderly, sometimes chaotic) class discussions. Such times are, however, distinct from the many instances during which students must raise their hands, for the many practical, logistic pieces of a school day. There are different norms, and different procedures, for different school and learning activities. You will present, explain, and teach the appropriate behaviors for the different activities in your classroom.

Chapter 5: Routines & Procedures

Numbering Students

Assigning numbers to students is a simple way of ordering many things inside a classroom: wardrobe hooks, books, computer sessions, etc. Assign each of your thirty-two students numbers 1 through 32. This is their number for the year.

Rather than labeling wardrobe closet hooks with names, label these items with numbers. This way, if kids are removed from your class and/or others are added, you do not have to re-label the hooks. The numbered hooks can also be used the next years; you'll just re-assign names to the numbers. If your class is given a set of special-interest books to use for a month, number the books and give the corresponding book to the kid with the same number. There are many things which are numbered which will find their way into your room. Numbering students fits into classroom routines effortlessly.

Student numbers is also a great way of keeping track of kids in less-controlled settings (the gym, the yard, when several classes are outside, etc.) and on trips. It is far easier to have the students count-off than it is to get them into a group and count them. Kids will memorize whose number is whose rather quickly. If a number is not called, the class will be able to tell you which kid is missing.

Chapter 5: Routines & Procedures

Student Jobs

Assigning jobs to students can make a classroom run efficiently. Student Jobs can significantly reduce time lost on paperwork and minor but time-consuming tasks. Student jobs can also be great ways to involve children and to reward them. There are many things that even the youngest children can do and that they *love* to do (filing papers, distributing materials, etc.). The more effectively these tasks are delegated, the more time teachers have for their most important duty – teaching!

I recommend having only a few student jobs. It is best if you create jobs that are important to you – that you feel are necessary to the smooth running of your classroom. This is for several reasons: (1) Monitoring jobs does take time (and you do not want to waste time on jobs that do not improve the classroom); (2) Students need to value the jobs, and that is difficult if there are many jobs, or if the individual jobs require little action or responsibility); (3) Having responsibility within the classroom fosters a sense of ownership and community.

This means that there will always be fewer kids who have jobs than who do not during any given job-cycle. And this also means that you need to be mindful of the passage of time and change the jobs regularly (so that most kids get a chance at each job during the course of the year). If the jobs are substantive, and kids actually have to *do* something, they will feel as if they are contributing in a meaningful way to the classroom; this increases the desirability of the jobs.

Following are the Student Jobs that I recommend for most classrooms:
- Attendance Monitor
- Line Leaders (2)
- Door Openers (2)
- Caboose
- Librarian
- Office Monitor
- Paper Passer & Collector
- Table Monitors or Group Captains (4-6)
- Assistant Teacher

Student Jobs need to be posted. The display for student jobs should be prominent; you want the kids to know that these jobs are important to you. I created a "student Job" wall (see Classroom Decoration). On it, I put small hooks, with labels beneath, each with the name of the different jobs. I purchased medium-sized tags (made of oak-tag, see "Price Tags" in the Shopping List section), on which I wrote every student's name. The tags were affixed on the hook for the different jobs. I had an extra hook at the bottom of the display titles, "Temporarily Un-employed," and this was for the students who did not have jobs for that job-cycle.

Some teachers change jobs every week, but I felt this was too time-consuming – as well as unnecessary. I preferred to change student jobs every three-four weeks. Remove all student job tags. The tags of children who just held jobs should be put aside. The others tags go in a bowl. Pick them out randomly. As each child's name is picked, s/he decides which job s/he would like, barring any that s/he has previously held. Occasionally, a child may opt to "pass" as the job s/he most wants has already been taken in that round.

Some children will not be able to do certain jobs, because of their behavior and/or attitude. Some specifics are discussed in the sections below. Explain this limitation to students up-front Make sure to include your reasons for limiting the jobs. Limiting access to some jobs can make them even more desirable and can serve as an incentive for children to behave better, be on time, get along with others, etc.

Attendance Monitor
See Attendance. This child's responsibility is two-fold: s/he records the attendance on the chalkboard and brings the attendance paperwork to the office (or wherever it goes). This child has to be a responsible child who is rarely absent and never late. In kindergarten and 1st grade, the Attendance Monitor does not mark attendance but does bring the attendance documentation to the office. If the Attendance Monitor is absent, the Assistant Teacher assumes these responsibilities for the day.

Door Openers (2)
These children step away from the line, rush ahead, and open the doors for the class. When the class has passed through, the Line Leaders rush to catch up and return to their line-spaces. This is a favorite job, as the kids have some autonomy (they may go up an alternate stairwell to get to the doors prior to the class, etc). Line Leaders must be instructed to hold the doors for any adults who happen to be passing through the hallway as well. If a Door Opener is absent, the Assistant Teacher covers.

Chapter 5: Routines & Procedures

Line Leaders (2)
These children, generally one boy and one girl, head up the two lines.
This job is a perennial favorite, especially for the tall kids who usually
stand in the back of the line (many schools preference that classes line up
in size-order). The Line Leaders can help significantly with orderly hall
passage. When you give instructions in the hall ("Walk to the next door"),
it is these kids to whom you are speaking. Tell the Line Leaders explicitly
never to listen to anyone else. This avoids other kids yelling at them ("Go
ahead, you know we're supposed to go ahead!"). If the Line Leaders do not
hear you, they should not move. Make note of the kids who lead the lines
very well, as you may choose them to be your Line Leaders for walks
outside of the school and field trips. If the Line Leaders are absent, the #2
kids (those who normally stand second in line) assume the
responsibilities for the day.

Caboose
The Caboose stands at the back of the line. As you walk through the hall
and pause to make sure everyone is together, it is this child you look for.
If s/he is there, you know you have got the whole class. If the Caboose is
missing, you know you need to wait. The Caboose must be instructed to
wait for kids who are stopping to tie their shoes or for kids who have
tripped, etc. Short kids, who usually stand at the front of the line, love
this job. The Caboose and Line-Leaders play important parts in Line-Up
and Hall Passage procedures. Make note of which kids are very good
Cabooses, as one of them will be the Caboose on trips. The Caboose is an
especially important job while on a trip. A good Caboose will help keep
the group together and will alert you if there is a problem in the line. If
the Caboose is absent, another child who has been the Caboose (or the
Assistant Teacher) takes these responsibilities for the day.

Librarian
This child straightens out the classroom library periodically. It is often a
coveted position, as the Librarian can go to the library whenever s/he
wants (providing class-work is completed). It is also a really important
job, as a classroom library can get *so* messy *so* quickly. You must take
time at the beginning of the year to explain (explicitly) what you want the
Librarian to do. If the Librarian is absent for a day, no-one does this job
(unless the library gets really messy – then assign the Assistant Teacher
to tidy up).

Chapter 5: Routines & Procedures

Office Monitor
This child is the one who goes to the office for all the reasons that kids have to go to the office, except for attendance procedures. This is a job that cannot be given to just any child; it must be someone you are fairly confidant will behave alone in the halls. If the Office Monitor is absent, the Assistant Teacher assumes these responsibilities for the day.

Paper Passer & Collector
This child passes out and collects all papers. The Paper Passer often works with the Table Monitors. When there are papers to be handed out, the Paper-Passer hands them out or gives papers for the table to the Table Monitors, who pass them out individually. The process is similar, but in reverse, to collect papers (see Paper - Collection and Distribution). If the Paper Passer is absent, the Assistant Teacher assumes these responsibilities for the day.

Table Monitors (5-6)
These children, one at each table or group, coordinate papers, supplies, etc. for his/her table-mates. This reduces the amount of movement in the classroom. When it is art time, the Table Monitors get the art boxes. When it is time to get social studies texts, the Table Monitors get enough for their table, etc. The Table Monitors return all materials to the proper places at the end of lessons too. These kids often work in tandem with the Paper-Passer. Table Monitors can also help you by checking work at his/her table. To save time, you can ask the Table Monitors to let you know when everyone has finished a certain task: "Table Monitors, please give me a thumbs-up when everyone has finished copying the homework." This job rotates among the kids at the table. If the table monitor is absent, the kid to his/her left assumes these responsibilities.

And the grand-daddy of them all . . . .

Assistant Teacher
This child can help with *everything*. The Assistant Teacher can mark points on the Point Chart, tell the line-leaders to proceed (if you are called away momentarily), give the vocabulary quiz, get items for you from your bag or desk, file or organize papers, and so much more. The extent of the responsibilities given to an Assistant Teacher will depend on the age of the students as well as your comfort level and style. The Assistant Teacher also assumes most other jobs when there are absences. Because this is such an involved position, I do not assign an Assistant Teacher until the fifth or sixth weeks of school. The Assistant Teacher

has fewer responsibilities in 1st and 2nd grades and it does not exist in kindergarten classes.

This job, more than any other, can only be assigned to children whose behavior is impeccable and who is rarely absent or late. It also has to be a child who will not be overly bossy, who will be respectful towards others, and who other kids like. The Assistant Teacher is the most coveted job. My goal each year was to help each child be able to hold this position at some point in the year. This was not always possible, but I tried. It is important to explain that this is your expectation. As the year progressed, I spoke to individual students about what they need to do/ change to be the Assistant Teacher.

Note: It was never the top student nor the best-behaved child who made the most effective Assistant Teacher. The best Assistant Teacher was just a reasonably good kid who really wanted the position and had to work for it.

When re-assigning the jobs, you'll know which children you consider to be eligible to be the Assistant Teacher. It might be a good idea, especially if you anticipate some problems, to review the requirements for the Assistant Teacher position. Another option is to just assign this job first, before moving on with the regular job assignment procedure.

For Kindergarten and 1st Grade Teachers
Kindergarteners should not walk in the halls alone. Attendance and office monitors should be assigned in pairs. First graders should ultimately be able to handle these jobs singly, but it is advisable to begin the year with pairs.

For the Out-of-Classroom Teacher
Out-of-classroom teachers also need help with logistics, much of which can be aided by student jobs. The problem, of course, is that out-of-classroom teachers see so many children, and they do not generally know all names. In addition, out-of-classroom do not have the same intimacy with the kids. For this reason, I recommend that the out-of-classroom teacher has fewer jobs. If you assign children numbers (see "Numbering Students") you can assign jobs by the numbers. For example, in all classes, #6 is the Attendance Monitor, #23 is the Librarian, etc.

Out-of-classroom teachers who see classes only once per week will rotate student jobs once per month. If you see classes several times per week,

rotate the jobs every two-three weeks. Prep teachers with their own rooms should have the following jobs:
• Attendance Monitor
• Librarian (or Supply Monitor)
• Office Monitor
• Paper Passer & Collector
• Table Monitors (5-6)

For out-of-classroom teachers without their own rooms, the following jobs are generally sufficient:
• Attendance Monitor (only if necessary: see "Administrative Logistics")
• Office Monitor
• Paper Passer & Collector

Chapter 5: Routines & Procedures

Pencils

"I don't have a pencil!"
"I lost my pencil!"
" I want the *blue* pencil!"
"S/he has *all* the sharp pencils!"
"My pencil broke!"
"S/he has *my* pencil!"

A teacher's day is punctuated by comments like those above. Some kids will not bring any pencils; others will bring dozens (which they may or may not be willing to share). Some students will bring mechanical pencils that will be disassembled within seconds of arriving in your classroom. Pencils will be broken, eaten, and thrown, but, unless you establish good pencil practices, they will not be used for writing lessons.

<u>Organizing Pencils</u>
Most pencil problems are about getting and keeping pencils and sharpening them. The following are three reliable methods for organizing pencils:

Dull & Sharp: Get two containers. Label one "dull" and one "sharp" (empty coffee tins are fine for this). Before class, sharpen several dozen pencils. Place all the sharpened pencils point-up in the "sharp" container. During the course of the day, when a child needs a new pencil, s/he holds his pencil in the air without saying anything. You give permission (or not) and the child can go to the containers and switch pencils. Do not let kids do this without your input, or going to the pencil containers can become a reason to get out of their seats and run around the room. Also, you need to determine if one or more kids are pressing so hard that the pencil point breaks regularly (this is normal for new writers and reasonably common through 2nd grade). Older children may do this on purpose, for the express purpose of being able to get a new pencil.

Pencil Exchange: Keep a collection of sharpened pencils in your desk, inaccessible to the kids. If a kid needs to borrow a pencil, take something as collateral. Many teachers make kids pay for pencils; this works, but I do not like to encourage kids bringing money to school. Some teachers have kids turn in a shoe – they get the shoe back when the pencil is returned. But you run into jokes about the kid and his/her feet. I am not certain if the trouble is worth it, though many teachers swear by the shoe-trade. My favorite "collateral" is the backpack. The kid cannot go home without it – and so, during pack-up time, you do the switch – the pencil for the backpack.

Three Pencils: All kids are required to, at all times, have three sharpened pencils in their desks. The teacher has to do periodic checks and reward the kid and/or the group for proper pencil maintenance (see Point Chart). This assures that kids have pencils, and that if, somehow, one kid loses all three of his/hers, there are other kids at the table who can loan one. This method will not take effect until after the first weekend (so that parents have had time to buy pencils). You will need to establish the policy, send home supply notes, allow time for parents to go shopping, and then reinforce the practice. You will also need a stash of pencils to get the class through the first week or so.

Sharpening Pencils
Sharpening pencils causes problems no matter how you decide to do it. To a large extent, it is a matter of choosing the lesser of multiple evils.

- Hand-Crank Sharpener: If your classroom has a hand-crank pencil sharpener, you should establish certain times during the day when kids can sharpen pencils. This is best done in the morning, during morning unpacking, afternoon packing-up, or during the transitions before or after lunch. Have one table at a time go to the sharpener; award points for tables that behave well while sharpening. In addition, award a bonus point for any table that is especially quick to finish at the sharpener.

- Electric Sharpener: Children should not have free access to an electric pencil sharpener; they will break it. In addition, if you allow children to use the sharpener, you will hear that grating whrrr all day. I preferred to sharpen pencils myself (after-all, I paid for the pencil sharpener, so I cared that it last as long as possible). While grading papers, or some other writing activity, I would sit near the sharpener and sharpen a few pencils every few minutes. During the course of the day, when the kids were working on an assignment, I would sharpen a few more pencils.

Note: Even the best, newest sharpener cannot sharpen more than ten pencils at a time without over-heating. It is best to sit next to the sharpener while you are doing something else (grading papers, writing lesson plans, etc) – and sharpen a handful of pencils every 15 minutes or so, giving the machine adequate time to cool down.

Chapter 5: Routines & Procedures

You may choose to purchase a hand-crank rather than an electric pencil sharpener. They are only nominally cheaper, but they do last longer (an electric will last one school-year if you monitor its use carefully; a hand-crank sharpener will last forever). A hand-crank sharpener has to be properly installed; this might not be worth the hassle.

At this point, people often ask my thoughts on small individual hand-held pencil sharpeners. I don;t like them, and I never allowed them in the classroom. My reason for this was primarily to avoid mess. If students use little hand-held sharpeners, the shavings will inevitably gather in their desks (and get on papers) or on the floor and be traipsed about the room. It is also not uncommon for one child to dump a mini-sharpener full of shavings onto the head of another.

There are teachers who feel differently; they purchase (or otherwise secure) quality small sharpeners, with reliable shaving-catcher parts, and they keep one on each table. Students may then sharpen pencils when they want, at their own tables.

For the Out-of-Classroom Teacher

This is an instance where out-of-classroom teachers have few options compared to classroom teachers. Of the above pencil options, the only one that is possible is #2, Pencil-Exchange. You cannot, however, exchange backpacks because you are probably not going to be around at pack-up or dismissal time. You can exchange something else of value, if you wish (i.e. baseball cap, toy, box of crayons, etc).

As an out-of-classroom teacher, I always did one of two things:
- I carried extra pencils. If a kid needed one, I wrote down his/her name and gave him/her one. I always stopped class a few minutes before the end of the period (for the Point Chart, see Classroom Management). At this time, I would make sure to collect all my loaned pencils.
- I carried no extra pencils. I insisted that kids find someone with an extra pencil and borrow it. Someone always has an extra pencil. I would also make sure to reward groups where everyone was prepared (again, the Point Chart) so it behooved the whole group to make sure each student had what was needed.

I preferred the second of the above options. It does cause a fair bit of grumbling in the beginning, but that goes away. This method forces children to take more responsibility for their behavior, which takes some of the pressure off the teacher. In addition, if you are an out-of-classroom teacher who travels room-to-room (as I was), it is difficult to carry additional materials.

Chapter 5: Routines & Procedures

Line-Up

Putting children in line is one of the most difficult things for new teachers – and one that is rarely taught in teacher preparation programs. Having kids in calm, organized line has benefits both within and outside of the classroom. Kids who enter a room in order tend to be quicker to get to work; classes who pass through the hallways quietly tend to be recognized be other teachers and administrators; orderly classes are less draining on teachers; the list is endless. Conversely, when teachers are unable to get a line together, they often experience organizational and instructional failures in many other areas of teaching. Their students spend less time in on-task activities. In addition, administrators tend to come down harshly on teachers whose students are disruptive in the halls and/or stairs; these classes struggle with transitions; again, the list is endless. A class that moves through the hallways quietly and tidily makes a teacher's life far more pleasant.

To Size or Not to Size?
Some schools stipulate how children are to be lined up. One example (and the most common) is two parallel lines, one of girls and one of boys, in size-order, with the shortest kids fronting the line and the tallest bringing up the back. Many people do not like the idea of grouping kids by gender, height, etc. This is a fair criticism, and there may be psychological impacts for these kinds of categorizations (think of the tall girl who is always in the back and the short boy who is always in the front). The fact is, however, you may have little say in a school policy.

I always lined up my kids in size-order, with a boys and a girls line. It was required at my school, and I decided that it was not worth fighting over (see Note 1 below). There is a logic to size-order that should not be over-looked: a teacher, standing at the front of the line, can see all children, if they are standing in size-order. This is true, but good teachers tend to move around the line. Other options for lining up children include: alphabetically by first name, alphabetically by last name, by birthday, etc. The important thing is to have a set line order and to ensure that all children know their places. You will need to stress, explicitly and repeatedly, what you require of the students in terms of line and hall behavior. You also need to remind them of the line-up protocol and to monitor their behavior constantly and consistently. In the beginning, this is an exhausting (and voice-wearying) process, but it pays off remarkably.

Chapter 5: Routines & Procedures

What Makes a Good Line?

What are the things that are important (to you!) about a good line? These are mine:

- Quiet: I do not want to get yelled at or resented by other teachers or administrators for disrupting their lessons as my class moves through the halls. I also know that a class of kids cannot simply "turn off" the volume when they enter the room, so it is important that the kids are quiet upon arriving to the classroom.
- Safety: Many school accidents happen on the steps. The more orderly the class is, the less likely such accidents are to occur. Explaining accidents to parents, filling out multiple accident report forms, let alone comforting a crying, injured child – is a whole lot for a new teacher to have to handle.
- Compact: The class must remain close together; there is no way a teacher can effectively monitor a class that stretches out with huge spaces between students.

Clear Verbal Cues

Your initial effort in creating good line-up procedures will seem endless, and it will be exhausting and often tedious. You need to tell students explicitly how you want them to get on line and what you want them to do while on line, and you need to do this over and over, at least for the first few weeks (remember the throat drops I recommended?). Vague phrases like "Be good" do not mean anything to children. They hear phrases like that over and over again; but they do not think about what it means, and it does not affect their behavior. It is better to use specific examples of what you want the students to do. Kids are far more "concrete" than adults are, and the level of concreteness does not change substantially until junior high and high school. Following are some common cues for lining-up:

- "Hands at your sides": I do not like it when kids have their hands in their pockets. On a practical level, kids who have their hands in their pockets are likely fiddling with something they should not be. Also, if a kid stumbles, s/he is more able to catch her/himself if her/his hands are free.

- "No hair-styling": This should be covered by the above rule, but it is not. Girls love to play with each other's hair. You need to tell them that this is not acceptable behavior when on line or passing through the halls.

Chapter 5: Routines & Procedures

- "Faces forward": A child facing forward is less likely to be talking to another child. It is also a good practice for children to face in the direction that they are walking.

- "No leaning" (on walls, columns, each other, etc): Leaning looks sloppy and lazy; I do not tolerate it for that reason and I say so. In addition, kids who lean on the walls are more likely to damage bulletin boards, signs, or displays.

- "Shoulders straight and tall": This is the "visual" that I give to kids about posture and comportment. They tend to respond quickly when I say this.

- "Empty hands": Kids should not hold anything in their hands as they walk through the halls (see Note 2). You frequently see kids with pencils or pens. This is bad practice; they are simply too likely to drag them across the wall, marking the walls or displays as they pass. Even the "best" of kids find this irresistible.

- "Keep a tight line": I explain that "tight" means no space between kids. A teacher can easily monitor 30-35 kids in a tight line, but s/he can't effectively monitor even 15 spread out.

Procedure
Decide where in the room the students are going to line up. It should be the same place every time, and it should be inside your room. Some teachers have kids line up in the hallway, either because of the size of their classroom or the arrangement of furniture, but I prefer to have my class contained and visible. If you have room at the front or along the side of the room, use it. You might have the boys line up along one wall and the girls along the other (depending on space), forming a "V" or a right angle.

The first kids to be called are the Line Leaders and the Caboose (see Student Jobs). The rest of the class is called by group or table. This limits the number of kids moving about the room at one time. It also lets each successive group settle themselves into line before the next is called. Remind them to leave spaces for the other kids. If you do not do this, all the kids will push and shove to be at the front, even if they are the tallest or know they belong in the middle. Mnemonics are always helpful: "Leave spaces for size places" is my favorite for line-up. Children love rhymes; they remember them quickly and tend to repeat them.

Chapter 5: Routines & Procedures

Explain what you do as you do it: "I am going to call one table to get on line. We'll all watch to see how well each group does this." As different groups move to the line-up area, go through the list of rules: "Are all faces forward? Are all mouths closed? Is everyone standing tall? Any hands in pockets? Do we have a tight line?" Award one point on the Point Chart as each group successfully melds in with the line.

For the first few weeks of school, you need to remind the students constantly to behave appropriately and you need to monitor them – in line and in all other activities/locations. You do not, and should not, raise your voice. Rather, talk through the rules and reminders. After the second or third line-up, you should take a moment to ask kids if they remember all the rules about line-up. Doing this involves the students and gets them to focus on the rules and their actions. If you give points on the Point Chart for accurate answers, they are rewarded for reinforcing your rules.

For the Out-of-Classroom Teacher
The line-up procedure is the same for all teachers. Because out-of-classroom teachers see less of any one group of kids, they will have less time to practice and reinforce routines. It is one of the challenges of being an out-of-classroom teacher. But remember: the classroom teacher is teaching rules and procedures the rest of the time.

Note 1: I did try to fight the size-order mandate my first year as a third grade teacher. I presented an alternate system to my class and they liked it and everything went smoothly for the first few days. One day, while my class was with another staff member, she ordered them to get into size-order lines. The class told the staff member that we do not use size-order lines. One child attempted to explain the system that we had for lining-up in our class. The staff member yelled at my class anyway. I then implemented size-order lines. I realized that, while I may have had valid reasons for lining-up the class the way I had (and that they had appreciated it), the students would pay a price, due to a rigid colleague. My philosophy was not worth it, and it certainly was not fair to the children.

Note 2: Your students may have to go to other classrooms for special services or classes (math coaching, writing or ESL tutorial, etc.). In these cases, you will have to send children through the halls with pencils and notebooks. Tell them how to hold pencils while walking through the halls: they should hold the pencil in a closed fist, with the eraser up and the point down. It is virtually impossible to write on the walls with a pencil in this position (it is also fairly difficult to jab another child while holding a pencil in this manner). In the beginning, as with all things, you need to make sure the kids are doing this properly, until it becomes habit.

Chapter 5: Routines & Procedures

Hall Passage

Passing through school hallways can take – and waste – a good deal of time. A well-behaved class of students can get from the library to their class, climbing four flights of stairs, in five-six minutes. Another class can travel the same distance but take more than 15 minutes. The teacher of the second class may lose upwards of 30-50 minutes of instructional time each day. Teachers simply cannot afford to lose this much teaching time. In addition, if chaos erupts in the halls, it can take a teacher upwards of ten (even 20!) minutes, once back in the classroom, to settle the kids down to be able to learn. If the class made the transition calmly and orderly, the settle-down time can be just a minute or two. If class lines are set up properly, passing through the halls is relatively simple. Without good line-up protocol, passing through the halls is extremely difficult. The order of these two sections is intentional.

Baby Steps
The most important thing in teaching correct hall passage, as in most school procedures, is to proceed in stages. It is easier to catch errors and correct them if they do not go on unchecked for too long.

Tell the line leaders to take the class just outside the door to the fire extinguisher (or some other easy-to-identify hall landmark). Follow the class and check that they are in compliance with all the line-up rules. Go over the rules in the hall, as necessary. If students are not following your hallways rules, remind them, using positive language: "Smiling mouths!" instead of "No talking!" When they are composed to your satisfaction, have the line leaders take the class to the next point (the stairwell, Ms. Roer's door, etc.). The class is never to move without your specific directions. At each point, review their behavior before proceeding. For the first few weeks, all hall passage is done in this way, with many small steps and lots of stops for reviewing and checking and praising behavior. Within a few weeks, the stages are longer and the checks are quicker.

Stairs
Walking through the stairwells causes *heaps* of problems, and stairs can be dangerous. The majority of school accidents happen on the stairs. Presenting injured kids to parents is no fun; nor is explaining the situation to your supervisor or filling out accident report forms. Many schools have designated "up" and "down" stairs and/or stairwells

designated for certain grades. Make sure to ask a senior teacher about any such policies. The following are my stairwell rules:

- One hand must be on the banister at all times. This causes kids to face in the correct direction and reduces the incidences of misbehaviors and the likelihood of accidents.
- The class takes only one flight of stairs at a time. You will monitor behavior at each landing before proceeding.
- The kids at the front of the line must go no further than the top, or bottom, stair, rather than being able to continue onto the landing. This keeps the group tight and leaves the landing clear. This is something that you must explain (and repeat a *lot*); it is also something to discuss and stress with the Line Leaders.
- The two lines of your class must remain close to the walls of the stairwell. Occasionally, a teacher or some students will come the wrong way on the steps and they will want to pass through your line. This is much easier if your kids are used to leaving room for passage.

Hallway Situations & Surprises

Things will happen in the hallway that can throw order into disorder. Preparing the children ahead of time and discussing appropriate responses will help when such unexpected things arise. Here are several of the more common hallway situations or surprises and how to prepare for them:

- About Face: There will be occasions when your whole class has to turn around and go the other way. This is not hard if you have practiced with your class. Explain the process and then practice. Kids are to remain in their size-places but turn around. The line leaders now are the cabooses, and the cabooses are now the line leaders. This is a temporary thing – and you'll tolerate no whining about the change of jobs (say this explicitly).

- Doors: Kids should stop just before a door or doorway. Invariably, someone will come rushing out of that door and bash into your kids. You must tell your class that they must stop one yard in front of or beyond a door (show them what a yard is), and you must explain why this is so.

- Another Class: Your class will come upon an unruly class from time to time. If your class is orderly and proceeding calmly, they will be irritated at the noise and disorder of this other class. You need to discuss with them this eventuality and how you expect them to behave.

Chapter 5: Routines & Procedures

It will score no points if your class badmouths the other kids or the teacher (even if this is a valid response & reflects your thoughts). When my class ran into poorly behaved classes, I had my class freeze and let the other class pass us.

- Former Teachers: The most orderly of lines falls apart when a former teacher passes by. Students are so excited to see and greet their former teachers and they forget the rules. Since you know this will happen, you can prepare for it, so that your lines don't fall apart entirely. First, greet the person yourself: "Ms. Stone, I know that several of my students had you in 1st grade. They talk about you a lot." Next, give the students an acceptable way to greet an adult in the hall: they may wave, they may smile, they may give a special silent cheer (devise one), but they may not yell out. Do make sure to tell your students that, under no circumstances, are they to leave the line and run up to the teacher.

Former students: the opposite of the above scenario will happen to you, starting in your second year: past students will see you in the hall when you are with your current class. They may want to run up to you or hug you. You should greet them pleasantly but formally and not allow them to hug you (but you should invite them to stop by the classroom after school to visit).

Water Fountains: They crop up menacingly in the halls when the class is on its way to the library or the lunch room. Calm, reasonable children are all-of-a-sudden dying of thirst. If you turn your back, they turn the spigot, sometimes not to drink from it, but just for the sheer joy of turning a spigot. They also like to put their finger at the spigot when they turn the knob so water shoots into the air (or at another child). There is rarely a dry floor in the area around a water-fountain, and children walk through these puddles so they can make that irritating squrrrk-squrrrk sound with their shoes. Rarely does a child actually *drink* out of a water fountain. Talk about water fountains ahead of time and tell the kids that they may drink from the fountain *only* on bathroom trips. During regular hall passage, you must teach the kids to "steer" around water fountains. Tell students that making the squrrrk noise with their shoes is punishable by death.

Egregious Behavior: What do you do when a couple of kids race by your perfect lines screaming at the top of their lungs? This is tough. As a teacher, you want to speak to those kids. You also want your kids to know that that kind of behavior is inappropriate, whether the student is from your class or not. At the same time, you have your own kids to worry about and a schedule to follow. A dilemma. If the kids stopped or slowed near our class, I scolded those children then. If not, I would get the kids' names (your kids are likely to know this, as well as their teacher and classroom). I would speak to that teacher and ask to speak with those kids. I try not to let things slide – with my students or others'. I found that I became known for this, and kids who routinely misbehaved tended not to do so around me or my classroom. Do not routinely ignore misbehaviors from other students. It bothers your kids, and it sends the message that you only have to behave in Ms. McGown's classroom. You want your kids to believe that polite, appropriate behavior is important for everyone, at all times.

Accidents: You will have kids get injured eventually. Usually (& thankfully!) it is not serious or life-threatening, just painful and disruptive. While practicing and reinforcing good hallway behavior will lessen the chance of this, stuff happens. Discuss this with the kids – include this as part of your rationale for demanding exemplary hallway behavior. Talk about what you will do if a child were injured while passing through the halls or stairwells: the Office Monitor will go to the office to get a supervisor; the Assistant Teacher will watch the class; and you will sit down with the injured child (see Student Jobs).

Principal or Assistant Principal: Speak to the kids about being especially well-behaved when an administrator passes by. It is just awful when the kids are unruly in front of a supervisor. Conversely, a class that behaves well in the hallways and stairwells scores points with the administration.

<u>Before Field Trips</u>
A teacher cannot take a class on a field trip, until she or he is absolutely certain that the kids can and will conduct themselves in an appropriate way. Explain this to kids: "I want to be proud of you; I want people to look at you when we're out and think 'What a super class that is!' And, of course, I want everyone to be safe. So, I'm promising you that we will not take one step out of this building until I am absolutely confident in your ability to line-up properly and walk together safely." It might sound like bribery, or a threat, but it is not. As a new or developing teacher, you will not want to take a class of children out of the school if you have concerns for their safety. Be honest and straightforward with the kids about the rules and the rationale, and they will not feel you are being dishonest or manipulating them.

Chapter 5: Routines & Procedures

For the Out-of-Classroom Teacher

In most situations, out-of-classroom teachers do not walk classes through the halls as frequently as classroom teachers. But many out-of-classroom teachers do have to do so periodically, and every staff member eventually has to lead a class through the hall. If you have not discussed protocol with the kids at all, this is likely to be rather unpleasant.

Many out-of-classroom teachers regularly walk some classes through the halls. Their schedule requires them to bring a certain class to lunch or to pick up another class from the library. You may learn of this when you receive your schedule at the start of the year. Try to speak to a senior teacher, or a mentor, if you have one, about these kinds of details and the expectations for you, as an out-of-classroom teacher.

Out-of-classroom teachers should go over many of the same rules and procedures as a classroom teacher does. The fact is, however, that some out-of-classroom teachers may see a class only once per week. In these cases, you cannot spend the same amount of time on routines, and you also do not need all the same routines that a classroom teacher does. For classes that you expect to bring through the halls, you need to review the above guidelines. You will also need to practice hall behavior. Depending on the behavior of the class, and how they respond to you, you will determine how frequently to practice. As an out-of-classroom teacher, I always spent the second session with any class walking through the halls and up and down the stairs. The kids found this tiring (as did I) but it gave me time to review the proper behaviors for hall passage. There generally were few problems. If problems persisted, I would spend another session, or half-session, practicing with the students in the halls.

Chapter 5: Routines & Procedures

Bathrooming

After your first week in the classroom, you will wish kids were born without bladders. Orchestrating and scheduling bathroom trips will take much more effort than you could ever have imagined. In addition, the teaching-time that is lost due to bathroom trips and bathroom issues is frustrating. Like so many other things, however, a solid, predictable routine will help immeasurably. Your school may have specific policies about bathrooming; make sure to speak to a teacher on your grade, or another out-of-classroom teacher, to find out what requirements exist.

There are two main ways to bathroom a class:
1) Individually (or in pairs);
2) Whole group (as a class)

It is often a matter of school policy which way kids are bathroomed. Some schools insist that all the lower grades go to the bathroom as a class. Some schools insist that classes are bathroomed as a group in the beginning of the year, to help model and enforce proper hallway behavior. Some schools feel that group-bathrooming takes up too much instructional time. Some schools and districts require that students outside of the classroom are always in pairs, as a safety precaution. If your school has particular mandates about bathroom procedures, then that is what you will be doing. If not, the age and maturity of the students can dictate the bathroom procedure. For grades K through 1, teachers should bathroom the class as a group for the entire year. For grades 2 and up, teachers should bathroom the class as a group for the first month or so, and then by "bathroom teams" (see below).

Bathroom trips are really the same as Hall Passage. If you have set up your lines well, and if you have emphasized appropriate hallway behavior thoroughly, there is not much more to making a trip to the bathroom. Once you are at the bathroom, however, it's another story.

Whole Group
Try not to take your class to the bathroom when another class is there. If your school has a bathroom schedule, stick to it. If you know there is a certain time when other classes go to the bathroom, go at a different time. You will waste too much time at the bathroom if there are other classes there. Also, there is no way you can control the behavior of other classes, and it will frustrate you (and your kids) if other students break rules

while your kids are behaving well. If you get to the bathroom, and another class is already there, I recommend that you either: (a) go to a different bathroom in the school or (b) return to the class, and go to the bathroom a short while later.

By Two's and Three's
Allow only two boys and three girls into the bathroom at a time. Tell students that they are to be quick. Explicitly tell them they are to go in, take care of business, wash hands, come out, and then get a drink from the fountain. When they return to the line, they are to go to the back of the line, and the line then advances to the original starting point. When the Line Leaders appear at the front of the line, the teacher knows that everyone has been to the bathroom. The class is then in the correct line order, ready to proceed.

If the kids behave reasonably well, you may be able to let 3-4 kids into the bathroom at a time. This will speed things up, but I recommend it only if your kids are consistently orderly in the hall.

Don't Enter the Bathroom
Teachers should avoid entering the children's bathrooms, even when children are loud, misbehaving, or stalling. Entering the bathroom can open teachers up to unfathomable problems, including charges of sexual impropriety. I do not mean to sound reactionary or frightening, but these things do happen. You should avoid being anywhere where children are not fully dressed. This is especially important (though not fair) for male teachers. If you must enter a bathroom, have one or two reliable students walk in with you, so they can serve as witnesses if anything untoward arises.

Water Fountains
Kids go to the water fountain after they have been to the bathroom. There are usually water fountains near the bathrooms; kids should get a drink, after the bathroom, before they go to the back of the line. If the water fountains are not near the bathroom, then bathroom trips have two parts; bathroom first, water fountain second.

Later in the year, when kids go to the bathroom in teams or pairs, the bathroom trips also require a stop at the water fountain after the bathroom. If one child is not thirsty, s/he must still accompany the kid on his/her bathroom team or pair to the water fountain.

Chapter 5: Routines & Procedures

Kindergarten through Grades 1 or 2

Classes in the early grades should always be bathroomed as a group. These ages are new to school schedules and limitations, so it is a good idea to bathroom them frequently. This means at least 2-3 times per day the first month or so. Never take earlier grades less than twice per day. Younger children often move through the bathroom process more slowly. They may have a hard time with the flush, cannot reach the faucets, etc. Whenever possible, schedule bathroom trips with another adult available to help (e.g., teacher's aide, parent volunteer, an agreeable out-of-classroom teacher). Second grade students can usually be treated like the upper grades. Occasionally, however, you'll have an immature group. Plan for your group, not the norm for the age.

Younger children often have problems with fasteners – zippers, belts, over-all hooks, etc. The teacher's reflex is to zip the zipper, hook the hook, or buckle the belt. This should not be a problem, but it can be, especially for male teachers (again, unfair). Encourage children ask one another for help with clothing fasteners. Where there is a recurring problem with a child (or children) being able to fasten their own clothes, you'll need to speak to the parent to help the child learn to button or un-button, hook a belt, etc or to dress the child without tricky fasteners. Such conversations can be daunting, especially for a new or young teacher, so speak with an experienced colleague first.

After the First Month: Bathroom Teams

There are many systems for sending students to the bathroom. Many teachers just let kids go when they ask. I find that I do not like being interrupted all day, and that, if I am not monitoring who is gone when, the same kids will go over and over, and they might be gone much longer than they should be.

I developed a "team" system that I found very useful. These Bathroom Teams are small groups of kids (two or three) matched such that they could generally be relied upon to behave well together while in the hall. Group students judiciously: a mix of rambunctious and quiet, goody-goody and not. I posted a small chart that looked like this:

Chapter 5: Routines & Procedures

Bathroom Teams

	Girls	Boys
A	Evelina, Dioska, Jannedieth	Giovanny, Roderick
B	Maoly, Michelle, Victoria	Carlos, Marcus, Roosevelt
C	Rubianna, Crist, Cynthia H.	Jose, Randy
D	Alexandra, Cynthia C, Emmy	Christopher, Hussein
E	Emmily, Ericka, Michelle	Alfred, Wilbin

Decide when in the day you want kids to start going to the bathroom. Third or fourth periods are often good for this (there is generally no reason for students to go to the bathroom the first two periods of the day as they just arrived). It is a good idea to tell the children that you do not expect anyone to have to go to the bathroom early in the morning and that they should make sure to go at home in the morning, before they leave for school.

I generally wait until the lesson is underway for third period. When students have started to do the independent-work part of the lesson, I monitor to see that everyone is proceeding well. I then begin to send Bathroom Teams: (A) team goes first. When they return, they silently go to the kids on the next (B) team and tap them on the shoulders. These teams go to the bathroom and repeat the process with the C team. To vary it (and to be fair), you should rotate the starting teams, but you must explain this (after team E, team A goes). Once the kids have mastered this process, it is effortless. You only need to send the first group. After that, the kids do the work. Since each team is out of the classroom approximately the same amount of time, everyone has roughly the same time for the independent work (ie, no one child will have missed more class time than another).

In my classes, we instituted Bathroom Teams the second month of school. Everyone goes to the bathroom third period and then right after lunch (the second bathroom trip may be done as a whole class, on the return trip from the cafeteria). The rule is that no-one goes to the bathroom at any other time. Make sure to stipulate which bathroom and which water fountain the kids are to use. Kids sometimes go "sight-seeing," and no teacher scores points having his/her 2nd graders on the 5th grade hall.

The Pee-Pee Dance
This is a pet-peeve of mine. The Pee-Pee Dance is the little jerky-jumpy dance that kids do to indicate that they wish to go to the bathroom. Kids learn, at an early age that, by doing the Pee-Pee dance and scrunching up their faces, teachers will allow them to go to the bathroom without hesitation. It is especially effective with new teachers and substitutes. When performed in combination with grabbing or pointing to their groin, it is a sure winner. I have seen the Pee-Pee Dance performed by students in 7th and 8th grades. I hate the Pee-Pee dance; it is unattractive and inappropriate.

The Pee-Pee Dance was a topic for the first day of school, along with my prohibition of it. I announced that I never expected to see the Pee-Pee Dance and that any kid who performed it would not be able to go to the bathroom, no matter how dire the situation. I explained that we are old enough to know and use words to express our needs. On the rare occasion that I witnessed the Pee-Pee Dance, I followed through and did not allow that child to go to the bathroom, for at least a few minutes.

Going Alone
Many schools have rules about whether students can go to the bathroom alone. This is generally predicated on issues of safety (real or perceived). The worry is that someone in the school (a teacher, a visitor, etc) could easily corner a lone child, but would not be able to do so (easily) if children are in pairs or small groups. If there is no such rule in your school, you should speak to veteran teachers about practice. In addition, you will have to make a judgment call, about what you think is appropriate for your students (considering age, the grades in the school, issues at the school, etc) when you set your own policy.

Yourself
One of the biggest surprises for new teachers is the loss of personal freedom. Teaching is not like "regular" jobs; teachers cannot make a quick call, grab a coffee or a snack, and TEACHERS CANNOT GO TO THE BATHROOM WHEN THEY WANT. Cut down on coffee and soda consumption and never pass a bathroom without using it (prep period, lunch, etc.).

Chapter 5: Routines & Procedures

Paper, Collection & Distribution

Much of a teacher's day is spent giving out, collecting, and sorting papers. Having a system to do this cuts down on wasted time and the feeling and appearance of disorder. Of all the routines, this is one of the easiest to establish. Distributing and collecting papers should be handled almost entirely by the Table Monitors and the Paper-Passer (see Student Jobs). When there are papers to be handed out, the Paper-Passer gives papers for the table to the Table Monitors, who pass them out individually. It is a similar practice in reverse to collect papers.

Because paper distribution does not seem very important when compared to the other things a new teacher has to navigate, it often gets overlooked. It is very easy (and tempting) to let a random child hand out papers – or the first child who volunteers. This does not set a good tone for the classroom, and the lack of an established routine can descend to chaos. When in doubt, implement a routine or procedure. As time passes, and you find a routine unnecessary, you can always do away with it. It is not as easy to move in the opposite direction regarding a classroom routine.

Papers with obvious grades or scores should be handled more discretely. Kids can be mean; in addition, they may make comments with no ill intention or awareness that another child may find hurtful. In these cases, the teacher should hand out the papers or call kids individually to pick up their papers.

Chapter 5: Routines & Procedures

Journal Writing

Keeping journals is a part of many literacy programs. Journal writing is also an effective way of getting children to write creatively. Unfortunately, few teachers execute journal writing well, so it becomes a chore. Because it is often set up without thought, kids rarely enjoy it, so very little meaningful writing gets done. Teachers do not usually understand what they have done wrong or what they could do differently. Instead, they just begin to dread the journal writing periods as much as their students do. The good news is that it is easy to make journal writing effective, productive, and fun.

Prompts
You cannot tell a child to "just write about anything." They will not be able to think of a single thing. Instead, you must give compelling, provocative, *detailed* writing prompts. Many times, you will have a discussion about the prompt or question first. In this way, you illicit responses and get kids excited and thinking about ideas. Even the more cautious children will be motivated by the ideas others offer.

Good prompts are engaging and creative. Over time, you will develop your own (it is fairly easy to do so); there are many websites that offer journal writing ideas for teachers. Some examples of my favorite journal-writing prompts are:
- Imagine that this classroom broke away from the school building and went sailing through outer-space. What kinds of things might we see out our windows?
- Describe your pencil in detail (hint: if it were in a bucket of pencils, someone should be able to recognize it from your description).
- Write about a time when you were really angry, so angry that you thought you might explode.
- What if you were as small as a mouse? How would your life be different? (hints: describe some things that would be hard for you to do; what would be easy to do?)
- Tell about a time when you were really sad.
- If your favorite t-shirt could talk, what do you think it would say?
- Look at your left hand and describe it in detail.
- Write about a time you laughed so hard you started crying.

I used prompts like these for the first months of school. Usually, at some point, November-ish (two months into the year), a child would ask if s/he could write about something else. Since one of my goals is independent self-directed writing, this was perfect! I allowed the child to write whatever s/he wanted; other children would begin to ask the same (not all, but some), and I would encourage this. I did, however, continue to provide interesting prompts, for the class.

See Chapter 10, Day 1 & Week 1, for a winning first journal activity.

Grammar
Every teacher has different rules and expectations about written student work. For journal-writing, my feeling is that kids should write freely and unencumbered. There are children who will get so caught up in spelling or punctuation that they will not write anything. There are kids are fearful of taking risks and making mistakes. I always told the students that there is no way to be "wrong" in their journals. I explained spelling and grammar do not count: "Just write what you feel and guess about the spelling." It takes some kids a while to "let go" of the rules; some never do. Most, however, embrace the chance to write and love the freedom.

Checking Journals
Some teachers feel that children's free-writing journals should not be graded; others feel that all student work should be reviewed and marked (if not graded). My believe is that student journals should not be graded but they should be read carefully. I always used a brightly-colored magic marker and wrote brief comments: "Boy, that sounds like fun! I really love roller-coasters!" "I wish I could have done that – but I think I would have been scared!" "That must have made you really angry – I know I would have been angry." Depending on the content, I write a little more or less. The important thing is to write *something* every time the kids write a journal entry. I rotated marker colors each time. This made the notebooks quite pretty; the kids loved this. Being a teacher a teacher and a grammar nerd, I was unable to pass on teachable moments. As the year progressed, I often included soft comments about grammar, spelling, style, etc.

When to Read/Check Journals
I generally checked homework while the kids were writing in their journals (see Homework). Morning was my preferred time for checking homework and journal writing, but the imposed schedule at your school may dictate this. Sometimes, journal writing was just before or after lunch or at another time (ie, whenever I could fit it in).

Chapter 5: Routines & Procedures

Frightening Revelations & Honesty
Kids reveal remarkable things in their journals. It is in journals that you
are likely to learn of a parents' divorce, a fight with a sibling or friend,
the death of a relative, a parent losing a job, abuse, etc. It is important
that you assure the kids that what they write in the journals is private,
that you will read it – but no-one else will. They should feel safe in
confiding in you. Explain to the students that you will never allow
another person to read a journal without the student's express
permission. Before Parent-Teacher conferences, put all the journals out of
sight. When a kid writes something especially cute or funny, and you
want to photocopy it or share it with others (this *will* happen), make sure
to ask the child for permission.

For Kindergarten and 1st Grade Teachers
Children in the early grades are not yet (usually) writers. There are
several strategies to encourage journal "writing." One is to give a similar
prompt and to have the kids draw a picture in response. As the children
are drawing, the teacher (and the aide or assistant teacher, if available)
walks around the room and has the kids "narrate" the picture. The
teacher writes what the child says and then reads it, inviting the child to
"read" also.

For the Out-of-Classroom Teacher
Out-of-classroom teachers do not usually have journal writing sessions as
a regular part of their classes. Since these teachers often see groups of
students only a few times per week, they must emphasize their own
subject/curriculum. In the cases where out-of-classroom teachers work
with the same group several times per week, they may choose to
implement journal writing. Out-of-classroom teachers should follow the
same procedures as described above.

Chapter 5: Routines & Procedures

Morning Routines (K & 1)

Most teachers have morning routines for their students but teachers of kindergarten and first grade classrooms often follow very structured morning routines. The early grades are the first years of formal education, and establishing the routine of school is top-priority. At these ages, too, children really like the same thing to happen the same way every day (think how many times small children like to have the same book read to them). These routines vary from school-to-school and teacher-to-teacher, but they have many elements in common.

For kindergarten, morning activities generally happen on the rug or in the story center. For first grade classes, the children may stay at their tables or sit together on the rug, depending on the teacher's preferences and the space in the classroom.

Good Morning Song
Many early childhood teachers begin the morning with a "Good Morning" song. A quick internet search will offer many options. Good ones are those in which the children's names are used. This allows each child to be "honored" and attendance can be taken this way.

Calendar, Weather, and Special Days
The calendar is a common part of most early-childhood classroom morning routines. Kindergarten and first grade teachers have large, colorful chart-calendars for this activity. Attractive cut-outs with numbers are used to mark the individual days. Cut-outs of all different shapes are available in packages in teacher supply stores. Some teachers prefer number shapes to reinforce the numbers. Others prefer season-appropriate shapes on which they write the numbers (leaves in the autumn, snowmen in winter, etc.). Activities involving the calendar include: marking the day, counting the days until a special event (a kid's birthday, Halloween, etc.), recording the weather, counting the days of sun/rain/snow/etc. so far this week/month, etc.

Daily Journal
In most early childhood classes, a "daily journal" comes next. This is a structured, predictable review of the day. The teacher elicits comments from the students for the daily journal, which s/he records on the chalkboard or a large dry-erase board. These include the date, the day, the weather, special events, absences, etc. The teacher then reads it

aloud, having children chime in. The teacher may ask some students to volunteer to "read" the journal on their own.

Some kindergarten and first grade teachers have a corresponding "writing" activity. In kindergarten, this may be a photocopied sheet, on which kids trace over the date and draw a sun or clouds, depending on the weather. This is sufficient for kindergarten, early first grade and/or low-functioning first grade classes. Generally, however, first graders copy the daily journal, or parts of it, from the board into their journal notebooks. Depending on their writing ability, students may be invited to add to the class journal. Many second grade classes begin the year with a similar morning structure. Second graders should, however, progress to regular journal writing by the late fall.

Chapter 5: Routines & Procedures

Schedule Changes

Schedules change, and school schedules changes a lot. Unfortunately, they also do so with little warning. Schedule changes can put kids in bad moods, whether because of the loss of dependable routine or the cancellation of a favorite class. Teachers get frustrated because the changes are (usually) not their fault, yet they are left to deal with the result: grumbling, disappointed kids. There is nothing a teacher can do to prevent schedule changes. The teacher can, however, prepare the children to handle changes and disruptions well.

Early in the year, have a discussion about scheduling and schedule changes. Ask the children to discuss times in the past that something changed or was cancelled in school and how it made them feel. Talk about what you will do when the same thing happens this year. Simply letting the kids share their feelings and listening to them will help the class respond better when these things do happen. Tell the kids that when something fun is cancelled (an assembly, art class, etc.), that you will try to figure out something fun for them to do. Explain that it won't always be possible but that you'll try (and then do so!).

On days of big disappointments/changes, remind the class of the above discussion. Try to do something fun but very structured. Art projects that require concentration and focus are great for this (see Origami or Magic Pictures). It is important the activity be truly engaging but highly structured. If you are in the middle of a great read-aloud book, read a few extra chapters and have the kids write in response to the chapters and/or draw illustrations for the part you read.

Chapter 5: Routines & Procedures

Written Assignments

Teachers often complain about the appearance of student work. This is something the teacher can control. When written work is sub-par, it is because the teacher did not invest adequate time up-front to explain expectations and to monitor kids' progress and compliance. Many teachers often forget to review the basic elements of proper penmanship or handwriting. Other teachers assume that kids know more about grammar or spelling (or etc.) than they actually do. There is increasingly less emphasis on the "art" of writing beautifully; penmanship is not a focus as it once was. Few kids have ever been taught how letters are formed and how they should look. In addition, some kids get lazy over the summer and un-learn practices from the previous year. If you want your students to have good penmanship, if you want their written work to be attractive, then you have to make it a priority to teach the kids the necessary skills.

Baby Steps
In the beginning, every written assignment should be done in steps. Tell the kids that they will write each section as you direct them and that you will check for neatness and accuracy before proceeding to the next section. Warn them that you will make them erase and re-write their work, so it is best not to move ahead or to write too quickly. Explain that form and penmanship will be counted on all assignments.

The first few times the class writes an assignment, tell them you will be walking around checking that each section is written properly. Explain what "properly" is. This may include the following:
• Letters straight up-and-down;
• Capitals go to the top of the lines;
• Lower-case letters go to the middle of the line;
• No hearts or bubbles over "I"s;
• Skip lines when asked; etc.

On the first day, the first time the class picks up pencils, walk around and make sure that each one is holding the pencil properly. Have the students start the assignment with the proper heading. Walk around and check that each child's work is acceptable. If a child has not written neatly, have him/her erase that section and write it over. Try not to be negative or punitive. When the child has re-written the section, make sure to praise him/her, even if the work is still not up to your standard (baby steps, remember). If you ask the class to skip a space before writing the title or objective of the lesson, make sure that they have done so before moving onto the next step. Give points on the Point Chart to the tables whose members do each part correctly. It is reasonable to award six points during an initial writing lesson or assignment.

When students have written the heading to your satisfaction, move to the next part of the written assignment, circulating around the room and checking progress all the while. Do not let any infractions slide. Tell a kid to erase and re-write a tilted word, under-size capitals, or poorly-formed letters. After the heading, the kids will write the title of the lesson, or the objective. After you have checked to see that all written work looks good, ask the students what they think of how their assignments look. Praise them: "This is good stuff. This is what the work of smart kids looks like," etc.

You will need to model proper penmanship on the chalkboard. This takes practice; it is not as easy to write on a board as you think!

Mention, then reinforce good penmanship at the start of each written assignment. This will grow tedious, but you will see results. As students write, especially during the first few weeks of school, walk around and evaluate the writing. Emphasizing routines is the *most* important thing teachers do the first few weeks of school. Remind the students each time they begin a new assignment that proper writing is important and required.

As time passes, you will monitor this (and most other things) less often and more randomly. These practices become habit, and you can relax. If kids start getting lazy and work becomes sloppy, start monitoring more closely again.

<u>For Kindergarten and First Grade Teachers</u>
Bad writing habits are learned, and reinforced, when kids first begin to write. Kindergarten is generally a year when "anything goes," because teachers wish to be fully supportive and encouraging. Kindergarten students should be encouraged to respond, first by drawing pictures, and then with key words. In the beginning the emphasis should be on expressing oneself in words, and less on the shape of the letters. These young students should, however, as soon as they start to write with some fluency, be taught that there is a proper way to form letters. Children at

this age are very flexible, and they are keen to do things correctly (like the "big kids"). Teachers should use this to their advantage.

In first grade, the emphasis moves from pre-reading and pre-writing and emergent reading/writing activities to actual reading and writing. At this point, it is essential to monitor and correct poor handwriting. For kids with especially poor writing or hand-eye coordination, it may be necessary to photocopy early handwriting workbook pages for extra practice.

Chapter 5: Routines & Procedures

Do Now

Most lessons and activities start with a piece that requires students to work quietly for a short period of time. This Do Now serves several functions: It calms and focuses students; it engages them immediately so that time is not lost; it often provides a hook or connection to previous content so that students are ready for the new content or related activity. An organized teacher can quickly review the Do Now for a quick temperature-gauge or assessment. The Do Now becomes a predictable part of lessons and activities, and so becomes a part of effective classroom management.

Most published lessons (in teacher-guides, on the internet, etc) will include a Do Now (though it may have different names in different schools or settings). If you are working without a text and guide, you need to design a Do Now on your own. This is not hard to do. Keep in mind that Do Now's should:
- Take no more than five minutes;
- Have questions or problems of varying difficulty (each student should be able to answer *some* of the questions un-aided);
- Be immediately interesting and engaging so that the students will *want* to start the work; and
- Have explicit, clear instructions so the students *can* begin work on their own.

Students' Responsibility
A Do Now is not effective if the students do not know what they are supposed to do and do not take responsibility for doing it. As in everything else, the more explicit you are when explaining Do Now's, the more likely to have the students perform adequately and to your expectations. I never posted Do Now rules, I just explained them and reviewed them periodically.

Do Now rules:
1) Take out all materials necessary for the Do Now.
2) Prepare the paper(s) properly (heading, etc.).
3) Try to answer each question; leave no blanks.
4) If there is a question/problem you do not think you can answer, you must "pull" any information from the book/etc which may help you to answer it.

5) You may not raise your hand for help until you have done all of the above for each question.

How do these play out?
Let's say your students are working on some review questions from yesterday's reading. The questions are written on the board.
1) Students should take out the reading text, notebook, and a pencil.
2) They should start by writing the heading in the reading notebook.
3) If a student cannot answer one question, s/he should leave enough space so that he can write the answer in later when s/he has help.
4) For a question that a student cannot answer, s/he should write *something*; s/he must "pull" something from the text or question. An acceptable response may be: "It's about setting. I think that's where the story happens. I can't find where it says anything about the setting." Additional spaces should be left as per #3.
5) Circulate around the room and help children as necessary if they have completed the above steps.

Number 4 is the most important, and it is the hardest to teach. Children learn early that saying, "I can't do it," and, "I don't understand," will get them out of school-work. Often, those claims are simply habit and do not reflect ability or comprehension. They may be cop-outs for students who struggle; they are also a recourse for students who wish to avoid work (many of whom have been successful in doing so prior to your class!). Breaking these habits can be tough. You will have to teach what you mean by explicitly how to "pull" relevant information from a question.

Help!
There will be times during the year when you are overwhelmed and need some extra time: The principal may have just told you that s/he needs certain forms filled out on all students; your prep period was taken away unexpectedly, and you had planned to prepare for a meeting with a parent after school; you forgot about your bulletin board which is due up tomorrow. If your students have been trained to work quietly on a Do Now, you can occasionally buy some extra time with prepared questions or worksheets or review puzzles, as discussed in After-Lunch Chaos.

Chapter 5: Routines & Procedures

"I'm Done!" and the Class Law

"I'm done!"
"I'm finished!"
"What do I do now?"
"I finished first!"

Imagine hearing this 32 times each time you assign any written work. It is enough to make anyone run screaming from the classroom. It's frustration because you know, and the students probably know, that there are worthwhile things they could do when finished early. in addition, these comments interrupt important things you are likely doing – helping an individual student, working with a strategy group, writing a quick answer to a parent's note, etc. The Class Law is a strategy to address this recurring problem.

Some kids finish work before others. They will whine about wanting other things to do or they will misbehave because they are bored. Other kids will still be working on the assignment, perhaps needing additional support. New teachers have a hard time balancing the needs of both groups of students. Many new teachers tell the students to "find something" to do. The students generally will not do this (often because they do not have the maturity to pick something appropriate and follow through), and the teacher gets frustrated. Or the students may find something to do (something fun, like coloring), and the others who are not yet finished will get distracted. It is better, at least initially, not to give students open-ended instructions; concrete suggestions will get better results.

In my classroom, we had a policy about what students may do when finished with a given assignment or activity I called this the "Class Law," the "law" being "School is important so we don't waste time; we find something to do." I prepared a chart with alternative activities listed on it. As a class, we discussed the different things that students could do when they had finished an assignment. In the beginning of the year, the chart would have only two or three activities. We added activities to the list as the year progressed. You may also add activities as you become more confident in the students' ability to work on their own. Tables receive points if their members find appropriate things to do when they have finished the assignment. This causes kids at the table to encourage

Chapter 5: Routines & Procedures

kids who were finished to do the "right thing." It also allows the teacher calm time to work with the students who need extra help.

My Class Law list typically included:
- Read a book from the library
- Study vocabulary words
- Read a dictionary (see note below)
- Study the times tables
- Practice grammar from the green books (see note below)
- Read the newspaper (I always had daily newspapers on my desk)
- Work on a book report
- Practice handwriting
- Fact Cards (alone or in pairs)

Dictionaries and Green Books

My class had a set of great children's dictionaries. The kids enjoyed looking through the books. I encouraged them to collect "weird" words for the Cool Word Wall (see Classroom Decoration) or to surprise me in writing assignments. I also discovered a set of old-fashioned grammar texts in the school's supply room (they were green, so we called them the "green books"). For no reason that I could discern, my kids loved working from these books. Many schools have sets of books, sitting unused in a corner of a supply room or a veteran teacher's closet. Try to poke around and see what you can find. Sets of dictionaries (as well as various subject texts) are a great addition to all classrooms.

Thumbs-Up

Teachers do need to give students silent ways of conveying certain messages. This keeps the noise level down, and it gives the kids alternate ways of communicating. In the case of "I'm done!" and the "Class Law," many well-intentioned and focused students still want the teacher to know they've finished. To handle this, instruct students to flash a "thumbs-up" sign, rather than yelling out. For your part, you must train yourself to acknowledge this sign and respond (a nod, a pat on the head or shoulder, a quiet "Good Job," or a return of the thumbs-up sign). If you wish to tie this behavior – ie, not calling out – to the Point Chart, simply award points to tables shoe members remain quiet while transitioning from the lesson to the Class Law activities.

Chapter 5: Routines & Procedures

Homework

There are conflicting opinions about the effectiveness of homework as to whether it impacts student achievement and/or the degree to which it does. Some studies show no relationship between homework assignment and student achievement. Most classroom teachers, however, would not agree. While there may not be a accepted, proven connection between homework assignment and student achievement, regular homework does foster the establishment of home routines and good study habits. It is also a great way to involve parents in their children's education and schoolwork. You may find that parents expect their children to have homework and they may complain if you do not assign it or if you assign very little. Other parents may complain that you assign too much or that it is too difficult.

The fact is that the decision to assign or not to assign homework, and even how much to assign, may not be up to the individual teacher. Many schools and districts require homework, and many determine how often and how much homework is assigned. In some schools, teachers on the same grade may be required to assign similar (or identical) homework each day. Make sure to speak to a more experienced teacher on the grade to find out what requirements and limitations there are for your grade/subject. In all likelihood, you will assign homework, and you will probably have some leeway as to subjects and/or amounts of homework. The assignment, collection, and checking of homework pose many problems for new teachers.

Homework Notebook
I found it easiest for each student to have a homework notebook, and that the homework notebooks be the same. The homework notebook should be sturdy enough to survive the back-and-forth in book-bags and the abuse kids dole out. Sewn-binding composition books are preferable to spiral notebooks, because they are sturdier, and pages are less likely to fall out. Most teachers also need some kind of folder – for class notes, worksheets, etc. You need to make sure that students maintain the notebook according to your specifications (a sample homework notebook page is in Appendix II).

Will your students copy the homework or will you distribute pre-copied handouts with the weekly homework assignments listed?

Chapter 5: Routines & Procedures

Assigning homework can be done in two main ways: the teacher can prepare photocopied homework sheets ahead of time or the students can copy homework each day. There are pro's and con's to each:

• Teacher Homework Sheets: Prepared homework sheets can be very handy. Teachers who opt for this approach generally prepare the sheets for a full week. This takes a lot of time upfront, but it takes very little time or effort after that. Using prepared sheets does require that the teacher has all homework planned at least one week in advance (this mans s/he also has to have a good sense of all lessons for the week as well, since homework supports school-work). It also means that s/he cannot make last-minute changes – or that such last-minute changes need some back-tracking.

• Students Copying Homework: Having the students copy the homework each day forces them to take some responsibility for the task. Daily homework assignment also means that last-minute changes are easy to incorporate. On the other hand, having students copy the homework takes time, and if a child mis-copies, s/he may not do the homework (this can also be used as an excuse to get out of doing homework).

Increasingly schools rely on the internet to communicate with parents and families. In some cases, the school will mandate that the homework for the class or grade is posted each week on the school's website. This requires the teachers to prepare homework sheets ahead of time and post them on the internet.

I had the students copy the homework everyday from the chalkboard or the overhead projector. Copying homework was one of the procedures I taught and reinforced from the very first day. We practiced speed and efficiency; it rarely took more than five minutes for the homework to be copied. Because the students copied the homework everyday, I could make assignment changes easily as necessary.

While all homework assignments are copied in the homework notebook, some may also be completed in the homework notebook. Others must be completed in the appropriate workbook or on separate paper. On the sample homework assignment (see Appendix II), the first item is written in the homework notebook. The second item is completed in the math workbook. The third item is written on separate sheets of loose-leaf paper. The fourth item (the parent's signature) is written in the homework notebook. The procedure for each kind of homework assignment must be explained:

- Assignments written in the homework notebook are written on a separate page. The date is written at the top, in the wide space. Skip one line and then write the title of the assignment (e.g., "Vocabulary Words, Three Times Each"). If this assignment is numbered, the numbers are written to the left of the pink line, each one circled.
- Workbook pages completed as homework must have student's full name, date, and "Homework" written along the top. Most workbooks have spaces for the name and date.
- Homework assignments written on separate paper get a full heading (see Classroom Decoration). For subject, students write "Homework."

The parents *must* sign the homework notebook every night. Homework is not considered complete without this signature. This makes the homework notebook a great place to jot down a quick note to a parent, and parents should be encouraged to write notes to you in the homework notebook. Some students may have difficulty in getting a parent to sign the homework; they go to daycare in the afternoon, they are watched by an older sibling, etc. This was something I addressed on the first day of school (as I assigned homework the first day). If a parent is not available, the homework notebook must be signed by an uncle, aunt, big brother, big sister, grandma, etc.

I also had students whose parents neither spoke nor read English fluently; the students sometimes offered that, for this reason, their parents could not sign the homework. This was generally an excuse for not completing the homework and/or for not having it signed. Explain to your students: "All your parent (or uncle, aunt, big sister, grandpa, etc) needs to do is check that you made some kind of attempt for each part. S/he does not have to check that the work is correct." The first few times this came up in class, we discussed exactly what needed to be checked, and how a person who didn't speak English could still do it. It may be necessary for you to explain this to the parent(s) at some time as well.

Copying Homework
When should the class copy the homework assignment? Some teachers have the students copy it in the morning. I never liked this, because the homework assignment may change during the day; if we were not able to cover something or if I felt the kids had not mastered a concept sufficiently to work on their own, I might not want to include it in the homework (as I had originally planned). Many teachers have kids copy

the homework right before packing up for dismissal. I did not like this either do this, because it adds stress to an often chaotic time of day. I preferred to have the kids copy homework right after lunch. Copying the homework became my predictable, focusing, do now when the class returned from the cafeteria.

For teachers who prepare homework sheets ahead of time, they still need to review the homework with the class everyday. This ensures that the students know exactly what to do; it also allows them to ask any questions about the assignment.

Homework Content
Students should be able to complete homework assignments on their own. Teachers should not expect that there is a (capable) adult at home who will be able to help the child. It is not fair to assign homework that requires parental involvement. My feeling is that homework is best used as classroom review and response-writing. Homework content should be things which kids can comfortably handle on their own. In addition, there is not enough time for you to check complicated homework assignments.

The more-straightforward the assignment, the easier it is for you to check. Teachers who assign lengthy homework assignments either kill themselves trying to check it all or end up not checking it (which frustrates the students and defeats the purpose).

Checking Homework
This is where the fun really starts. Checking homework is terribly time-consuming. New teachers have a great deal of difficulty fitting it into the daily schedule. It can be a challenge for even the most experienced of teachers. I set up a routine from the second day of class.
1) Decide on your homework-checking time; make sure students know when it is due and when it will be checked.
2) Assign a written activity on which the kids can work quietly, on their own. My favorite assignment during homework-checking time was writing in journals (see Journal Writing).
3) Instruct the children how to display their homework so it is easiest for you to come around and check, while they are working at their desks. I required all homework books and materials be open to the page they completed for homework, in a stack, with the homework notebook open on top of the pile. Students may need help, at least initially, in working with so many things on their desks. They will get used to it, but in the beginning, they will find it cumbersome.

4) Walk around the room and check homework. Believe it or not, this will take very little time, generally half a minute per student. I used a bright-colored magic marker to check homework, a different color each day. The kids liked the colors, and it made their homework notebooks attractive. If a child had completed the assignment, or made a fair attempt, and had a parent's signature, s/he got a sticker for the Homework Chart. For the first few weeks or month of school, I give two stickers, one for the assignment and one for the signature. By the end of the first month, the reward became one sticker for the whole assignment (including the signature).

5) Your walk-around allows you to do two things: (a) you "check in" with each child; it's your "private" hello time; you'll be able to find out if a child is in a bad mood, has something exciting to share, etc, (b) you will discover common errors in the homework; if many students did not complete #5 on the math page, then you need to go over it; if many mis-spelled the same word the same way, you probably mis-spelled it when you wrote it on the board, etc.

Written Assignments/Essays

Written homework assignments are collected and checked separately. This is for two reasons: 1) A teacher cannot review adequately a written assignment in half a minute; and 2) Written assignments are generally on-going, part of the writing process, and cannot be "checked" in the same way that review assignments and workbook pages can be. I had the Table Monitors (see Student Jobs) collect the essay drafts from the table and give them to me. I then reviewed them at another time.

Fair Attempt

I expected all students to make a "fair attempt" on all homework assignments. It was okay if a child could not figure a certain answer, but s/he had to have tried. I had to explain this to students. Many kids have learned that "But I don't understand!" is a good way to get out of school work. "I don't understand" elicits some "softening" and/or pity on the part of the teacher; this often gets the child out of the assignment. This "habit" has to be unlearned. "I don't understand" cannot be accepted as an excuse for not trying.

Such excuses are commonly used when working on math word problems (many students do not like math word problems and will try to get out of doing them). A child may say that s/he didn't understand the word problem. I explain to the class that, when they get to a question or problem they think is hard, they must try. This means reading the question/problem and "pulling" pieces from it that may be necessary to solving it. In math word problems, this means pulling the (possible) relevant numbers, the operations, and the unit. Often, if a child does this, s/he will be able to solve the problem. If I see some kind of true effort, the child receives homework credit. I have had low- and high-level classes; after clearly explaining my expectations about fair attempts – including giving examples and answering student questions – all kids have been able to meet those expectations to get homework credit. The concept of "fair attempt" carries through all parts of my classroom, not just homework.

Homework Chart
The Homework Chart is a simple tool that I used to track homework completion. The rate of homework completion, in my classrooms, was extraordinarily high. On the first parent-teacher night, all my parents asked to see the "homework thing," because they had heard about it so much from their children. Most parents have not witnessed such interest or excitement about homework. When parent see the homework chart, they are always surprised – because it so simple and so unremarkable (and yet so effective!).

To make a Homework Chart, purchase pre-made grid-charts (poster size) available in teacher supply stores (see Physical Classroom). Print the names of the students down the left side of the chart. Across the top, write "Class 3-309 Homework Race." When students complete homework assignments, they are invited to place a sticker onto the chart (each student should affix his/her own stickers). After a pre-determined amount of time (no more than two weeks in the beginning and 3-4 as the year progresses), you will review the chart to see which kids have "won," by counting which students have the most stickers to-date. After the first "race," you will mark a line down the chart and start over. This means that each student, regardless of his/her work previously, has an equal chance in winning the next round. This is very important, because it maintains motivation and interest. Some of the "slower" children, especially those who have not had much "winning" in their academic past, may not understand this. You will have to bring them up to the chart and explain it to them individually (otherwise they may lose motivation for completing homework assignments).

You may use different things to award the winners; I used pre-printed ribbons that said "Class 3-309 Homework Champion" (see Shopping List). At the end of the day on homework race days, we had a small ceremony for the homework winners. Each student came to the front, and I pinned a ribbon on his/her chest. The rest of the class applauded.

For the Kindergarten Teacher
Kindergarten teachers can use the Homework Chart, but they do not need to culminate with a homework ribbon. At this age, the visible row of stickers on the Homework Chart is enough.

For the Out-of-Classroom Teacher
Most out-of-classroom teachers do not routinely assign homework to students. The Homework Chart is simply not necessary for these teachers.

Chapter 5: Routines & Procedures

Cleaning Up

It helps very much to have a clean room. Children and teachers tend to feel more comfortable, and be more productive, in a well-organized environment. Teachers who have messy unorganized rooms tend to get less accomplished (as do their students). If you implement a system for organizing and tidying the classroom regularly, and if you take a few minutes everyday before you leave to neaten up your desk, you feel much better the next morning. Walking into a tidy, orderly room sets a positive tone for everyone.

The fact is, of course, that classrooms get messy, and someone has to clean them. This is much more complicated than it sounds (unless the teacher does it). Kids love to help, but they are not effective without explicit instructions. If you just instruct children to "help clean," you will generally end up having to re-do everything they did.

Desks & Desk Areas

For the first couple of days, you must check desks regularly. Tell the students that there should be nothing unnecessary in the desks and that all books and notebooks should be in neat piles inside the desks. There should also be nothing on the floor around the desks. Tables with neat desks and a clear floor earn points on the Point Chart (see Classroom Management). As the year progresses, you will check desks every couple of days or weeks or when you see they are getting messy. At these times, you will have classroom cleaning sessions. I often played some music and made it into a clean up "party."

Periodically, the desks and desk areas will get really messy, and a spot-check will not do. At these times, you will have to coordinate a full-out "desk-dump." You will need to explain to students what they need to do:

1) Have kids take *everything* out of their desks and pile it on top of their desks.
2) If the desks are filled with ucky stuff (crumbs, pencil shavings, etc.), you'll have to pick up the desk and turn it over. Do not allow a student to do this.
3) Throw away all garbage or scrap papers.
4) Quizzes and school papers should be turned into the teacher and filed properly; the Assistant Teacher may be able to help with this (see Student Jobs).

5) *Superfluous* items go into the backpack; tell students that these items should be taken out of the backpack that evening at home (superfluous was a word all my students knew; they could explain that it means extra and unnecessary).
6) Look through each of the books and notebooks for papers stuffed in between the pages. Have the child throw out or turn in as appropriate.
7) Replace books and notebooks in the desks.
8) The Table Monitor sweeps the area around the table (see Student Jobs).

The tops of desks will also get dirty. This is the purpose of the spray cleaner (see Shopping List). I avoided using the spray when the whole class was present, because it was possible that someone would get squirted in the eye. Instead, I would have a couple of kids help during lunch or after school. I always did the spraying (I was always worried about cleaner getting in an eye), but they followed me with paper towels to scrub and wipe. We did this once every two weeks and after all parties and messy projects.

Garbage Bin
The class garbage bin is an open and constant invitation for kids to get out of their seats or to set things soaring through the air. Teachers seem unwilling to check this behavior, because the kids are being responsible and helpful, right? Nope. The garbage the child is throwing away is often a paper s/he intentionally crumpled up to *make* garbage to be able to get out of his/her seat.

Set garbage rules:
• Students may not get out of their seats during lessons to throw away garbage. All garbage should be kept in students' desks until an appropriate time; it can be thrown away on the students' way out of the classroom, during clean-up, or during some other time the teacher determines.
• Any sticky garbage must be wrapped in a piece of scrap paper.
• Students must take the most direct route from their desk to the garbage bin.
• There are no Michael Jordan's in room 309 (substitute the name of any popular non-retired basketball player here). No 3-point shots allowed.

Chapter 5: Routines & Procedures

Chalkboard

The chalkboard needs to get wiped down periodically, or it becomes really hard to read. Children *love* washing the board (water!) but they invariably do it poorly. Make sure they follow these rules:
1) Fill a bucket with water.
2) Remove all charts and magnets from the chalkboard.
3) Wet and squeeze out two sponges.
4) Helpers must wipe the chalkboard in one direction only (top to bottom), with a damp sponge.
5) Watch that the kids do not wipe in circles, or the board will be a mess when it dries (hardly better than when you started).
6) If you have a large board, you may have two helpers working at once, each starting from one end of the board, working toward the middle.
7) After the board has been wiped down once, the helpers must rinse out their sponges completely and re-fill the bucket with fresh water. They then repeat the process. Three times is generally sufficient.
8) Many teachers want the boards washed every week; I found every two-three weeks to be sufficient.

Floor

The floor should be swept a couple times per week. This can be a separate job for a student (see Student Jobs). I often had the Librarian do it, since s/he had to sweep the library area anyway.

When to Clean?

Students enjoy cleaning the classroom. I often combined room-cleaning with some other house-keeping activities, like filing book reports and other finished work, returning class-library books, collecting permission slips, etc. (see Student Work). Such a house-keeping period might be in lieu of a free period, but the students never minded and the room got cleaned. I scheduled "big" room-cleaning periods about every three-four weeks. As the year progressed, I sometimes played music and allowed snacks, and we called it a "Clean-Up Party."

Chapter 5: Routines & Procedures

Probability Bowl

The "probability bowl" is a multi-functional item. It can fairly pick a child to answer a question, bring something to the office, etc. It is also a simple way to assign work groups or pairs. The bowl itself is just a medium-sized kitchen storage container, in which are placed slips of paper with each of the students' names written. To choose students, the teacher shakes the bowl and picks names without looking. Since the probability bowl is totally random, it is absolutely fair (as my students say, "The bowl is fair"). This bowl comes in handy, in terms of management, for four main kinds of situations:

1) To pick a volunteer: An announcement comes over the PA, "Teachers please send a monitor to the office to pick up letters that must go home today." At that moment, chaos erupts, as each of 32 children scream to run the errand." Once you have assigned student jobs, this chaos can be avoided. But what if the Office Monitor is absent or in the bathroom? The probability bowl helps the teacher choose a student fairly and maintain calm in the classroom.

2) Special Activities and Games: A teacher can turn reviewing for a test into a game by using the probability bowl. Since the bowl introduces an element of chance, a rote activity becomes a game. The teacher can pick students from the probability bowl to answer review questions; correct answers earn a point for the table.

3) Time Filler: Sometimes teachers find they have a few extra minutes. This time can be turned into a quick review or game with the aid of the probability bowl (see Fact Cards).

4) Assigning pairs or triads (threes): While teachers often have pre-set pairs or triads for certain activities (reading buddies, math groups, etc), there are many times when assigning random pairs or triads is necessary. Students will often complain about working in certain groupings ("But I worked with him last time!" "Why can't I ever work with ----?" etc.). Whatever the complaint, kids feel that the teacher has pointedly chosen the specific grouping. If, however, the bowl "picks" the pair/triad, there are far fewer complaints. It's as if they see the bowl as a higher, objective authority (the fact is, too, that the bowl is fully objective – and it rarely puts the same kids together on subsequent days).

Chapter 5: Routines & Procedures

Math Connection - Probability
Students tend to be introduced to the concept of probability in the second or third grades. It is a hard concept to teach (how many adults do you know who can explain it well?). Children find probability confusing, as there are no "definite" answers. Probability generally shows up in math curricula every year through high school, with increasingly in-depth exploration. The probability bowl is a great introduction to probability. I use the term "probability bowl" long before I begin a discussion on probability. When I do first mention probability in terms of mathematics, the students recognize the word, from the bowl, and they understand the relation of chance and fair; and we start our discussion from there.

For the Out-of-Classroom Teacher
Out-of-classroom teachers who travel room-to-room do not generally need a probability bowl. Teachers with their own rooms should make class sets of name-cards and keep them in little zipper-seal plastic bags. As different classes enter the room, switch the names in the probability bowl. Presto!

Chapter 5: Routines & Procedures

Quizzes/Tests

Teachers give informal tests and quizzes regularly, and formal standardized tests, both practice and real, periodically. Ever more emphasis is placed on how students perform on these various assessments. It is imperative, therefore, to establish routines that focus the students and help them perform as well as possible. These routines should be established early in the year, from the first quiz. The testing routines must be reinforced at every test or quiz, even minor ones.

As in many classroom routines, the teacher must explain the rationale behind the testing routines. This can be covered in a give-and-take brainstorm session with the children ("Why is testing important?" "What makes you feel better when you take a test?" "What can we do to help each other do better on tests and quizzes?" etc.). This discussion should happen during the first week of school and before the first quiz or test. Teachers will re-visit this discussion during the year, especially prior to big tests.

Review all <u>testing rules</u>:
• No talking during tests;
• No looking at another's paper; and
• No bathroom or water fountain trips during tests.

Make a list of all <u>testing routines</u>:
• Desks are moved so that each child has adequate space and none can look at others' papers;
• Desks are cleared of everything except two sharpened pencils and an eraser; and
• Students must have something to do (something quiet) when they have finished the test – a library book, their journal, an unfinished book report, etc. This item should be placed on the floor next to the student.

There will be additional routines, depending on the kind and length of test being administered. These may also be rules or practices mandated by school policy. It is important to speak to a supervisor or senior teacher about testing policies, especially for any school, district, or city/state tests.

Chapter 5: Routines & Procedures

Oral Tests

Many quizzes and tests are given orally, most commonly Spelling/Vocabulary tests and various subject short-answer tests and quizzes. Teachers like oral tests, because they do not require formatting or photocopying. Giving oral tests can be frustrating, however, if the teacher does not review the procedure ahead of time:

1) Students must prepare their test paper (heading, etc.). They then put their pencils down and wait for the teacher to read any instructions.
2) The teacher reads these instructions twice and asks the students if they have questions. The teacher must then review the oral test routine: "I'll read each question twice and give you some time to respond. I will then move to the next question. If you've not yet written an answer, leave that space blank. After I've read all the questions twice, I'll go back and read through each of the questions a final time. I will not read any questions after that." This might seem harsh, but listening and appropriate response-time is important, and it is something children must learn (see note).
3) Children write "(1)" on their papers and put their pencils down. The teacher reads the first question twice. Children should listen the first time, and they start writing the second time.
4) Children respond. When they are done, they write "(2)" on their paper and put their pencils down. The teacher knows to proceed when all pencils are down.
5) The teacher reads the second question twice, making sure to preface each time with "Question # 2."
6) Children respond, write "(3)" and put their pencils down when they have finished.
7) This pattern repeats until the entire quiz/test had been administered.
8) The teacher then reads each question aloud *once* for children who have missed a question and for all children to review their answers.

Big Tests

There are timed and un-timed tests. For long tests that are un-timed, I recommend having students take short breaks to stand up and stretch. It helps clears their minds and to make them feel better. We do this as a class. In addition, I often bring in a small, sweet snack (a cookie or a gummy candy) to distribute during the middle of a long test. I feel this lowers anxiety and raises morale (the testing season can be really hard on kids).

Chapter 5: Routines & Procedures

<u>Testing and Special-Needs Populations</u>
Special-needs students and Special Education classes often need more time to process information, figure responses, and to questions. For these students or groups, the testing routine may have to be tailored. A senior teacher, a Special Education teacher, or a supervisor should be able to offer guidance on the testing requirements for special-needs students.

Read-Alouds

All children enjoy being read to, regardless of how old or how "cool" they are. I am not talking about reading that is part of an assignment or material that will be tested; I am talking about reading for the enjoyment of reading. I am talking about reading aloud a great story and inviting children to listen to "get lost" in the story, to be swept up be adventure. Unfortunately, except for the early childhood grades, reading aloud to children has fallen out of favor. Teachers tend to allow little, if any, class-time for reading aloud. This means that many children miss out on the sheer joy of reading. For children who are struggling readers, this is especially detrimental as their only relationship with reading is so often negative.

Kids benefit from being read-aloud to in numerous ways:
• Children who are weak or reluctant readers are able to follow a story
• Children learn that reading can be entertaining
• A shared story is a uniting experience; the class is in this imaginary "adventure" together, they can talk and wonder about it together

Any teacher can make Read-Alouds part of their day. With just ten minutes everyday or every other day, a teacher can read a chapter book over the course of of six or seven weeks. With a minimum of effort, a teacher can take his/her students on wonderful, imaginary adventures. These Read-Alouds can also save a teacher "in a pinch": a prep teacher is absent, you had nothing planned; the class arrived to the computer lab before the tech teacher was ready; the class finished an activity in less time that you had allotted; etc. In each of these situations, the prepared teacher could read aloud to the students, and lose little instructional time.

I feel that Read-Alouds should be primarily for fun. While the kids will learn from them, these stories should not be tied to assignments and lessons. This is a time to introduce (or emphasize) the fun of reading. There may be be extension activities based on the story, but that should not be the focus of the reading.

<u>When to Read Aloud</u>
It is good to have a fixed-time for reading aloud to the class. Immediately after lunch is often good, as it relaxes the children and helps them be more focused for the afternoon lessons. Right before lunch is another good

Chapter 5: Routines & Procedures

time; they go off to lunch talking about what might happen next in the story. Just before dismissal is also good; reading becomes a reward for cleaning-up and packing-up quickly.

Preparation: Before you Start
ALWAYS read the book first! Preferably twice or more. This familiarizes you with the content of the story and the sequence of events. This enables you to anticipate unfamiliar words, know when to pause for clarification, generate good questions, and plan where to stop. It also eliminates the surprise of strong language or sensitive topics or events.

In addition:
• Pick a book you love – perhaps one that was read to you when you were young.
• Pick a book that is unfamiliar to the students; this is a great time to read those books that are now considered "old-fashioned." Do not pick a book that they are likely to already have heard about or had read to them. EXPAND their experiences!
• Books with short chapters are great, as it is easy to squeeze a whole chapter in between classroom lessons or activities.

What to Read
There are so many guidelines for choosing engaging meaningful books and stories for children of all ages. One can pick books based on endless criteria - one's own favorites, classics, real-life conflicts, Newbery or Caldecott winners, historical tie-in, setting, etc. Internet searches for "Favorite Children's Books," "Librarians' Recommendations for Children," "Middle School Novels," "Forgotten Children's Literature" will keep you busy for lifetimes!

My Read-Aloud Favorites
As a classroom teacher, during the course of a full school-year, I found time to read five "chapter books" aloud. The following were some of my favorites:
• *Charlie & the Chocolate Factory*, Roald Dahl, grades 3-6
• *Charlotte's Web*, E. B. White, grades 2-4
• *Half-Magic*, Edward Eager, grades 3-6
• *The Wizard of Oz*, Frank Baum, grades 3-6
• *Mrs. Frisby and the Rats of NIMH*, Scott O'Brien, grades 3-7
• *Escape from Witch Mountain*, grades 4-7 (out of print)
• *The Girl Who Owned a City*, grades 5-8 (this book can be scary to younger students)

Chapter 5: Routines & Procedures

- *My Father's Dragon*, Ruth Stiles Gannett, grades pre-K-3

Some longer books are not chapter books; rather they contain a series of adventures around a central character or group of characters. These are great in-between books – for times when you've finished one chapter book but are not ready to start a new one. Some of my favorites are:
- *(Introducing) Mrs. Piggly-Wiggly*, Betty MacDonald, grades 1-5
- *Encyclopedia Brown*, Donald J. Sobol, grades 3-5
- *The Stories Julian Tells*, Anne Cameron, grades 1-4

No teacher is worth anything if s/he does not read some Dr. Seuss (Theodore Geisel) every year!

Kindergarten & First Grade Teachers

These ages need to be read to, and regularly, but they do not usually have the stamina for longer books and for books stretching over days and weeks. Kindergarteners and first graders should be read to several times each day, from a variety of picture and story books, including non-fiction books. The reading sessions should not last longer than 15 minutes. Short chapter books may be appropriate for the early grades, but this will depend on the group. Some kindergarten classes will be able to sit for a chapter books (and retain the story-line, one chapter to the next); and some will not. Many first grade classes will be able to follow shorter and simpler chapter books.

Chapter 5: Routines & Procedures

Study Habits

New teachers are often disappointed with the grades on quizzes and tests. Teachers send the students home to study the vocabulary words, or the state capitals, or simplifying algebraic equations. The students do study, yet they do poorly on the tests. The teachers are both frustrated and mystified. The answer is simple: the kids did not score well, because they do not know how to study; this is probably because they do not have good study habits.

Teachers cannot assume that students know how to study. Even if the students are older and accomplished, they still may not have good study habits. If you are working with younger students, or if you have a lower-performing group, it is very likely that they never learned how to study. Depending on the situation in the homes, the students may or may not learn good study habits from their parents. You are going to have to teach students how to study.

Before the first vocabulary quiz, study aloud with the class. Model for them how you study yourself:
1) "First I read the word to myself." Have everyone do it together.
2) "Then I spell it aloud while I'm looking at it." Have everyone do it together.
3) Talk aloud to yourself about the tricky spelling parts: "Gosh, I have to remember the silent 'e' in that word." Ask kids to share the parts of words they think may be tricky to remember.
4) "Now, I'm going to read the word aloud and then cover the word and see if I can remember how to spell it." Model yourself with one word, and then have volunteers try this with the same word.
5) Do the same thing with other words.
6) Review all the steps.
7) Go to the chart of this week's vocabulary words and mark on the chart the problem spots the students have identified.
8) Tell the students that they will need to repeat this procedure when they study the words.

To study the multiplication tables:
1) First write down the table being studied (1x through 12x). You will write this on the board.
2) "Look at the numbers while reading each one slowly." Model this.

3) "Now, look at the board and say the first three. Close your eyes, and repeat those same three numbers again."
4) "Do the same thing but with the first four." Model this.
5) "Continue adding another number each time."
6) Do this aloud with the class for several rounds. You may think it is dull and repetitive, but it effectively re-enforces good study habits. Your students will not find the practice dull.
7) At one point, make an intentional error: "Oh, I missed one. I better go back and practice some more." Then go back over the steps.

The above steps outline one way of approaching independent studying. It can be very effective to study with a partner (it's also more fun that way!). Instruct students on how to "quiz" one another on vocabulary words, math facts, etc. Model how they can help one another while studying and how they should prompt one another for correct answers – ie, not just giving the correct answers. This is something you can "role play" with volunteers in front of the class.

These are just two examples of effective study procedures. You may have a different method; if so, that is what you should use with your students. Depending on the subject(s) you teach and the age and level of your students, you may develop and introduce many different study procedures. The important thing is not to assume that they know how to study. Instead, take the time to go over each procedure, to allow students time to practice during class, and to reinforce periodically.

Chapter 5: Routines & Procedures

Vocabulary/Spelling Words

Most elementary teachers have a weekly list of spelling or vocabulary words and a corresponding weekly quiz. Some schools have mandated lists of words, which all teachers on a the same grade use at the same time. Sometimes, these words are pulled from a reading unit; sometimes the words will have certain phonetic similarities (double letters, blends, etc). Other schools require that each grade has a certain number of words (e.g., ten words for first grade, 12 for second, 20 for third, etc.). In some schools, teachers have full freedom to determine the words, as well as how they are presented and tested. It is important for new teachers to check with supervisors or veteran teachers for any requirements at their school.

Spelling vs. Vocabulary
Strictly speaking, spelling lists are used to teach spelling, whereas vocabulary lists are used to teach new words, definitions, and spelling. For first and second grades (and kindergarten, in certain cases), spelling lists are preferred. Spelling words in these early grades generally share characteristics that stress phonetics, patterns, and sight-word recognition (words ending in "at," words with "th," etc.). These lists, and the quizzes, are meant to build the spelling and word-comfort of emergent readers.

By the time children are in third grade, they have usually developed some reading skills and a sense of words, spelling patterns, and usage. They also understand how different words express different ideas and feelings. Children at these ages usually find words, especially unusual or long words, interesting. Because of this, I preferred to *combine* spelling skills with meaning. My class had vocabulary words instead of spelling words, and kids had to learn to spell the words, memorize the meaning, and use them in good sentences. I feel this increases spelling, literacy, *and* vocabulary.

New teachers may opt to begin with spelling words even if they prefer the idea of vocabulary words, simply because it is easier to organize spelling assignments and to give spelling quizzes. In addition, the spelling list/ spelling quiz format is more common, so kids tend to be familiar with it. As the year progresses, you can switch to vocabulary lists, if you wish.

Chapter 5: Routines & Procedures

Whether you assign "spelling" or "vocabulary" words, you will need to develop a routine for the words, including class-work, homework, study habits, and testing. Most teachers follow the same routine every week.

My routine generally followed:
- Monday Class: Read through the words. Have class repeat words after you, for proper pronunciation. For vocabulary words, discuss the definition. If the words are from a story or came up during class, invite kids to explain the definitions in "their own words."
- Monday Homework: Write each word 3-5 times, making sure to spell each one correctly.
- Tuesday Class: Read through words again. Ask students to point out words they think are difficult to spell and why they are difficult. On the newsprint chart of words, highlight the tricky parts of those words.
- Tuesday Homework: Write *meaningful* sentences with the words. If you don't emphasize "meaningful," you get "The girl is irascible" or "Where is the isthmus?" neither of which require thought or understanding. I challenged the kids: "You can cram as *many* words as you want into a single sentence, as long as you've used each one intelligently." Or: "Make me laugh, and you get a special sticker." The kids had a blast with that and often came up with clever, creative sentences.
- Wednesday Class: Have children share their favorite sentences aloud with the class. Stellar examples get posted on the Spelling/Vocabulary display.
- Wednesday Homework: Study words. You must teach kids how to study vocabulary or spelling words (see Study Habits).
- Thursday Class: Review for quiz/test tomorrow. Written options are crossword puzzles or unscramble sheets. There are teacher websites that have templates for creating word puzzles. Later in the year, spelling bees are good, but kids (especially those who "get out") are likely to grow bored and misbehave. One option is to have a spelling bee by table, with each kid at one table giving one letter of the word. The table gets a point on the Point Chart if the word is correctly spelled (see Bees).
- Thursday Homework: Word Search. Prepare a word-search with the week's words. There are computer programs that create word search grids based on the words entered.
- Friday Class: Quiz.

A vocabulary quiz can take many forms. You may give the words, and the students must spell each correctly, as well as provide a definition.

Another is to give the definition and the students must write the correct word. Change the format periodically and have fun with the options!

Chapter 5: Routines & Procedures

Fact Cards

"Fact Cards" are exactly what they sound like - cards that have pieces of information on them (much like "flash cards"). Prepare index cards with questions on one side and the answer or "fact" on the other. These cards should have facts or concepts that the class has studied or learned. The cards can be about anything: the capitals of states, spelling words, the order of operations (mathematics), the population of New Guinea; any fact or concept that the class has studied or discussed can go on a Fact Card.

Fact Cards can be used in a variety of times, and for a variety of reasons in the classroom: review for an upcoming assessment, part of a game, individual review, as a filler, if an activity/etc has been cancelled, etc. The Fact Cards can also be used by the children to quiz each other when they've finished the class-work (see Class Law).

Using these cards in conjunction with the Probability Bowl makes an easy game that is also valuable review. Pick a name from the Probability Bowl. That kid gets to try to answer the question on the card. If s/he gets it right, the table gets a point on the Point Chart. If s/he doesn't, you can put the card aside or pull another name from the Bowl (see Probability Bowl).

Note: Ask the question to the class *before* you draw the name. Doing this encourages all students to try to recall the answer. If you call out the student's name first, the other students may "turn off" and not think about the answer at all. This is true for all questioning activities.

For all Grade Levels
This activity can be amended for all grades even kindergarten. The questions, of course, will be very much simpler: "Where did the Man in the Yellow Hat get George?"

For the Out-of-Classroom Teacher
Few activities translate as well as this to the structure and limitations of the out-of-classroom teacher. These cards are easy to prepare no matter how many different level students you work with. All ages and levels benefit from the review and everyone enjoys the game of it.

Contracts (Student)

A behavior contract is a signed document between a teacher and student. The behavior contract should not re-state all the regular school rules. Instead, it should include a few rules which are important to you, that you enforce in your classroom, and which the parents can directly influence. These rules should cover behaviors which cause the most irritation and significant classroom disruptions.

All class rules should be introduced and discussed the first or second day of school as part of a lesson. Behavior contracts, if a teacher wishes to use them, should be introduced and discussed shortly after that. Each child signs a copy of the contract, acknowledging that s/he understands the rules and intends to follow them. These signed contracts are then filed (along with any saved notes, Anecdotals, etc). Contracts should also be sent home to the parents for their signature (see Appendix II). These signed contracts come in handy as the year proceeds and kids test the rules. Always bring the signed contracts (and other relevant notes, anecdotals, etc) to meetings with parents or administrators about specific children.

Individual Behavior Contracts
There may be instances when a teacher wishes to create a contract with one student, generally due to repeated and consistent behavior issues. These contracts are different than the all-class contracts discussed above. In individual contracts, the purpose is to address specific behavior concerns with one student and to provide support in changing the behavior. To do this, the teacher must meet with the student to discuss the issues. The teacher must invite input from the child about his/her behaviors, what the child thinks might help him/her, etc. The teacher then generates the contract with the student, and both sign the document (see Discipline Management).

With individual behavior contracts, the parent is often (though not always) involved. The contract often stipulates a regular check-in to monitor progress. The teacher must make sure to follow the stipulations of the contract carefully and to meet with the student regularly. There are many template behavior contracts available on the internet.

Sample behavior contracts, for parents and students, are included in Appendix II.

Chapter 5: Routines & Procedures

Transitions (Arrival, Dismissal, & Lunch)

A transition is any shift in the day, when a group of students must change from one activity to another. The school day is studded with transitions: morning arrival, switching from math to science, going to art, returning from the library, going to and from the cafeteria, afternoon dismissal, etc. Some transitions involve changing classrooms and passing through the halls, and some are contained within a classroom. The good thing is that you do not have to learn anything else to handle transitions. One of the hardest things for teachers to master is managing groups of children through transitions. Mastering transitions requires implementing several of the routines already discussed as well as strategic use of the Point Chart. The various routines and procedures that you have established for other purposes are all that are required for handling transitions effectively (see Classroom Management, Quiet/Attention, Line-Up, Hall Passage, and Do Now).

Arrival
In some schools, students go to their classrooms individually. In others, the teacher picks up the class from a common area, like the yard or the auditorium, and s/he brings the students to the classroom. You will not have any choice in this.
- If the students come up to you, make sure to have a clear Do Now on the board. This gives each student something to do when they enter the room, rather than talking and playing.
- If you pick up the class, walk through the halls as outlined in Hall Passage. If the class seems especially loud or unruly, walk more slowly, to give them time to settle down. When you have arrived at the classroom, wait for the class to settle, before sending the students into the room. Whatever you do, make sure not to allow students in the room when they are loud and/or unruly; you do not want them to associate that behavior (or attitude) with your classroom. Send students in by table, awarding points for quiet, well-behaved tables. The Do Now should already be on the board.
- Unpacking: In the beginning, the students should go right to their seats, unpack homework from backpacks, place the backpacks on the floor next to their chairs, sit down and begin the Do Now. You will call students to put away their jackets and backpacks table-by-table. Once the class has adapted to the routines, you may have them combine steps – ie, have them unpack and put their backpacks and coats away in the same step and start the Do Now, all at the same time.

Chapter 5: Routines & Procedures

Book-bags on Chairs

There will be times when the students will need to keep their book-bags at their desks rather than in the wardrobe or closet. The temptation is to have students hang them on the back of the chair. Book-bags are heavy and can topple a chair (when a child gets up or shifts in the chair, the whole thing goes over, making a huge racket and, occasionally, hitting another child). Instead, have the students put their jackets on the chairs and the book-bags on the floor next to their desks.

Lunch

School cafeterias are chaotic. They are often under-staffed, and the staff they have may not be fully qualified to monitor children (parent volunteers, school aides, etc). In addition, each adult in the cafeteria may be responsible for 100 kids (which is a stretch for even the most qualified individual!). Teachers usually hate to be in the cafeteria – and so do many children Anything a teacher can do to encourage some order will be appreciated by everyone:

- Know the rules of the cafeteria and the procedure for picking up lunches and milks and disposing of garbage; review these with the students before lunch. Don't leave it all to the lunch staff.
- Remind the kids to thank the lunch servers.
- Tell the students there is no eating or drinking while walking. Once seated, open a napkin, and then begin eating. This is polite and it helps to avoid spills.
- Make sure your students are calm before entering the lunchroom.
- When the teacher enters the cafeteria to pick up the class, the students are not supposed to jump up. Establish some hand signals – one to indicate it is time to stand, another to call the boys to get on line, another for the girls, etc.

And for your own benefit:

- If the class is unruly after lunch, do not return right to the class. Walk through an extra hall or up and down an extra stairwell until the students have calmed down (see After-Lunch Chaos).

Dismissal

Dismissal is not just arrival in reverse. It is harder; the kids are tired, you are tired, and no one has the patience and energy they did in the morning. In addition, teachers tend to rush pack-up and dismissal, glossing over last-minute announcements or homework reminders, which can contribute to chaos.

Chapter 5: Routines & Procedures

Dismissal *can* run smoothly if you follow these recommendations:
- NEVER RUSH! Leave adequate time for tidying the desks and chairs, collecting papers, packing-up, and lining-up. It is preferable to leave the class a few minutes early and arrive for dismissal a few minutes early (see Cleaning Up).
- Make sure that homework is copied earlier in the day; if you wait until the very end of the day, some students may not finish copying the assignment (see Homework).
- If you must schedule homework-copying at the end of the day, make sure to allow sufficient time.
- Before students get backpacks and jackets, have them stack on their desks all that they need for the homework assignment. Have the Table Monitors check that each child has all s/he needs (see Homework).
- My favorite end-of-day schedule was to pack-up, minus jackets, fifteen minutes early. The kids would then sit back down, with their jackets on the back of their chairs and their backpacks on the floor next to them. I would dim the lights and read a section of our chapter book to them (see Read-Alouds).

Buddy-Pack

At least once a week, two minutes before the end of the day, when the students have their jackets and backpacks on, an announcement will come over the PA, "All Classroom teachers please send a monitor to the office for notes that must go home today." This is frustrating for teachers, as it throws a wrench into the calm end-of-day routine. The kids (knowing the notes must go into their homework folders) start pulling off backpacks; the sleeves of their jackets will get stuck in the backpack straps, so those come off too. Throw in a tangle of scarves, lost hats, and at least one kid who got hit by a swinging backpack, and it's a mess.

Being aware of this (common) eventuality, preparing for it, and practicing with the students, makes all the difference! Since you've assigned student jobs, the Office Monitor zooms out to pick up the letters. But how do you avoid the above-described backpack-jacket chaos and get the letters into the backpacks smoothly? Enter the Buddy-Pack: Students will buddy-up, in pre-established pairs; each kid takes the note for the other kid and they take turns opening the *other's* backpack, finding the homework folder, and placing the note/letter there (at today's page). We practice this from the first week.

Chapter 5: Routines & Procedures

<u>Good-Bye</u>
Different districts and schools have different regulations about how closely children are monitored upon leaving school. Ask a senior teacher what is the policy and the practice at your school. For example, children through fourth grades may not be permitted to leave school unescorted; they must be picked up by a designated adult. A child also may not be released to anyone other than the designated adult without prior written explanation from a parent or guardian. Teachers follow these rules with varying degrees of care; it really is worth an extra moment of caution for all your students to be safe (this is one of the many situations when I consider how I would like teachers to handle my own children).

Explain your procedure and the rationale: I told the children that they were never to run off without saying good-bye. When a child saw his/her pick-up person, s/he was to tell me, "Ms. McGown, My mom's there in the red hat" (the child would point in the direction of the mother). The child then had to wait for me to see the parent and say, "Okay." Occasionally, this meant I had to wait a little extra at the end of the day – until all children were picked up (or until I was able to turn those kids over to the designated person); I felt that it was entirely part of my responsibility, as the students' de-facto parent by day. I never imagined this was not what all teachers were doing, but I had many parents thank me for being so vigilant with their children.

6

Discipline Management

Chapter 6: Discipline Management

About this Chapter

Despite the most effective classroom management techniques, there are times when things do not go well in the classroom. On these occasions, teachers must resort to strategies beyond the established management systems. This does not mean the teacher has failed; it does not indicate poor management, or weak teaching, or horrible children. It is just that nothing works perfectly all the time. In the best of classes, and among the best of children, with the most experienced and effective teachers, there will be times – class periods, days, or even weeks – when things seem to unravel. This section outlines several effective strategies for dealing with these occasions.

The strategies described here are not to be used *in place* of effective management systems or behavior modification programs. They are to be used in conjunction *with* those strategies. It is important to keep in mind that, even though the classroom strategies may seem not to be working for a period, it is essential to maintain all the established routines. Continue using the Point Chart and continue sending Good Kid Letters (and the like) *while* you are implementing the various discipline measures outlined in this chapter.

Chapter 6: Discipline Management

After-Lunch Chaos

In my work with new teachers, a frequent and specific request I hear is for assistance in handling students and teaching right after lunch. New teachers helplessly watch their carefully-crafted lessons fall apart because the kids have just returned from lunch. The period following lunch can be chaotic. Mornings tend to go relatively smoothly, in most classrooms, regardless of the grade, subject, or teacher. Once lunch has come and gone, however, things often change. Students can be loud and unruly; they may be unresponsive and uncooperative. They may not seem to want to do any work, and the incentives that worked before lunch seem to have no effect after. In addition, later in the day, the teacher is also tired (it is amazing how much half a day of teaching can wipe one out!). Many teachers, including experienced ones, become frustrated because they feel powerless and lose so much teaching time. The key to avoiding "after lunch chaos" is, like so many things, planning carefully and thoughtfully.

From the first day, it is important to implement a tight, predictable routine for the period immediately following lunch. In the early grades (Pre-K-2nd), teachers often enforce a quiet "nap" time, when lights are turned down/off and children must lay their heads on the desks for several minutes. Children do not necessarily have to sleep, but they are meant to have some quiet time, both to allow them some restful down-time and to help bring calm and order to the afternoon classroom. Some Pre-K and K classrooms still have full nap times with mats or cots. This is great – for both the teacher and the kids. Naps are not appropriate for, nor generally well-received by, children over the age of eight or nine. Teachers in these grades need other strategies.

Some teachers schedule journal writing after lunch. This can work to focus and calm the class, if the prompts are sufficiently provocative (See Journal Writing). Many teachers opt to have math after lunch because math is, by nature, more structured than other subjects. Still other teachers read aloud to their class right after lunch, to calm them for the rest of the day's lessons. These strategies will work much of the time, but on the days that they don't . . . .

Review Worksheets
The strategy is simple. Present kids with structured easy-to-do work while you catch your breath.

Chapter 6: Discipline Management

Make several class sets of photocopies of worksheets. These should not be "busy work"; rather, they should be well thought-out and relevant review materials. Mathematics worksheets tend to be the easiest to prepare and are generally well-received. Based on the level of your students, you will need to develop appropriate worksheets. Keep in mind: if the class is unruly and/or unresponsive, you do not want to invite questions or discussions. Any worksheets you design, therefore, must be self-explanatory, so that students can get to work without your guidance. The level of difficulty should start just below or at that of your students – difficult enough to be compelling but simple enough to be satisfying. These sheets should be review work, reinforcing previously taught skills and concepts. Students should not need any verbal instruction or clarification. Instructions should be should be minimal, simple, and clear.

Worksheets for addressing After-lunch Chaos should take no less than 5-8 minutes for grades 2-3 and no less than 7-10 minutes for grades 4 and up. The number of problems and the level of difficulty will depend on the level of the children. Some general recommendations are:
- 2nd grade 15-20 addition problems
- 3rd & 4th grade 30 addition, 20 subtraction, 10-15 multiplication problems, or 30-40 multiplication facts
- 5th -7th 15-40 problems depending on operation and difficulty

There are many websites with ready-made worksheets. On a number of them, you can enter subjects, level, and the site will generate a worksheet. Teachers must always review any ready-made products to make sure they are appropriate for their students (it is alarming how many teachers fail to do this).

Other options for worksheets are: grammar (eg, circle the verbs, give the irregular plural forms), dictionary skills (guide-words, synonyms, etc.), reading/literacy (short-answer questions from a recent reading), alphabetization, etc. Teachers should always have several sets of these worksheets prepared in a folder. Again, I must emphasize that these should not be time-filling busy-work. There is not enough time in the teaching day for kids to do work that is not useful.

There will be days when you know the kids are going to be "loose" after lunch. On these days, place worksheets on each desk while the kids are at lunch. On the chalkboard, write: "Welcome Back from Lunch. Please Work Silently on the Math Review Worksheet." As the class enters the room, point to the board. Your goal is to keep noise to a minimum. For the most part, the students will begin working on the sheets without (much) delay or comment. Allow at least five minutes but no more than ten – enough time for you to see that they are calm, to get yourself centered, and to be ready to deliver a lesson. You can have the students do the remainder of the worksheet for homework. This will have an added benefit the next time you have review worksheets after lunch; students will work harder on the worksheets to avoid additional homework.

There will also be days when the teacher does not expect the class to be "loose" or unruly. The teacher goes to pick up the class from lunch, and s/he gets a bad feeling. On these occasions, the teacher can ask the Assistant Teacher (see Student Jobs) go to the class room ahead of everyone and pull out a stack of the prepared worksheets and place them on every desk. If the students return from lunch on their own (or are accompanied by another person) the teacher will not have the same "advance warning" about the mood or tone of the class. This can take you by surprise. Be prepared. As soon you have realized that there is something amiss with the group, stop what you are doing and get a stack of the review worksheets; have the Paper-Passer hand out the sheets. Calmly write the directions on the board; you may say, "Let's do a few minutes' of review first." Try very hard to say very *little* during this time. The point is to create some space, some order, some calm. Anything you say, when you are at (or beyond!) your limit, or when the kids are unruly or unresponsive, is not going to contribute positively. Avoid yelling; simply write directions on the board, and point to them.

When you feel the class has settled down and you are ready to teach, call time. Some students may complain as they were not yet able to finish. Try not to respond and not to engage anyone (the goal, after-all, of this after-lunch activity, is to reduce any unnecessary noise and negativity). The majority of the class will now be ready for the lesson, as the quiet work will have calmed them. Tell the class that the remaining problems/questions on the worksheets will be for homework. Some kids will whine, but more will accept it. Make sure to collect the completed worksheets the next day. If you do not do this, the students will view the sheets as "busy-work," and they will not be as likely not to complete them the next time (there *will* be another time when you are faced with After-Lunch Chaos). In addition, assuming you have designed quality worksheets, not checking them is a loss of valuable assessment.

Some schools or districts have rigid or scripted curricula. The above technique for reducing After-Lunch Chaos does not necessarily fit in with a scripted curriculum. Can you use it anyway? My response is, yes. When countered on this, I argue that an inexperienced teacher who is overwhelmed or uncertain about how to handle a classroom situation is likely to lose valuable instructional time. If the teacher opts to *plan* to lose just five-ten minutes, so that s/he can get back on track, that is a good use of time, and it does not mean a loss of instruction. If you are able to control and reduce After-lunch Chaos effectively, you will have lost very little time. In doing so, you now have order in a class, where before you had none. You might not have been able to accomplish anything before calming down the class (and yourself), and now you can.

It is also worth noting that administrators do not often visit classrooms after lunch. They know that the kids are often relatively loud and rambunctious at that time and they want no part of it. If a supervisor does enter the classroom during this time, explain that you're doing a quick mini-review (which you are). It is unlikely that anyone will react negatively, especially if the kids are focused and calm right after lunch.

For the Out-of-Classroom Teacher

An out-of-classroom teacher uses the same practice to reduce after-lunch chaos for the same reasons and in the same manner as classroom teachers. These teachers can prepare review worksheets for their subjects. Out-of-classroom teachers may also speak to the classroom teachers for input on subjects for review or reinforcement.

Chapter 6: Discipline Management

Tickets

The school-year has cycles. There will be times when the students behave much more than they misbehave; and there will be times when the same students misbehave far more than they behave. Occasionally a few students will become unacceptably difficult. In many cases, these students may be ones who have had behavioral issues all along. Sometimes, it is a student who has had not problems during the year. And then something happens – too much test preparation, a spate of bad weather that cancels recess or gym repeatedly, a full moon, etc. While many of the students may remain on-task in the classroom, and they may still respond adequately to the Point Chart (or whatever systems you have implemented), some students may have or continue to have difficulties with self-control. This is most noticeable during less-structured times – in the hallways, during gym, on the stairwells, in the cafeteria, after lunch, etc. Students often bring out-of-classroom moods into the classroom, so these misbehaviors will likely affect the mood of the classroom.

For times like this, an additional strategy may be necessary. Tickets are simple items (I cut mine from index cards) that are distributed to the children whose behavior needs adjustment. I explained the process of the tickets to the whole class. I did not want the tickets to be a secret, punitive process. In addition, the system benefits if the rest of the class is invested in its success. Each child must realize that s/he benefits from the tickets system. Explain that a child must surrender a ticket whenever a teacher speaks to a student about behavior. At the end of the day, the tickets are counted. The goal for each child is to keep as many tickets as possible each day. The teacher must decide what will be an appropriate reward for the highest number of tickets retained. I allowed the winning child to pick a special sticker from the special sticker collection

I have found "tickets" to be very effective. Have a discussion with the whole class. Pick a calm time; early in the morning is good. Be straightforward: "We've got a new problem. Some of you have started to be really disruptive in the halls and it's affecting us in the classroom." Watch carefully that no-one points at or teases the kids who have been misbehaving. Make sure to award points on the Point Chart accordingly. The targeted children should not feel attacked – by you or their classmates. The message needs to be that the problem is a *shared* one and that everyone needs to work together to address it. The kids in question are likely to speak up (they know who they are). Allow them to talk about their behavior and to own up to the different incidences there have been each day. Make sure to praise them for their honesty. It is important to keep this conversation even and calm. This is not a time for punitive measures or chastisement; it is a time for information gathering and non-judgmental group discussion.

There might be some resistance because these "bad" kids get a chance each day to win a prize and the rest of the class does not. Have a discussion with the whole class about how this will benefit everyone: "Doesn't it bug you when kids are rude and loud in the halls? Don't you hate it when our class gets yelled at by other teachers?" You need to get them to acknowledge that the "injustice" is worth it. Once they do, then tell them that there will be a reward. Each Friday of Tickets, there will be a luncheon party for the rest of the class (without the ticket kids). Everyone in the class who is supportive of the process and of the kids will be able have lunch in the classroom with the teacher, where there will be games and music. The targeted kids, and any kids who haven't been supportive of the tickets system, remain in the cafeteria for the lunch period.

To make the tickets, use index cards cut into quarters, allow for 10-15 tickets per child. I wrote "3-309" on each ticket. Give out tickets each day, slowly decreasing the number every few days. Start by giving more tickets than you think is necessary. You do not want any child to lose all tickets on the first day. This will demoralize him/her. The first few days, issue 15, then 12, then 9, etc. Stop using the tickets when you feel the kids have, on average, and relatively-speaking, calmed down. Every time I have resorted to using tickets, it has only lasted two-three weeks. Interestingly, it has been the targeted kids themselves that have asked for it to stop. The prizes and/or acknowledgment or praise at the end of the day did not outweigh the students' being singled out and missing the parties. At the conclusion of the ticketing period, I had one final Friday luncheon, and the whole class joined me (see Fun Fridays) – exhausting!

It may happen that one or two of the targeted children start behaving well more quickly than the rest of the group. That child may ask to join the weekly party; s/he cannot. You are combating more than the individual misbehaviors; it is the larger issues of poor judgment, following others, and not thinking for oneself. Explain this: "Yes, I see you've shaped up the quickest, and that is really cool. But you took part in that insanity, for way too long, just like the others. You are as responsible as they are. Next time they get kooky this way, make better choices - walk away and don't get involved."

Tickets should not be issued any earlier than the third month of school. Until that time, it may be, especially for new and developing teachers, that your systems are not full established – ie, the children are "loose" not because they need additional guidance and discipline, but because your systems need more time to "stick." I never used tickets until after the December break.

For Lower Elementary Classes
This is not a system for the lower grades. It involves a higher level of maturity than small children can handle. Depending on the maturity of second graders, you may use tickets with them. It is an ideal system for third-sixth grades.

For the Out-of-Classroom Teacher
Tickets can be effective for out-of-classroom teachers, but the system has to be altered for the irregularity of the schedule. An out-of-classroom teacher who sees the class every day or several times per week can use tickets; one who sees classes just once per week will have difficulty implementing the system (the children are likely to lose the tickets between classes). The out-of-classroom teacher will likely have children retain tickets over several days, before counting for prizes or praise.

Chapter 6: Discipline Management

Time-Out Essays

A time-out is exactly what it sounds like - time for the child (and the surrounding children, along with the teacher), to take some time away from the stimulation or frustration of the setting. The time-out essay is something the child writes to reflect on what has occurred. A time-out essay may be assigned anytime that a single child is being disruptive or rude or when the teacher feels a child needs time away from the group (sometimes, a child may decide that s/he needs time away from the group and/or wishes to express his/her feelings about the event/setting).

The time-out essay is a written activity; this means it is reflective and educational, rather than punitive. The time-out essay gives a child the opportunity to reflect and to write; it gives him/her some time away from the group – some quiet time. It also allows the child to vent, which is sometimes necessary. The time-out essay also allows a child to acknowledge mistakes and to apologize. The process of writing the time-out essay generally calms children down as well, so after the essay is written, the child is better focused and ready to join the group. In addition, the essay reduces or eliminates the yelling to which a teacher might otherwise resort.

Prepare time-out essay forms ahead of time. The form should have space for the name and date, the prompts for recall and reflection, and lines for the child to write on. During the first or second week of class, hand out a set of time-out essays for the kids to read and discuss. Explain when you will use the essay forms and what you expect from the students. Make sure to explain that spelling will not be counted on a time-out essay. It is important to discuss the expected behaviors of the kids who did not misbehave and did not receive a time-out essay; they are not allowed to tease, point, or be negative in any way (see Purple Snit). The essay form must be fully completed before the student can re-join the group.

During this initial orientation discussion, it is fun and effective to role-play some common misbehavior and ask students to offer what they would write for that misbehavior. This is a good time to explain words on your form that may be new to your students. Elicit many different responses from students, so they are not overwhelmed when they have to complete a time-out essay during the year.

Chapter 6: Discipline Management

Keep all time-out essays. They are great informal records of classroom conduct. When meeting with a parent or administrator, make sure to have all time-out essays and similar documentation available.

Take time-out essays forms on class trips and to special events. Tell the kids that you have the essay forms and that unacceptable behavior may require a time-out essay.

For Lower Elementary Classes

The time-out essay can be used for any group that has solid reading and writing skills. In a first-grade class, you may use the essay, but you will have to adjust the prompts to reflect the level of emerging writers.

For the Out-of-Classroom Teacher

The time-out essay can be used for any teacher, in any setting, in which the students can read and write. The out-of-classroom teacher should use time-out essays, as necessary, in the manner outlined above.

A sample time-out essay is in Appendix II.

7

Parents

Chapter 7: Parents

About this Chapter

Teachers have very different expectations about parents and the degree to which parents and families will be involved – and should be – in the school and classroom community. Some teachers expect to see parents frequently; others assume parents will be ancillary to the activities in the classroom. Both situations are possible. Parental involvement will vary significantly and for a variety of reasons. It often varies by community; in some communities, parental involvement is very high, and in others, it is low. The level of parental involvement tends to reflect socio-economic lines, wealthier parents tend to be more involved in their children's schools, and poorer families tend to be less involved. But this is just a generalization; teachers report great involvement in the poorest communities and fully absent parents in high income communities.

Many teachers spend a lot of time complaining about the parents of the students they teach: "If only the parents were involved more, or disciplined their child more, or helped with homework more, or . . . it would be so much easier to teach." This is true; parental involvement and support contribute greatly to a child's academic success. *Parental involvement is not, however, a requirement for student success.* Moreover, having involved parents was not a guarantee when you signed on to be a teacher. This is not to say that teachers should not reach out to parents regularly and enthusiastically. It does not mean that teachers should not embrace parental interest and input. Parents can be an important part of a child's education, and teachers can impact parental relationships positively; teachers must do all they can to involve parents. Teachers cannot, however, allow a parent's lack of involvement to be an excuse for a child's lack of achievement. *It is a teacher's job to educate the children in the classroom regardless of parental involvement.*

In situations of low parental involvement, many new and developing teachers tend to attribute this to a lack of interest on the part of the parent. This is never the case. In most situations, when families are not involved or are not communicative, there are a variety of practical and valid reasons. While a teacher wants to encourage parental involvement, s/he must respect the choices that the families make, even if the teacher does not or cannot understand the underlying rationale. The teacher who responds critically towards parents, who acts as if the parents do not care about the child's schooling, and/or whose language, tone, or behaviors convey this message, will only alienate the parent, and potentially hurt the child. This generally causes even greater parental disconnect and absence.

It is important to note that parents will often participate and cooperate in school activities to the extent that they feel capable, comfortable, and welcomed. An important responsibility of the teacher, therefore, is to make parents feel capable, comfortable, and welcome. Teachers must acknowledge that parents are the primary educators of their students. Teachers must work to make sure that the parents know the teacher respects their role, accepts parents as valuable partners in their students' education, and believe that parents have a great deal to contribute.

Many veteran teachers have pre-conceived notions about parents and students; do *not* listen to jaded teachers complain. All parents love their children and want the best for them. Parents also want their children to have good teachers and to learn a lot. For the most part, parents and teachers want exactly the same thing for children. Parents and teachers often fail to connect because of different cultural, linguistic, or socio-economic backgrounds. It is the teacher's job to work to bridge these differences and to reach out and involve parents. All parents can be effective partners in their child's education.

Chapter 7: Parents

Community Presence

Teachers should make their presence known – to the parents and within the local community. This is especially true for teachers who live in a community far away from and/or very different from the community in which they teach, or for teachers of a different race and/or cultural background than students in the school. While a walk through a neighborhood or a stroll through a local shop will not provide in-depth knowledge of different cultures, these exposures do help develop awareness. In addition, the teacher who rushes to the car, bus, or train at the ring of the dismissal bell gives a powerful and negative message to parents, children, and community members: this is not a community that I care about or where I want to spend any extra time.

Get to know the community of the school. Walk around the neighborhood, buy groceries there occasionally, browse through local shops. Teachers should also make an effort to attend neighborhood or cultural events, weekend fairs, etc. Not only is there a lot to be learned by spending "real" time in the students' neighborhood, but doing so gives teacher credibility with the parents, community, *and* the children.

Chapter 7: Parents

Initial Contacts & Letters

Many parents hear from teachers only when their child does something wrong. Teachers do not customarily contact teachers for positive or "neutral" reasons. Break this pattern!

From the start, teachers should communicate with parents, and these early outreaches should be positive (or neutral). There are plenty of opportunities to send positive or neutral communications in the first month of school: welcome notes, topics to be covered in class, invitations to visit the school, etc. By making multiple contacts with parents early in the year, teachers start to foster a positive relationship with the parents. Setting up regular, non-negative communication with the parents also helps teachers navigate their first parent-teacher conferences, reducing much of the anxiety of the conferences – for the parent and the teacher.

Teachers should prepare a set of "standard" letters, to be sent to parents at specific points of the year. The general content does not change much year-to-year, so it makes sense and saves time to have the templates readily available on the computer. Your school may have required family letters. Make sure to speak to a veteran teacher for advice on school practice. The following are my recommendations on family communications:

- Before the first day: It is a good idea to contact parents before the first day of school. A good practice is for classroom teachers to call the homes of all students the evening before the first day of school. This is a friendly call – to touch-base with the parent and to remind him/her about the first day and the time that school starts. Introduce yourself, say hello, and ask for a parent (or grandparent, uncle, aunt, or, if necessary, an older brother or sister). Explain why you are calling, give the necessary information, answer any questions, and sign off.
- First day of school: Send a Welcome Letter home the first day of school along with the Supply List (see Appendix II).
- First week of school: Send a note home with the class rules; include a behavior contract if you are using one (see Classroom Management and Appendix II).
- Second week of school: Within the first two weeks of school, send a note home outlining the procedure for parents to make appointments to speak with you (see Classroom Management and Appendix II).

Chapter 7: Parents

- <u>Third Week of School</u>: Send "neighborhood" or "local" permission slips home (see Special Activities).
- <u>First month letter</u>: At the end of the first month of school, send home a letter that acknowledges whole-class accomplishments to-date and invites parents to celebrate their child's participation (see Appendix II).
- <u>Fifth/Sixth Week</u>: Send Good Kid Letters (see Classroom Management, Routines & Procedures, and Appendix II).

Any letters sent to parents during the first month should be whole-class letters. The tone of these letters should be friendly; they should be informative, celebratory, etc. Letters for the first month should be addressed to "Parents of Class 3-309." This is to avoid any parent feeling that s/he, or his/her child, is being singled out.

For the Out-of-Classroom Teacher

Out-of-classroom teachers may send each of the letters mentioned above, except the Supply List, as the needs of an out-of-classroom teacher (except for art) are generally not distinct from the classroom teacher. Typically, the out-of-classroom teacher requires an additional folder or notebook for his/her subject/class. This can be mentioned in the Welcome Letter. Alternately, out-of-classroom teachers may ask for their required supplies to be included in the supply letter of the homeroom teacher.

Chapter 7: Parents

Language & Translation

In most school communities, there are parents who do not speak English or do not speak it well. These parents may be embarrassed to speak with the teacher, to attend meetings, or to ask questions. Parents whose language skills in English are weak often get a reputation of non-involvement. It is usually their discomfort, however, not their lack of interest, which causes their absence. It would be nice if we all spoke many languages, but we do not. At some point in your teaching career, you will need to work with a parent whose language of comfort is not yours.

There are a number of things a teacher can do to help parents feel comfortable and to increase their involvement:
- Smile openly and greet the parent warmly and sincerely every time you see him/her. Do not avoid speaking to a parent because s/he does not speak English. A warm "Hello, Ms. Somebody, it's wonderful to see you," is understood by everyone.
- Learn a few words of greeting in the languages represented in your classroom. No-one expects you to become fluent in Ukrainian, Croatian, or Spanish simply because you're a teacher, but "Hello, how are you?" in the parent's language scores points and opens doors.
- Children are natural translators. You will learn that the students of non-native English speakers are quite adept at translating for their parents. In some cases, very young children have accompanied parents on appointments to government agencies, an immigration office, etc. The same children can translate conversations between you and the parent. I am often asked at this point about the possibility of a child intentionally mis-translating the conversation; I have *never* known this to happen.
- Find faculty members who know the parent's home language and may be willing to join a meeting to help with translation.
- Show interest in the languages and cultures represented in the class. This does not have to be an over-the-top all-consuming project. It also should not be an appearances-only posting of travel posters. A few genuine inquiries about the language, the country, the culture, etc. can show that you are open and interested.
- There are great children's books about other peoples and cultures or that that reference other languages and cultures. Find good books that do this, and share them with the class.
- Include language dictionaries in the classroom library.

Chapter 7: Parents

- If the neighborhood has restaurants or stands that serve food of the countries represented in your class, eat there from time to time. My kids were consistently amazed that I *chose* to eat food from the neighborhood. The kids told their parents, many of whom asked if this were true; the parents and families were thrilled that I enjoyed food from "their country."

Translating School Documents & Letters
There are different thoughts on whether to translate letters to parents for whom English is not the primary language or the language of comfort. This decision will depend on a number of variables – your school community, the practices of other teachers, and your own language background. I cannot dictate one protocol that will work for all teachers in all school communities, or that will feel right for all individuals. I will, however, explain what I did, and what I found to be effective.

I did not translate any class letters. The main reason for this was the potential loss of nuance or emphasis in translation. Furthermore, it is very common to have several non-English home languages represented in a single class; it is not reasonable to translate a letter into multiple languages. But more importantly, having the letters in English put valuable responsibility onto the students. Whenever I sent a letter home, I first used the letter as a reading/literacy lesson during the school-day. I distributed the letters just as I did any reading handout or article. Students had time to read the letter silently in class. For weak readers or younger students, I asked that they look through the letter for words they recognize. I would then read the letter aloud, asking that kids follow along. I might have volunteers re-read parts, and then we would discuss the letter. I answered all questions about the content of the letter. I told them, explicitly, that they would have to be able to answer all the same questions when their parents asked them. In the homework notebook for that day, one entry would be: "Explain 'Class Rules Letter' to parents" (see Homework). I found that this took care of the translation issue *and* encouraged practical reading skills.

I also learned that every non-native English-speaking family has someone who is the designated official translator. This person was often a family member, but it might also be a helpful neighbor. If you are working with immigrant families, remember that they have had to navigate confusing and form-ridden bureaucracies. Each family of immigrants has found someone to help them understand and complete forms. I asked my students about this once, and they all offered, without hesitation, the name of the person who had helped their parents with immigration and governmental forms. These same individuals can help parents with school notices as necessary.

Some schools will require that class notes are translated into the languages represented in the class (in these schools, school-wide notes will be translated). In most cases, such schools will provide sheets with common phrases in the various school languages. In some cases, there may be individuals (other teachers, office staff, parent volunteers, etc) who help teachers translate communications. If this describes the situation in your school, then you will be required to translate your documents (regardless of your thoughts about the process). If you can find someone who speaks that language with whom you can work whenever you have to translate something, you'll feel a greater comfort that the translated document reflects your tone.

Chapter 7: Parents

Parent-Teacher Conferences

There is little that creates more anxiety for new teachers than the first parent-teacher conferences. My graduate students are worried about this a full year before they enter the classroom! Even experienced teachers do not relish an evening of meeting with worried parents. Since misery loves company, it may be helpful to note that this anxiety is often shared by both the teacher and the parent.

New teachers often feel unsure and think the parents will see right through their lack of experience. Teachers who are struggling through bumpy first years worry that parents will question their ability. In addition, many new teachers are younger than the parents of the children they teach; this makes them feel especially insecure when addressing parents. The parents, on the other hand, are also worried about the conferences. If the child is not a strong student, that parent is expecting to hear a *stranger* tell them what is *wrong* with their child. It is very important to keep this in mind: no matter what a child's scores, nor how poorly s/he behaves, nor any of the other issues commonly addressed in parent-teacher meetings, it is painful for a parent to hear negative things about his/her child. The child represents all the hopes and wishes of that parent. Don't forget this when you speak to a parent.

Some schools have specific guidelines for parent-teacher conferences. It is imperative that you speak to a veteran teacher so that you know of any required school practices.

While Parent-Teacher conferences can be difficult for all participants, there are several things that make them easier:
• Establishing and maintaining regular contact with parents
• Keeping clear, accurate records of performance, grades, absences, etc.
• Preparing the students
• Preparing the classroom

Letters and Parents
The communications described in the previous section will pave the way for a pleasant and productive relationship with parents. Such regular communication makes the teacher less a "stranger," and it makes both the teacher and the parents less wary of one another. These outreaches help to ensure that the first parent-teacher conferences go well.

Chapter 7: Parents

<u>Record-Keeping</u>
Parents are most interested in knowing TWO things: (1) how their child is doing and (2) what they can do to help. The teacher must have a comprehensive record of each child's grades, assignments, participation, and behavior (see Grade-Keeping), and be ready to discuss each aspect.

New teachers find report cards daunting, especially the first go-round. It is imperative to speak to senior teachers to learn what policies exist at your school about report cards (see Report Cards & Grade-Keeping). Writing report cards, especially the first few times, will take a significant amount of time. Plan enough time for this, so you do not have to rush.

<u>Prepare the Children</u>
Kids are also anxious about the parent-teacher conferences. They want the parent to hear good things about them from the teacher (even your best students worry about what you will say about them). They also want the teacher to like their parents. Students who do not perform well in school will be even more concerned. Students who did not have a good relationship with last year's teacher will have special worries. Just because you know that you are going to say good things to a particular parent; do not assume the child knows this. Kids are as baffled by adults as we are by them.

In the weeks before the parent-teacher conferences, I had a discussion with the class, during which I invited the students to talk about the things they were worried about, in regards to the conferences. Some were worried that parents might embarrass them; some were worried about what I would tell parents. To alleviate their worries, I invited a discussion of what they thought I would tell the parents. The students were always very honest, and they offered, in front of the class, honest estimations of their struggles (they were less adept at discussing their strengths and accomplishments). They would share with the group that they knew I was going to say that they talked too much, or that they forgot homework sometimes, etc. Almost without fail, the students would not list anything they did well. I had to push them to articulate their strengths. This class discussion was a good temperature-gauge for me, as it gave me a clear idea of their self-views.

During this class discussion, I told the children that the things we had just spoken about were the things that I would be writing in report cards and sharing with parents. This was very good for the students, because this removed the element of surprise: they walked away knowing what I would share, positives and negatives. The children often shared this information with the parents ahead of time, so there were very few surprises at the conferences. This relieved a great deal of unnecessary and unproductive anxiety of everybody's part.

Special Projects for Parent-Teacher Conferences
I always planned fun activities with the class in the weeks before the first parent-teacher conferences. This was to involve the children, allay their fears, and decorate the room.

Two of the perennial favorites were:
• Kids' Letter to Parents: The students wrote letters to their parents, outlining their strengths and areas for improvement in school, including behavior and homework. The kids were usually harsher on themselves then I ever was. On the afternoon or evening of the conferences, I set these letters on the kids' desks and invited the parents to read them before they spoke with me. Since the letters were in the kid's own hand, any difficult news was easier to "take." In addition, the letters provided a comfortable introduction to the topics I felt the parent(s) and I needed to discuss.

• "Things Your Parents do that Embarrass You": Kids are often embarrassed about how their parents may behave when they visit the class. I used this as a writing/art activity prompt. I invited the students to write about the things that their parents do in public that embarrass them (kissing the kids in public, saying "Oh my Darling" out loud, fixing their hair, etc). I then had the students draw accompanying pictures. These were done on pre-cut circles of drawing paper. The kids then drew light red-lines diagonally through the pictures (like "No Smoking" signs). The students loved the activity, and the parents giggled when they saw the display.

Displayed Work
Make sure that the classroom has attractive work, from *all* children, displayed on the walls and bulletin boards. You should start at least a month before the conferences to assign and collect art projects, decorated essays, etc.

Before the conferences, I always made sure to do the following:
• Special displays: Bulletin boards were up-to-date, with good work, colorful trim, etc.

Chapter 7: Parents

- <u>Select work on desk</u>: I let children choose favorite work or projects to display on their desks during the parents' visits. The "Letter to the Parents" (above) should be on the top of this pile.
- <u>Display Texts/etc</u>: At several places in the room, I displayed the collection of texts that we were using this year, so parents could look through them.

Other things that to prepare/update:
- <u>Tests and quizzes</u>: These should be in a folder to be shared individually with each parent.
- <u>Standardized test scores</u>: I put these on a grid, where the students' names could be hidden. I would show the parent his/her child's scores in comparison to the class.
- <u>Book reports</u>: Good examples should be on the child's desk.
- <u>Homework Chart</u>: Make sure to have parents look at the homework chart (see Homework). If the parent comes with a student, the student can explain how it works.
- <u>Siblings</u>: Parents may bring younger siblings, and it helps to have an area in the back of the room with building blocks or crayons and paper.

<u>The Night Before</u>
Expect to be nervous, so you may not sleep well. Try to get to bed early, so you are as well-rested as possible. On the day of the conferences, wear clothes that make you feel confident. If you look really young, dress as conservatively and "mature" as you can. People judge others by their clothes (right or not), and a tie or tailored skirt can set a positive, professional tone.

<u>Early in the Day</u>
- Arrange with another teacher, or a supervisor, what you will do if a contentious situation arises. There may be school-wide policies for this; speak to a senior teacher.
- Prepare a sign-in sheet to keep track of who attended and to make sure you speak to each parent in order.
- Set up the children's desks, with the materials you have prepared.

<u>The Conference Itself</u>
When speaking with the parents, start with the positive. Wherever possible, this positive should be academic. You may also include other positive attributes or behaviors, but they should be secondary to academic strengths or accomplishments.

Chapter 7: Parents

Once you have discussed the child's strengths or accomplishments, the heart of the conference must focus on areas for improvement for the child. If this is a long list, choose the most important, so as not to overwhelm or discourage the parent. You should include in the conference one *specific and concrete* directive that the parent can do to support the child's progress. The purpose of this directive is twofold:

1) Classroom instruction can be positively impacted when the parent supports it. A child simply *is* more likely to memorize his/her multiplication tables if an adult is helping him/her in the evenings.
2) The parent will feel involved and empowered if s/he knows there is something specific s/he can do to support the learning of his/her child.

Keep an eye on the Clock

Make sure to watch the time. Most schools have a recommended time for the individual conferences. Make sure to follow this; you cannot allow time to run out without having spoken to each of the parents, for at least the minimum length of time. There will be parents who want to take more time with you; this can be difficult to navigate. Tell parents they may wait to speak to you after you have finished speaking with the other parents. You may have to be firm about this, working to remain as pleasant and professional as you can.

It may help to have a paper listing your available times over the next week or two. Parents who want to speak with you at greater length can sign up for one of these times.

After the Conference

Make sure to send thank-you notes to the parents who attended the session.

Chapter 7: Parents

Throughout the Year

Teachers must establish and then maintain regular communication with parents throughout the school-year. A few letters in the beginning of the year, with no follow up, is not sufficient. Nor is it acceptable for a teacher to send notes only during key times during the school-year. It is a teacher's responsibility to keep the parents informed, but it is also his/her responsibility to make sure they feel involved with the school and the classroom. A teacher who does not keep in touch with the parents is not doing his or her job and s/he loses a potential resource and ally.

Communications with parents do not have to take one specific format. It becomes a matter of preference on the part of the teacher and available resources. One of the easiest options is to send a monthly or bi-weekly class newsletter. This "publication" will include testing dates, thematic units, class accomplishments, upcoming events, etc. Once you have developed the format, you will have a template you can use for subsequent issues. After a few "editions," it will become quite simple to update the document each time.

Another popular option is to create a class website (or a webpage, on a school's website). This should be done only if you are confident that all families have computer access at home. Class websites offer a great deal of flexibility, and there are no printing or distribution costs. Websites or webpages can include many more items, because there is no limit regarding paper, copying, etc. There can be student pages, photos, etc.

Some teachers have a parent "tea" every month or six weeks. On these afternoons, the teacher prepares refreshments (coffee and cookies) and invites parents to visit the classroom. There does not need to be any structure to these afternoons; they just provide a friendly forum for parents to meet with one another and with the teacher. Alternately, sessions like these can be planned for specific reasons or events – explaining the upcoming tests to parents, a health or fitness seminar, a publishing party, etc. In any event, the point is to share information and to keep communication open and welcoming.

8

Special
Activities

Chapter 8: Special Activities

About this Chapter

During the course of a school-year, there are many major events – holidays, school and class achievements, milestones, etc. There are also smaller events that deserve notice – a unit completed, the first snowstorm, a long weekend, etc. Each of these should be acknowledged and maybe celebrated. A party may be appropriate, but so might an afternoon game or special video. The activities and issues described in this section are for such events. They are a great deal of fun; more importantly, each one has solid educational objectives.

Some schools have policies about classroom games or special events, as well as the consumption of food. Make sure you learn what, if any, limitations and rules exist at your school. Administrators are generally fine with occasional classroom games, providing students do not get too loud or unruly. The activities and games listed in this section are my favorites, as well as the favorites of my former students. They are also activities that have been well-received by administrators.

Chapter 8: Special Activities

Food in School

There will be numerous occasions during the school-year in which students will have food in the classroom. This can go very smoothly, but it can also be problematic; it depends on the planning and thought a teacher puts in ahead of time.

Food Rules
The teacher must have clear rules about food in the room, and s/he must carefully supervise any food-containing activities. It is much easier (and more pleasant) to avoid a mess than it is to clean one up. In addition, some schools have recurring problems with pests, and food in the classrooms contributes to this. Some classes will have sinks in the room, but many will not. Since you do not want to be left cleaning up after a special event (nor do you want to risk the ire of the custodian), a few simple rules are necessary.

The same rules that Mom enforced at home apply in the classroom. I explained these rules to the students before the first party or special activity, and we reviewed them before any subsequent food-filled events:
1) Eat and drink only when seated.
2) Hold all plates, trays, and cups with two hands.
3) Have a napkin out and unfolded before you begin to eat.
4) Unfinished beverages must be poured down a sink, not dumped in the class garbage can (this might necessitate a trip to the bathroom).
5) Wipe the area where you were eating, even if you did not spill anything.

"Seated" has specific a definition in a classroom: when using chairs, "seated" means the whole butt (or "both butts") on the chair; when sitting on the floor, "seated" means cross-legged (what we used to call "Indian-style and is now in elementary classrooms often called "Criss-cross applesauce"). Both of these ways of sitting are very stable; it is difficult to move much if one is sitting squarely on the chair or on the floor. This means it is also difficult to spill beverages or snacks!

Sometimes a teacher will invite a few students to eat lunch in the classroom with the teacher. This can be a reward. It can also be to help the teacher with a project in the classroom (changing bulletin boards, etc). If the invited students eat the school lunches, this means that they must bring the school lunch trays from the cafeteria/kitchen to the classroom. This is a process that takes some care and monitoring, especially if stairs are involved. The teacher needs to make sure that everyone walks slowly, holding the trays carefully (again, as Mom says, "Use two hands!"). In addition, some students will want to eat as they walk. They cannot do this; the teacher must remind them to wait until they are in the classroom and seated before they may start eating.

<u>Kinds of Foods</u>
Part of the fun of parties is sharing special treats – often sodas and snacks. There are very mixed feelings about what constitutes appropriate in-school treats. Some teachers do not want to allow any un-healthful snacks in their classrooms, and some schools have policies about what outside foods are permitted in the school building. Policies limiting food and treats are becoming more common and stricter, in response to the increase of childhood obesity and related health issues. Many schools may have strict policies on a day-to-day basis, but loose policies for special occasions. Interestingly, I have not found parents to express concern about treats during school parties and special events.

So where does this leave you? The first thing any teacher needs to do when planning a party or class celebration is to learn the school policy about parties and snacks. This will dictate your options. Assuming that the school allows some flexibility in for parties, you need to make decisions based on your own views. I allowed treats for all class parties and special events, and I did not limit it to "healthful" foods only. Parties in Class 3-309 always had an assortment of sodas, chips, and cookies. But I monitored this carefully – to ensure that children shared the different goodies and did not overeat. At a typical all-class party, we would consume just two 2-litre bottles of soda, two large bags of chips, and one package of cookies or candies. This never seemed excessive to me (see Birthdays & Parties).

<u>Food Allergies & Etc</u>
Teachers often ask me about children's food allergies. I have found that parents tell the teacher on the first day of school of any serious health issues. In addition, the school nurse will inform the teacher of any extenuating medical concerns among the student body. It is worth noting that children with serious conditions, even very young children, know that they cannot eat certain things. Children with serious allergies or diabetes know at a very young age what happens if they eat the wrong foods, and they are very good about it (unimaginably so, to us adults). They do not want to feel ill, and they do not want to go to the hospital. If

you do have doubts, or if you have questions about foods or allergies, make sure to speak to a veteran teacher or the school nurse.

Chapter 8: Special Activities

Birthdays & Parties

Birthdays are a *big* deal to kids. They expect a fuss to be made over them for their birthdays. This is true for young children, and it is true for older children (remember your own childhood birthdays!). A birthday is a child's own day, a day that s/he is special. Adults don't always realize this; teachers of elementary school students need to acknowledge birthdays and help make children feel special.

Most new teachers agree with the above, but they wonder how to fit it in with all the other demands of teaching. They also wonder about how to fit it all in – 30 kids means 30 parties? Can I lose that much teaching time? What about kids who have birthdays on weekends or over vacations? What about summer birthdays? How can I afford all this?

Parties With Parents
Some teachers leave birthdays up to the parents. They tell the parents that birthdays are up to them; parents can plan to come in, purchase goodies, and celebrate the birthday during school. This is a popular option, and it is very easy, but I do not think it is a good one. Not all parents will participate, and the kids whose parents do not (or cannot) plan parties for them will feel badly. Furthermore, you will have little control over what happens for the party that the parent plans. A parent could say s/he is coming at 11am and not show until noon. Some parents will give no notice about coming and show up with party supplies and a slew of relatives and multiple video cameras. The class might be in the computer room with the technology teacher, and you have to scramble to get the students back into the classroom for this impromptu party, irritating everyone along the way (from the technology teacher, to the custodian, to the parent). It's even possible that a parent who was expected to come in and bring party supplies does not show up. Then you are left with 30 disappointed moppets (and nothing planned!). I am painting a grim, and some would argue an unfair, picture. Many teachers have had wonderful experiences with cooperative, organized, helpful parents and enjoyable, fun birthday parties. But each of the above scenarios I outlined above happened to teachers in my school every year.

My Solution: Five Parties
I had five birthday parties during the course of the school-year. They fell at the following times: end of October, before Christmas/December break, mid-February, mid- or late-February (generally before the Winter Break).

Chapter 8: Special Activities

April or May (before the Easter/Spring break), and in June. While these parties did align with major holidays (Halloween, Christmas/Hanukah/Kwanza, Valentine's Day, and Easter/Passover), it is a good practice to avoid celebrating specific holidays. There are often several cultural backgrounds, religions, etc in a single class; as a general rule (unless teaching in a religious school), it is a good idea to have non-religious parties or special events. It is worth noting that many schools or districts have explicit rules against certain kinds of parties or celebrating certain holidays. My five parties were: a Fall Party (or October Party), a Holiday Party, a Winter party, a Spring Party, and an End-of-School Party.

I solve the birthday "problem" by combining birthdays at each of these parties. Any child who has a birthday in the two months prior to one of the parties will be celebrated at that party (ie, all children with birthdays in September or October will be celebrated at the October party; all children with November or December birthdays will be celebrated at the December party, etc). Within the first few days of school, you will explain this to the class (it ties in well with a math activity, see Day 1 & Day 2). Children whose birthdays fall in July or August may pick which party they want to join.

Timing
Parties are best scheduled after lunch (some schools have policies requiring this). It is good if dismissal immediately follows the party, as the children are likely to be too excited to do much else. Depending on the activities involved, a party will last an hour or an hour and a half. The cake (candles, singing, cutting, and eating) takes 15-20 minutes. Clean-up will take 10-15 minutes. This allows approximately an hour for party games or special activities.

No Birthdays Allowed
There are some children whose religions do not allow the acknowledgment or celebration of birthdays. The child and the parent will share this information. It can be tough as a teacher; you want to respect the religion of all children, but you do not want any child to be left out. Speak to last year's teacher to see how s/he handled the child's birthday. Sometimes, parents with these views are flexible about what happens in schools; sometimes they are not. If you sense that a parent will have problems with the party, speak to him/her, and ask what the preferences are. A parent might offer to pick up the kid after lunch on party days. S/he might allow the child to remain with you, but request that the child not participate. S/he might ask that the child be sent to

another room during the party. No matter what your personal views are on this, you must honor the parent's wishes.

<u>Party Activities</u>
New teachers often make the mistake of not planning adequately for parties. They think they can tell the kids to bring in some "games" and perhaps some "music" and all will go well: "We'll just have free time!" Ugh! Parties can be a great deal of fun, but they only work with thorough planning and foresight.

Party activities may be limited by school rules or the administration's preferences. Find out about this ahead of time; ask a senior teacher what is expected and allowed. For the first party, do not plan an "active" party. You do not know the kids well enough to know how they will behave during a party. In addition, new teachers generally do not have the experience and confidence to be able to remain calm and in control during rowdy activities.

Calm party activities include: videos, whole-class games (where everyone stays in their seat), and special art projects (like origami). As the year passes, and your confidence grows, traditional party games are a great deal of fun.

For the majority of the birthday parties in my classroom, I showed a movie. It was never just any video; I always chose a video that corresponded to a read-aloud book that we had recently finished (see Read-Alouds). The children are always enthusiastic about a movie, even more so because they enjoyed the book. If the video is a musical, or contains several songs, we learned all of the songs ahead of time; this added to student interest and engagement. A video also segued into various comparative lessons/activities. We would talk about the difference with books and movies; we would talk about which we liked better and what might have done differently if we were making the film. Sometimes we did larger project/activities based on the book-movie connection.

It is not necessary to pick a video that corresponds to a shared book. You may show a video on its own. Make sure, however, that it is a quality video (party time should not be "lost" time). The video should be one the students have not seen; it should add to their knowledge. Older "classic" films are often great choices. Be aware that children do not easily sit for prolonged periods of time. a limit of 30-45 minutes is appropriate for

Chapter 8: Special Activities

preK-2 and an hour and a half for upper elementary grades. Longer movies may be shown over successive days. Interestingly, if you are showing a video that corresponds to a book, the sitting time of the students is greatly increased.

Who brings what?
The children (parents) are responsible for snacks. Each child must bring one thing – a bottle of soda, a pack of chips, a package of cookies, or a bag of candy. Make sure to give the class advance notice, so that they can remind their parents. I have never had parents, even ones with very little money, fail to contribute something. At the same time, I never made a point of discussing or tracking who brought what.

As the snacks trickle in, you need to store them. Soda bottles can line the floor of the closet or the back of the room. Munchies need more attention, as they can attract pests. I brought in a large canister (the kind that comes with flavored popcorn) for candy and cookies. Bags of chips were clothes-pinned to clotheslines I strung along one wall of the room (to keep them out of reach of mice).

The teacher brings the dry goods – paper cups and paper towels or napkins. If cake is being served, you will also need small plates and plastic forks or spoons. The teacher brings in the cake.

Ice
There is no ice! Tell the kids this in advance, and allow no discussion, and there will not be a problem: "If you can't drink the soda room temperature, then you don't have to drink any." In my years of teaching, not one child (or parent) ever minded room-temperature sodas.

Serving Food
In addition to the "Food Rules" already mentioned above (see Food in School), the following are my recommended routines for serving food in class:
1) Get two large-sized garbage bags ahead of time (the custodian will be able to provide these).
2) Get two rolls of paper towels (the custodian may be able to provide these).
3) Discuss with the class, before the party, how food will be served at the party.

4) On the morning of the party, decide as a class which of the accumulated snacks will be served at this party (much more will have come in than any class can eat - or should eat – at a single party).
5) Review how the food will be served and shared: everyone will be able to take a little from each bag, but no-one may take too much. I found the class to be quite good about this – when it was discussed ahead of time. They appreciated being able to make the snack decisions, and they were quite good about sharing at the party.
6) Everyone goes to the bathroom before the party. If the party follows lunch, stop by the bathroom on the way to the room from the cafeteria. Except for extenuating circumstances, children should not leave the room during the party.
7) Arrange cups on a table off to the side of the room. The teacher pours the soda, cups half-full.
8) Invite groups of children to come and get a cup. Remind them to hold the cups with both hands and not to take a sip until they are seated. They return to their tables or to the video-watching or activity area. Once children have sodas and are seated, they do not move again.
9) Award points (see Point Chart) to groups who do all this in an orderly manner.
10) The Paper Passer-Outer (see Student Jobs) should hand out double paper towel squares to each child, as well as leaving a few extras out in case of spills.
11) Bring out the cake (see below), light the candles, sing, etc.
12) Cut pieces of cake (or etc) and distribute with forks or spoons (if necessary – I'm a fan of eating cake with fingers).
13) Once you main activity of the party starts (video or whatever), you begin handing out the snack bags. Children will take small handfuls of whatever interests them, place their portions on the paper towel, and pass the bags on.
14) If kids want more soda, they are to silently raise their hand, and the teacher comes around for re-fills. This may seem labor-intensive (and a bit like being an un-tipped waiter), but it avoids spills and messes.
15) When the party is over, call the class by groups to throw away their cups and papers and wrappers, etc. Un-finished beverages will need to be tipped into a sink, which may necessitate trips to the bathroom or water fountain. Award points for orderly behavior during clean-up.

Cake

Children expect a cake for birthday parties. There are several affordable options. One is to go to one of those giant wholesale groceries and order a sheet cake (well under $20, enough to feed 32). Have them write on it:

Chapter 8: Special Activities

"Class 3-309 Birthdays" and the names of the kids whose birthdays are being celebrated at the party. You can bake your own cake, if you are the baking type. This can get expensive, and it is time-consuming (new teachers tend to have little money and less time). My solution (taken from a colleague): make a giant crispy-rice cereal treat. Follow the recipe on the side of the package. I found that three times the standard recipe was adequate for 30 of us. It took about 35 minutes.

If you make a crispy-rice treat, or if you bake a cake, you need to decorate it yourself. Buy a tube of frosting with writing tips (the same tube will last you the whole school-year). Writing with frosting is not as easy as it looks; you'll need to practice (on a plate) a few times before you write on your first cake. I also recommend some sprinkles or special-shape candies. Specialty baking or candy-making shops have wonderful collections of special occasion sprinkles; the kids love them!

You can also dye the crispy-rice treat or the cake with food-coloring. Kids love things luridly-colored. One of those little food-coloring containers dumped into the cake batter or the marshmallow goo will delight the kids, even if you find the bright-green end-result hard to stomach.

Leftovers
With 32 kids each bringing in party contributions, there will be bags of snacks leftover. I would serve these during special activities in the times between parties – during an afternoon art project, following a spelling bee, etc. Sharing some snacks made a regular classroom activity a mini-party.

For Out-of-Classroom Teachers
Some out-of-classroom teachers see upwards of 500 children every week. These teachers simply cannot acknowledge every child's birthday. Don't even try. When a child says it's his or her birthday, wish them a great day, and that's the end of it.

Other out-of-classroom teachers see fewer students and may wish to honor birthdays. One idea is to review the roster of the students and find the birthdays. Keep a list of birthdays and check it at the end of every month. For the next month, write little "Happy Birthdays" notes for each child who's having a birthday that month. Put the cards in a bundle in your desk, in chronological order. Check the bundle in the mornings and give out cards to the kids on their birthdays (before the weekend for weekend birthdays and before vacations for birthdays that fall over vacations). Make July and August cards and hand them out at the end of the year.

Chapter 8: Special Activities

Birthday Days

The question still remains: what will you do on a child's actual birthday. This is largely a matter of personal preference and style. Some teachers have a "Birthday Crown" or special hat that kids wear on their birthdays. That way, the birthday child feels special and, all day, anyone who passes wishes him or her a great birthday – lots of "Happy Birthday" wishes in a day! Some teachers opt to have the class sing "Happy Birthday" at the end of the day. Some teachers will give a small token at this time.

I kept it simple. In my class, I had several collections of special tokens and stickers (see Goodie Can). Some years, I had children come to take a gift from the Goodie Can. Other years, I would invite kids to take a special sticker from the special sticker collection. I did not ordinarily orchestrate a round of "Happy Birthday"; the students in the class tended to do this automatically. Children who had weekend birthdays would collect their goodie on Friday, and summer birthday kids would collect a goodie at the end of the school-year.

Another easy birthday practice is to write personalized notes to each child on his or her birthday. Give the card to the child at the end of the day, on Friday for weekend birthdays, on the day before vacations for holiday birthdays, and at the end of the year for summer birthdays. Children tend to receive very few personalized, written items – especially in this era of online communications. Mailed cards and birthday cards are nearly a thing of the past. A handwritten birthday card becomes ever so much more special and valued.

Some schools may have school-wide policies about birthdays; check on these before acknowledging or celebrating birthdays.

Out-of-Classroom Teachers
Please see above section, Birthdays & Parties

Chapter 8: Special Activities

Bees

Spelling Bees and Math Bees are educational activities that reinforce concepts/skills and which the students usually enjoy. Bees have been a part of school since the beginning of time, and not much has changed. Some people have negative associations with classroom bees, and this is unfortunate. Bees can provide an alternate and engaging activity for reinforcing, practicing, and demonstrating skill mastery. Like all special activities, the teacher must plan carefully – so that students remain engaged and enthusiastic.

Bees should be scheduled regularly, but no more than once every three weeks, so that they do not get "old." Teachers should schedule different types of bees; in addition to the common spelling bees, there can be math bees, social studies facts bees, etc. This ensures that different kids get a chance to "shine." I always allowed the winner to pick a prize from the Goodie Can (see Odds & Ends).

<u>Round Robin</u>
Teachers must establish the order in which students will speak or spell as part of a Bee. This sounds small, but children can be quick to claim that something is unfair. If it is not clear who follows whom, and if the same order is not maintained throughout the Bee, the students may get frustrated or complain. I set up a Round Robin system and posted it on a chart on the wall. The Round Robin chart does not list student's names, only tables or desks; this way it can be used for the whole year, regardless of any seating changes.

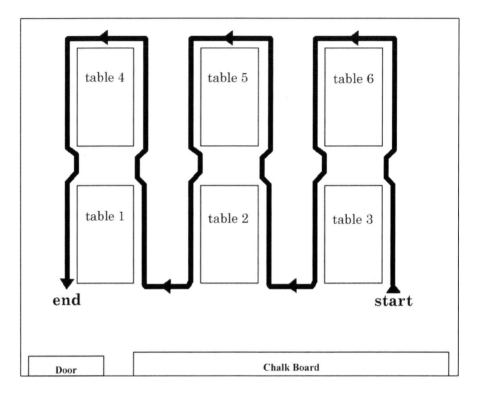

Bee Rules

When a conducting a spelling bee, the order of the words must be set ahead of time. Alternately, they may be chosen from a hat. What cannot happen is that teacher picks words as s/he goes along; teachers who do this may inadvertently call easier or harder words for some children, and they will (correctly) perceive this as unfair.

I instituted the same rules for classroom bees that are part of the National Spelling Bee. My students always enjoyed knowing they were doing it the "real way":

1) Pronounce the word: After the teacher says the word, the student must say it; s/he may say the word more than once.
2) Clarification: The student may ask for the definition or for the teacher to use the word in a sentence.
3) Spell the word: The student spells the word. S/he may start over, but s/he cannot change any of the letters s/he has already said.

Chapter 8: Special Activities

4) Repeat the word: The student repeats the word, indicating that s/he has finished.

If a student spells a word correctly, s/he remains in the competition. If a student misses a word, s/he sits down and is "out." As the group gets smaller, the remaining students may move to the front of the room, facing the other students. This makes the spellers nervous, but they enjoy being "on stage." This often helps the rest of the class to stay more focused and involved.

For non-spelling Bees, I followed the above rules as closely as possible (and appropriate), though the break-down of steps, or rules, do not "translate" well to all subjects:

5) Students may ask that a question, math problem, etc, be repeated.
6) For math questions, students may jot down numbers as they wish (this is not allowed if the bee is about multiplication or etc facts – ie, facts that I expect the kids to know by memory.)
7) Students may ask that the teacher defines certain terms or phrases in the question or problem.
8) The student indicates that s/he is finished by repeating the (essential parts of) question, along with the answer.

Bee Preparation
The preparation for Bees varies. Spelling Bees are easy to prepare: Simply create random-order lists of sight-words and/or spelling/vocabulary list words. A teacher who tracks these lists on the computer can easily pull up such a Bee list in seconds.

For Math Bees, SS Fact Bees, etc, the preparation is more involved (and time-consuming); the teacher must create lists of questions and answers. S/he must place them in an order (random is often best). If a teacher has created Fact Cards all along, s/he has only to grab a pile and use those as the questions for the Bee (see Fact Cards).

Avoiding Boredom & Misbehaviors
The children who get "out" early tend to get bored and may misbehave. My favorite antidote to that was to use the Probability Bowl (see Routines & Procedures). If a student missed a word or question, I pulled names from the Probability Bowl until I got one of a child who was already out. If that child could spell the missed word (or answers the question correctly), his/her table earned a point. The trick was that, at this stage, I

would not repeat the word or question, so the child had to be paying attention during the Bee.

<u>Doesn't the Same Kid Always Win?</u>
The above question is the reason that many people do not like bees; they think that the same kid or kids will always win. Moreover, many teachers feel that the this kid is one who already stands out for academic performance. I did not find this to be the case. My best writers, best mathematicians, best etc – were simply *not common winners* (typically) in the different bees. The think-on-your-feet quick-answer format of bees is quite different than the mathematic talent or writing talent that shines in other parts of the classroom. In fact, bees in the elementary classroom may provide opportunities for other skills (and other kids) to be recognized.

<u>For Out-of-Classroom Teachers & Other Subjects</u>
Bees can be used for all subjects. It is just a matter of preparing adequate Fact Cards, word lists, questions, etc.

Chapter 8: Special Activities

Two Games: Buzz & Categories

There are countless engaging educational games that whole classes or groups of students can play in the classroom. A quick internet search or a survey of veteran teachers will turn up more options than anyone can use. The two games listed here are ones that I used in every class I have ever taught – and that the children loved.

Buzz

Buzz is a math game that reinforces basic multiplication facts. Children must be familiar with the three multiplication tables or "counting by threes" prior to playing Buzz. The game can be used for ESL children who are learning to count in English. The game, with variations can be played in second through eighth grades (even my graduate students find it challenging!).

Explain that each child, in turn, will count off one-by-one, with the first child saying "one," the second "two," etc. If your room allows the students to form a large circle, then Buzz should be played that way. Otherwise, use the Round Robin Chart (see Bees). Practice counting one-by-one. This step is pretty easy, but the kids will enjoy "practicing" even something so easy, because it is part of a game.

The first time Buzz is played in class, write the three times table on the chalkboard and review it with the class (3, 6, 9, 12, 15, 18, 21, 24, 27, 30, 33, 36). Depending on the level of the students, this may take more or less time.

Explain that, in Buzz, students will count off as they just did, but they may not say any multiple of three (ie, any number in the three times – currently written on the chalkboard). This is a good time to practice again: have the kids count off, with each third child saying, "Buzz." This is practice (no-one will get "out" for a mistake); if anyone makes an error, that is okay. The next child simply starts over (with "1"). The counting proceeds: "One – Two – Buzz – Four – Five – Buzz – Seven . . ." If the class gets to 36, try to encourage successive children to figure what are the next numbers (they may count on their fingers: 39, 42, 45, etc). Go through the group at least twice.

Then introduce the trick: since this game is about three's, no-one can say any number that has a three in it, even if it is not a multiple of three.

Chapter 8: Special Activities

This may take a few minutes to clarify and explain. I usually wrote on the board the additional numbers that kids could not say – ie, 13, 23, 30-39, etc. Count off the numbers yourself so the kids hear the double-buzz pattern at 12-13 and 23-24. Have the class practice a few rounds.

Once play begins, a kid is "out" when s/he misses; a miss includes saying the wrong number, saying "buzz" instead of a number, and saying a number that should have been "buzzed." When a child misses and is out, the next child starts counting with "one." Play is continued until there is one child left standing; that child is the winner. A round of "Buzz" with 25-30 children generally takes 15-20 minutes. I allowed the winning child to pick a prize from the Goodie Can.

Like all games, play Buzz no more than once per month. Even if the children clamor to play again (the next day or the next week), do not allow it. Special activities need to remain special; this means occasional. If you play any game to often, no matter who much the students request it, they will grow tired of it.

For the Early Grades
Buzz is not appropriate for kindergarten or first grade. Some second grade classes might be able to handle it, depending on their proficiency in math and their maturity.

For Upper Grades, a Variation
If you are working with the upper grades or a high-performing class, you can make the game more complicated. Do this only after the class has played Buzz successfully, understands the math, and enjoys it. Please note again: I played this game in graduate classes, with graduate students, and they stumbled and laughed, just like the younger kids. The game is sufficiently challenging as it stands.

Introduce "Zap." Just as you "Buzz" for three's, you "Zap" for five's. This always gets messy, as the buzzes and the zaps frequently overlap: one – two – buzz – four – zap – buzz – seven – eight – buzz – zap. Few kids get very far, but they enjoy the challenge. An eighth grade class I worked with loved the Buzz-Zap combination.

For the Out-of-Classroom Teacher
Whether or not your subject is/includes mathematics, Buzz is a great game to have in your emergency tool-kit. If you are unexpectedly asked to

cover a fourth grade class last period on Friday afternoon, Buzz is a perfect solution.

Categories

Through all my years of teaching, Categories was everyone's favorite game, first through seventh grades. The object of Categories is to come up with items in designated categories that begin with a certain letter. Based on the chosen letter and the categories, this game is easily modified for different ages and levels. Categories is a bit difficult to explain and set up the first time; allow 30-40 minutes when you introduce the game and play it the first time.

Write three or four categories on the board. I wrote them across the top of the board so that I had plenty of board space left below. My standard categories were:
1) Food or drink
2) Game or sport
3) Geographic place names

Additional categories can be:
1) Science Words
2) Math Words
3) Historical Figures
4) Any subject of interest to your students

On one corner of the board, I would draw a square. In that square, I would write a letter (a consonant); use "B" the first time. Ask the class for B-words that correspond to each of the categories. This is fairly easy and straightforward, and you will get many responses:
• Beans, broccoli, banana, etc.
• Basketball, baseball, bingo, etc.
• Brooklyn, Brazil, Boston, etc.

Explain to the students that the game of Categories is not much more than what they have just done. They will work in teams (generally their tables) to come up with an answer for each of the categories using a new letter. While they may discuss multiple answers, the group must decide on a single answer. Spelling does not count; they simply have to be able to write the word clearly enough that they can read it and that the rest of the class will understand it. Groups will have 3-4 minutes to decide on a single answer for each of the categories.

Chapter 8: Special Activities

Each table will have a single piece of paper and one student will be the recorder; s/he will write down the answers. This job of writing will rotate for each round of the game. When a table has answers for all categories, the recorder turns the paper over and puts the pencil down. They then indicate they are finished by giving the thumbs-up sign (see Routines & Procedures).

Step-by-Step Procedure for Playing Categories
1) Have the Paper-Passer (see Student Jobs) hand out papers to each table. Ask that each table take 30 seconds to determine who will do the recording for this round. Award points to the tables which do this with a minimum of fuss (see Point Chart).
2) Have a sample answer-sheet prepared to hold up as a model for the class. The sheet will have a small box drawn at the top for the letter and numbers 1-3 below. Ask the recorders to hold up the papers to make sure that they have done it correctly.
3) Say: "You will work within your groups to come up with good answers for each category. I *strongly* encourage you to *whisper* as you discuss possible answers."
4) When all tables are ready to play, write a letter in the box on the chalkboard. Start with the easier letters, the common consonants: T, S, M, R, D, etc.
5) There will be a fair bit of noise the first time the class plays Categories. Do not worry about it. Walk around the room to make sure that every group is coming up with single answers and that there are no skirmishes regarding the recorder.

Groups should not be held to a time limit the first few rounds of Categories. Ensure that the students are focused and working quickly, but allow them to finish. *Say* there is a time limit, to keep the kids on task, but do not enforce it. After a few rounds, the students will be able to complete the task much quicker, and you will then hold them to a 2-3 minute limit, depending on the age and maturity of the students.

Tallying Points
There needs to be space on the board or on hanging newsprint paper to record the answers for each table. The teacher does this initially. Once the class has played Categories several times, and the rules and process are clear to everyone, you may have a student record points (the recorders come to the board and write the groups' answers).

Chapter 8: Special Activities

Each table will share their answer to each of the categories, and the teacher/recorder will write the answers on the board. Record the answers to one question at a time, moving through the tables. A table or group gets a point for each correct answer:

T	Table 1	Table 2	Table 3	Table 4	Table 5	Table 6
Food	tea	tea	taco	tomato	Tabasco	turkey
Game	tennis	Tic-tac-toe	tag	tennis	tag	track
Geo	Texas	Toronto	Tennessee	Toronto	Trenton	Tallahassee

Tables rarely leave blanks, so each table will get the maximum points possible (with three categories, that is three points per round). But then there are the "bonus points." Explain that *originality* earns extra points. Cross off all duplicate answers:

T	Table 1	Table 2	Table 3	Table 4	Table 5	Table 6
Food	~~tea~~	~~tea~~	taco	tomato	Tabasco	turkey
Game	~~tennis~~	Tic-tac-toe	~~tag~~	~~tennis~~	~~tag~~	track
Geo	Texas	~~Toronto~~	Tennessee	~~Toronto~~	Trenton	Tallahassee

Adding the regular points and the bonus points, the scores after the first ("T") round are: Tables 1, 2, 4 – 4 points, Tables 3, 5 – 5 points, and Table 6 is in the lead with 6 points. Some of the duplicate points will have been because students overheard others' answers and wrote them down. When you count up the bonus points, there is likely to be some whining: "They took our answer!" "We had that first!" Tell the class that they may take others' answers if they wish, though it will not help the groups earn the bonus points. Explain that each table has the greatest chance of earning bonus points if the members speak softly to "protect" their answers. This will ensure that subsequent rounds will, therefore, be much quieter.

Categories is a great game for a Thursday or Friday afternoon, after testing, or as part of a party or class celebration. Playing four rounds, after the introduction session, takes 30-35 minutes. Class 3-309 played Categories one a month.

Chapter 8: Special Activities

Two Art Activities: Magic Pictures & Origami

As in the above section on games, there is no end to the number of engaging art or arts and crafts projects for children. Good art projects can be simple, and they can be very involved. Some will require special items, and some will require only ordinary classroom or household products. Most of the lessons you teach across the curriculum – math, reading, science – lend themselves to engaging art activities. Veteran teachers, instructors' manuals, and internet can provide many ideas. The following two art projects were perennial favorites for students.

Magic Pictures

Magic Pictures is a calm, structured art project, for second through sixth grades. It takes 25-40 minutes.

The purpose of this activity is to make a "magic" picture. Each child will make his/her own picture, and each one will be different.

Materials:
- crayons (bright colors only)
- black crayons (or halves, one for each student)
- index cards, 5x7 inches
- newspaper
- toothpicks

Note: Crayon "nubs" (scraps) are great for this activity. In fact, this activity is a great way to use up crayon nubs; there is no reason to use new, pointy crayons.

1) Give each student an index card. Place the card on the newspaper, to protect the desks. Students are to make a design on the card, using only bright-colored crayons. They are to color every bit of the card. The kids must color over and over to make sure the whole thing is strongly and brightly colored. In all likelihood, their fingers will start to feel greasy, and their fingers might cramp a little. The students may even complain a little, but in my experience, these complaints are always good-natured. This part takes 10-20 minutes.

2) Distribute black crayons, one to each student. I generally used the left-over crayon nubs that I saved from previous years. Students must color *over* the beautifully-bright and painfully-done work. The

students will not believe that that is what they are supposed to do. They will have to press really hard, over and over, to cover all the underlying colors. I never tell them what the end-result will be, as it is such a lovely surprise. This part takes 10-15 minutes.

3) Students then use toothpicks (rounded ends are best) or pencils to "draw" a picture by scratching away the black. The resulting picture is made up of colorful lines and shapes on a black background. Students can "erase" by coloring over their scratched-away designs. This part takes 10-15 minutes.

I generally allowed the children to draw and re-draw designs on their magic pictures. While they were working, I walked around the room, talking to the students, asking them about their pictures, etc. It was a nice, calm "connecting" time.

Origami

Origami is the ancient Japanese art of paper-folding. There are countless books on origami, with detailed instructions for many paper designs. I do not think a teacher's library is complete without a book on origami. Children as young as four and five can master basic folds, and there are folds that professors at MIT practice. Origami takes focus, so it is a calm and structured activity. Teaching origami takes practice and planning on the part of the teacher, but it is worth the effort.

If you have never done any origami, you will need to teach yourself some basic folds first. Then practice doing the folds (without the book) one step at a time, until you can do the fold without thinking. Then do the fold again, explaining OUT LOUD exactly what you are doing so students will be able to follow. It will help if you can find a friend that you can teach – so that you get a sense of where the stumbles or frustrations are likely to be.

I always taught origami standing on a chair. The students had to watch me make the fold, without touching their own papers. I then un-did and repeated that one fold, so that the students were clear on what to do. I then invited them to do the same thing with their paper. The students would then hold their folded papers in the air, and a quick survey told me where there were problems.

Chapter 8: Special Activities

I then instructed students to put their papers down on the desk, while I did the next fold and repeated it. With every step, I walked around the room to see that the student folds were okay.

Start with a fold that is easier than you would predict would be appropriate; origami folds take longer to teach than the books indicate. Depending on how the students progress, you can choose harder or simpler folds for the next origami session. Origami requires square paper; you will have to buy origami paper (which is expensive). It is well worth the effort to find a shop that sells origami paper in bulk. Do not buy the mixed-sizes packages; you should have larger squares only (little hands will struggle with the tiny-sized squares).

Chapter 8: Special Activities

Song Lyrics

There are many ways that music can be a part of a classroom. Even without a music background (or any musical ability), a teacher can incorporate music into his/her classroom. Music lends itself to so many subjects – history and social studies, math, reading, etc. Lessons can be brought to life with music. This section is about one small aspect of teaching music – learning lyrics. I found this to be an enjoyable activity, and it is appropriate, with variations, for emergent readers right up to middle school. Using music and song lyrics is also very effective in helping English Language Learners (ELL) to use and practice English.

The first step is to pick several songs and to get the lyrics copied. A quick internet search will reveal songs for nearly every subject area, from every country, etc. When working with ESL/ELL students, I found that some of the 50's rock-n-roll classics were very successful. These songs have lively tunes, simple lyrics, and the topics were generally quite clean and school appropriate. Other popular choices were older "cowboy" songs and Broadway show tunes. Avoid recent popular music hits for two reasons; their lyrics can be off-color and inappropriate and they do not expose the children to anything new. Initially, the students might offer some resistance, as the music chosen is "so old-fashioned." Explain to the kids that you want them to hear all different kids of music. Tell them that some of this music is early rock-n-roll. All my students loved learning new songs, and any grumbling passed quickly.

When you give the lyrics to the class, read through them aloud once or twice slowly. Instruct the kids, even the non- or pre-readers to follow along with their fingers. It gives them the "feeling" of reading; and most of them will recognize certain words and letters. Explain the story behind the song and define unfamiliar words and out-of-date language. Have the class repeat after you any particularly tricky words or terms. Listen for correct pronunciation. Then have the class chorally repeat after you, one line at a time. It is important, especially in ESL activities, to give students multiple opportunities to respond as a chorus; this gives them confidence to participate, which they might not feel if called on to speak alone. Then have volunteers read lines or verses aloud individually.

This activity allows you to discuss the parts of a song – verses, the chorus, etc. Depending on the music education of your students, this may be new to them. Many songs have great rhyme schemes, and this is great for developing readers. Songs also are great examples of imagery, which is so important for young writers. You will also discuss the "creative" stressing and rhyming that the singer uses to make a rhyme "work" (half-rhymes, word choice, alliteration, etc). I once had a recently-arrived second grader in a bilingual class figure out that, in "That'll be the Day," Cupid shot a "dart" instead of an "arrow," because "arrow" does not rhyme with "heart."

When the class seems comfortable with the words, play the music. Tell them that they *may* just listen (i.e., that they do not have to sing along). Insist that they keep place on the sheet with their finger. Watch for this, as you walk around the room. Following the text encourages word-recognition and increases reading competence (it also helps the children remain focused).

I generally played a song 3-4 times. By the second time, all students were singing at least some of the song. This activity, from start to finish with one song, takes 20-25 minutes. When I had a series of songs (eg, for a unit), I would introduce one song on one day, have a day or two break, then introduce the second song and review the first.

It is important to link these songs to other lessons or activities. I found that songs were great motivators for writing activities. So many songs have great metaphors or similes, and they can serve as motivations for children to write their own. In "Blue Suede Shoes," children wrote about things they cared about as much Carl Perkins did about his shoes.

The National Anthem
Many children do not really know the National Anthem. And if they know the words, few understand the meaning of the words (let alone the context in which the song was written and then adopted as the anthem). I had a student ask one year if I would teach it to the class. This child was an immigrant, and she felt that it was disrespectful not to be able to sing the "country's song" (he words) when it was played. That year, I taught our class all the words to the National Anthem. We discussed what the words really meant, and the kids sang all the words proudly (and loudly) at subsequent school assemblies.

Movie Musicals
One popular activity for class parties is to show a video (see Birthday Parties). If the videos had songs, I would teach those songs in the weeks

leading up to the party. This increased excitement about the movie, as well as presenting an opportunity to practice reading and speaking.

Chapter 8: Special Activities

Awards Luncheon

There are many ways to celebrate the end of the school-year. Some schools will have all-school events or celebrations – field days, picnics, carnivals, etc. These events are wonderful, but I always liked having a more personalized event for my students and their families (in addition to any school-wide or grade-wide event). Our class event took the form of an Awards Luncheon.

The awards luncheon was held one of the last afternoons of the school-year. The luncheon was a "potluck," and parents were invited to prepare and bring favorite dishes. We designed invitations for family members, selected teachers, etc., and we delivered them a few weeks before the event.

At the awards ceremony, each child received at least one award. I chose mostly non-academic categories for the awards, because academic achievements are often acknowledged and/or celebrated in numerous other ways (honor rolls, school-wide awards, etc). Instead, I created fun categories that were specific to the group of children and the individual personalities. The awards themselves were pre-printed certificates, available in office supply stores. Some typical categories were:
- Class Comedian/Comedienne (best joke teller)
- Math Whiz
- Neatest Penmanship
- Book Report Champion
- Fastest Runner
- Buzz Champion (see Buzz)
- Coolest Vocabulary
- Geography Wizard or Cartographer (best map/geography knowledge)
- Class Artist (best drawer)
- Spelling Bee Champion
- Trivia Whiz

Many parents came to the awards luncheon, and they always brought more food than the class could eat. The parents brought friends, relatives, and neighbors. They brought video cameras. We generally had 60+ people squeezed into a classroom, with people sitting on desks, on radiators, on boxes, etc. It was always over 100 degrees (my school was not air-conditioned), yet no one minded. The awards luncheon was a wonderful way to celebrate a year.

9

Odds & Ends

Chapter 9: Odds & Ends

About this Chapter

This chapter contains a variety of tips and hits that did not fit squarely anywhere else in the book. They represent effective practices from my classroom.

Actions Speak Louder . . . (Always Say Thank You!)

It is very easy in during the school-day to say to a child, "Roosevelt, go get my plan-book for me." Roosevelt will not be bothered; he probably will not notice that you did not say, "Please." But that fact has registered, on some level, for Roosevelt and for the rest of the class. The same holds when a secretary or school aide delivers a document to your classroom; that person should be thanked. It has always amazed me the teachers who expect their students to say, "Please" and "Thank you," but who do not, themselves, regularly show such courtesy to the teachers around them – or to their students. If you want the students to internalize the courtesies you value and seek to teach them, then you must make sure to model the same behaviors within your classroom, at all times. Students must hear you say "please" and "thank you." These courtesies must be directed at everyone – the principal, other teachers, the custodian, etc. A positive classroom community starts with the teacher.

Book Reports

Most schools require that children read books and prepare written reports on their reading. Some students like reading and writing book reports, and some do not. Teachers have mixed feelings about book reports; they want students to read books and to think about them critically, as well as to record their thoughts in writing, but the reports teachers must read and grade can be repetitive and tedious. If a class has 30 students, and each student is required to write (for example) 25 reports, then the teacher must read 750 book reports during the academic year. If the students are not enthused about their writing projects, the end-product is likely to be un-inspiring, and this makes for dull reading and grading.

Teachers tend to remember the book reports from their own childhoods and assign similar projects. We do this without thinking, without being aware of our motivations. This is unfortunate, because there are so many more-interesting options for book reports. There are formats that satisfy the purpose of the assignment yet allow for increased individuality and creativity. It is in a teacher's best interest to assign a book-report format

that is enjoyable to read, and to offer several options, so that children
have choice. I found that when children have some say in their work, they
tend to be more enthusiastic about it. In addition, when pushed to think
and write from different perspectives, children often produce more
engaging, higher-quality work. Three of my favorite book report formats
are:

• Re-tell the story as if you are a character in the book, in the first-person
("Life was very hard on the prairie. Our neighbors lived very far away,
and I only had Mary to play with. . . .").
• Pretend you are the author and write what would happen in a sequel to
the book ("After Sam learned that he liked green eggs and ham, he
went on a vacation. He was very tired from trying to run away from the
guy with the green eggs and ham. . . .").
• Write a letter to one character in the book, asking about significant
events of the story ("Dear Wilbur: I would like to know if you have gone
to more fairs, and if you won any more prizes? Do you still see
Fern? . . .")

Clothes (Teachers')

Kids want teachers to look like teachers. Kids *deserve* to have teachers
who present themselves professionally and appropriately, in a way that is
respectful to the community, the school, and the teaching profession. For
men, this means tailored pants, a pressed button-shirt, and a tie. For
women, this means tailored pants or skirts and a pressed blouse or top.
No one should wear jeans, sneakers, sandals, or track suits, and no
clothes should be overly casual, tight, or revealing. This also means
covering any tattoos and removing piercing-jewelry except from the ears.

New teachers should dress especially carefully and conservatively. It may
not be fair, but appearance counts for a lot. As in any job, a new teacher
is "on probation." Depending on the policies at the school or district, the
probationary period can last a few months or a few years. This period
should be viewed as an extension of the job interview, and a new teacher
should dress as professionally as possible during this time. You do not
want to be the new teacher who is in short skirts or frayed jeans. I have
read countless administrators' evaluations of teachers, in which (a lack
of) appropriate dress was mentioned. Once a teacher has established him/
herself in the school, understands the administration and the community,
and has had successes in the classroom, s/he may make other choices or
statements.

Chapter 9: Odds & Ends

Computer & Internet

All teachers must have regular access to a computer with internet capabilities and a printer. Most states require that teachers are technologically competent and incorporate technology into their lessons, and school districts may have additional technology or computer requirements for their teachers.

The internet is a fabulous resource for teachers; lesson plans, unit plans, worksheets, games, etc. are all available on the internet. There are also countless sites that offer support and information to teachers, new and experienced. Lesson plans, letters, worksheets, etc. can be created, saved, and changed on a computer; this allows a teacher not to "re-invent the wheel" each term or year. A laptop is as essential a tool in the classroom as are textbooks, a pencil sharpener, and math manipulatives.

It is fully unacceptable in today's world not to be internet-connected and savvy. Teachers who do not use computers do a disservice to their students.

Exercise Breaks

With increasing emphasis on standardized tests and scores and decreased funding for "extras" like art, music, and physical education, children today rarely get enough exercise. This is unfortunate – both in terms of children's health and in terms of unused energy. Exercise breaks help the kids to work out excess energy and irritations. This can be especially helpful during high-stress periods in the year. A teacher can only do so much because of the teaching demands and the limited time in a school-day (and often the limited space as well). It is possible, however, to squeeze in mini bursts of exercise. The children enjoy the release, you will enjoy the break, and everyone benefits from some exercise.

As with all new activities, it is best to start with structured, limited-movement exercises. I recommend exercises where the feet do not move: arm-circles, arm and upper-body twists, neck-rolls, shoulder lifts, etc. As with all instruction, it is necessary to break the activity in steps, and to make sure that each child has mastered the individual pieces before moving on. Start by modeling the action. Have the kids repeat the actions while counting aloud. It is important that everyone does the correct number, counts out loud, and stays in rhythm with the rest of the class. If the class gets unruly, stop and have everyone sit down. If an individual child mid-behaves, s/he must sit out. As the kids master the various actions or exercises, add more complicated exercises. I found that exercise sessions of four-five minutes once or twice per day were a positive addition to the classroom.

Fonts

Teachers should have two fonts that they use consistently for school-related correspondence and documentation. Using a single font consistently helps to distinguish your correspondence from the many forms and letters that parents already receive. Pick one that will be your parent-font; it should be friendly but professional (serif, non-slanty, simple, etc), and all letters to parents should be written in this font.

For student documents (worksheets, homework, etc), the font must be one that is "comfortable" for students to read, not too artsy or stylized. For younger children, the font should resemble clear manuscript printing. One way to pick a font is to find one that has the "a" written in the way children write it: "a," not, "a" (many people call the former the "ball and stick a"). Comic Sans is a good student-fonts (though Comic Sans is NOT a professional font and it should not be used as your parent font). For students older than 2nd grade, you do not need to avoid the "a."

Signing letters: It is a generally forgotten fact that a person signing his/her name should not use a title. This is a matter of courtesy; the logic being that someone else should use a title when addressing you, but that you should not use a title for yourself. This means that a teacher, signing a letter home, should simply sign his/her full name. Take this as you wish.

Goodie Can

Teachers need a collection of prizes for special games, contests, or exemplary performance, and they need a sturdy container in which to keep them. Large novelty tins are perfect for this (gift-popcorn canisters, large Danish cookie tines, etc). The prizes I stocked in my goodie can did not cost a lot of money; many were free. As a teacher, you will become a bit of a scavenger, and you will become adept at scouting out good deals and free stuff. In addition, as you get to know children, you will begin to recognize things that appeal to them but are inexpensive (or free).

- The give-aways (sometimes called "swag") at conferences and trade-shows make great prizes – mini-flashlights, key chains, stress balls, highlighters, fancy pens or markers, etc. Ask friends who attend such events to collect items for your goodie can.

Chapter 9: Odds & Ends

- Art supply stores often sell decorated or colorful pencils at reasonable prizes.
- Party favors make great gifts, and they can be purchased in packs, very cheaply. Favorite party favors are: sliding number puzzles, flying whirligigs, and water-gun rings (confiscate if anyone gets squirted).
- Office supply shops sometimes have fancy pens, markers, and erasers on their clearance tables.
- Dollar stores often have a section of toys/favors that are reasonably-priced.

With some creativity, you can keep a goodie can filled with great stuff without breaking the bank!

Language (Yours)

Teachers should never use any bad language in school. This does not only mean the "f" word or the "sh" word. Avoiding the truly vulgar or profane is obvious. But there are a number of words which are fairly common-place, and therefore acceptable, but are offensive to many people. These include words like "damn," "hell," etc. In addition, there are other words which many people may think of as "neutral," but are offensive in a school setting; these include "stupid," "dummy," and "shut-up." No word that attacks another person should ever be used in school.

Many teachers use substitute words for those times when an expletive feels right but will not do. Grandma's "Oh, gumdrops!" though it feels silly, is perfect. Teachers should always err on the side of propriety and conservatism. The teachers' lounge is part of the school. Teachers should not say anything in the teachers' lounge that they would not say in front of administrators, parents, or their students.

And when you err . . .

Teachers are human, and rare is the teacher who has not uttered a "bad" word within their students' hearing. Acknowledge it, own up to the gaffe, and apologize. As necessary (often depending on the age of the students and/or if they are satisfied with your acknowledgment and apology), have a brief conversation with the students: Say that the word you said is inappropriate in school and that we all make mistakes. Allow comments from the students, to the degree that you feel is appropriate and productive.

Chapter 9: Odds & Ends

Lights-Out/Dimmed (Read-Alouds)

During read-alouds, it is quite nice to turn off all or some of the lights. This tends to settle everyone down, and it focuses them on the words you are reading. Turning some of the lights off during an independent work time can also create some calm in the classroom. Dimming the lights can be especially effective during tough transitions (see After Lunch Chaos).

Listening & Pencils

Children are generally incapable of listening if they have anything in their hands. This includes pencils. When giving assignment instructions or clarification, it is essential that the students put down their pencils and look at you. Repeat all oral instructions twice. Ask if there are any questions. Then allow the children to pick up their pencils and begin to work.

Manipulatives

"Manipulatives" refer to the physical items used during a lesson to reinforce educational concepts. Manipulatives are used in many subjects but are most common in mathematics (counting blocks, plastic geometric shapes, spin-dials, thermometers, etc.). Most manipulatives are fun to play with – as well as essential in helping children understand mathematical concepts and skills – counting, measuring, etc. Effective teachers must use mathematics in the teaching of mathematics, through elementary school and into middle school (there are university math professors who also use manipulatives!).

Unfortunately, teachers often give very little thought to planning the details of a lesson that incorporates manipulatives. Such teachers often find manipulative-lessons stressful – as the children seem to spend much of the time playing and/or otherwise mis-using the manipulatives. In addition, for these teachers, and these classes, it seems that the students do not "get much out of" working with the manipulatives (so why bother?). Using manipulatives *seems* so easy and straightforward ("I'll just hand out the spinner-clocks and let the kids play"). Unfortunately, like so many things in teaching, planning is essential; this is especially true for new teachers or for those who have not used manipulatives much (or with success) in the past. When planning a lesson with manipulatives, the teacher must plan each step, including specific instructions for the use of manipulatives and questions to ask throughout the lesson. Teachers guidebooks often outline lessons to details; the internet is a great source for lessons.

Chapter 9: Odds & Ends

Teachers must expect – and allow – children to be children. When the manipulatives are first distributed, the children will want to play with them. Many teachers will fight this; it is a fight that the teacher will not win. Expect the children to want to play with the items before they use them for the assigned purpose and plan for this ("Let's take a few minutes to build anything we want with the cuisenaire rods. Then I'll have you stop and give some more instructions"). If you do not give students a few minutes of free time with the items, they will *take it anyway*, and you will be frustrated.

Whenever I introduced a manipulative, I would hold one up and explain its purpose and use. I always asked for comments, if they kids had seen one before, etc. I would then tell the class that we would be using the item to help us with a math activity. Before we began the activity, I would tell the class that they would have three minutes to "play" with the items. I would explain that I would flick the lights when it was time to stop playing. Anyone who did not stop playing when the lights were flicked would lose their manipulative.

Moving Around the Room (Sitting in Kids' Desks)
Teachers should circulate in a classroom, rather than standing at the front all the time. This helps the teacher to interact with more students. It puts him/her in contact with different students (ie, not just those in the front or in the back). While circulating, a teacher can easily review students' work, encourage – or quiet – with a shoulder pat, etc. Rare is the effective teacher who sits at his or her desk for more than moments in a day (teaching is much more *physical* than most people think).

Moving around the room tends to reduce the noise or fidgeting that occurs frequently at the back of a classroom (or wherever that classroom's "problem" area/s are). Kids also tend to appreciate the proximity of the teacher. A brief stop at a desk or table gives a bit of "personal" attention, no matter how fleeting; it keeps a teacher in touch with the class and the individuals.

But sometimes a teacher has to sit. Rather than sitting in the teacher's desk, a teacher should sit at an empty desk or the desk an absent students. Alternately, the teacher can send one child to sit at the teacher desk, and the teacher can sit in that child's desk. This keeps the teacher "in the middle" of the action. Sitting with the kids gives the message that you are comfortable with them and that you like them. It also gives the teacher a different perspective (you see what the kids see). Make sure to

Chapter 9: Odds & Ends

sit in different spots, so as to get a view of all parts of the room. In addition, you'll find that everyone will want you to sit next to them.

Power of Music

People often say, "Music calms the savage beast. The comparison to elementary schools and students is easy to make, though not one we should say out loud. That being the case, music *can* be soothing, and children often respond very well to music.

After the active part of a lesson (the mini-lesson, or the whole-class instruction portion), when the children are starting to work independently, some soft music can be very effective in maintaining focus and calm. The music should be carefully chosen – interesting and soothing. Jazz, classical music, nature, international music, etc. are all good choices. Music can also be used that supports a social studies or history unit.

Purple Snits

The "purple snit" is a concept from my own childhood. The term was one my father used (and still uses) to describe a foul mood that children can get into – unresponsive, combative, contrary, and wholly un-like-able (adults are not exempt). In my household, anyone in a "purple snit" was meant to remove him/herself from the group, and take some time alone until s/he recovered. Everyone comes out of a snit eventually, but the process cannot be rushed.

The concept is not different in a classroom; kids get into snits, and nothing is going to help them recover but some quiet distance. Cajoling a child in a purple snit accomplishes nothing except to irritate him or her even more (and prolong the time that s/he is unreasonable and un-reachable). But I had a special rule that applied to such situations: if a child got himself into a purple snit, *no-one was allowed to bother him/her*. In fact, if one child bothered a child in a purple snit, such that the be-snitted child took some inappropriate action, *the bothering child got in trouble* (and *not* the kid in the snit). It simply is not fair for one naughty kid to pick on someone who is vulnerable and get away with it. In my class, we spoke about this at the beginning of the year, and the kids all thought it was great. They may be little, but they understood how it is irritating it is to be bothered when you are already in a bad mood.

Chapter 9: Odds & Ends

Signing letters

It is a generally forgotten fact that a person signing his/her name should not use a title. This is a matter of courtesy; the logic being that someone else should use a title when addressing you, but that you should not use a title for yourself. This means that a teacher, signing a letter home, should simply sign his/her full name. Take this as you wish.

Sitting in Kids' Desks

See Moving Around the Room.

Tape-Loops

Most student work (papers, art projects, etc) are hung up with tape. Scotch (clear) tape is used to repair rips; masking tape is for affixing items to walls.

To hang things on the wall, teachers generally make little tape-loops, stick them to the back of the project, and press the whole thing to the wall. This sounds fairly straight-forward; but 28 tissue-paper jack-o-lanterns need 112 tape-loops. That is a lot of looping (and a lot of time that can be used for many other things). Students are naturals in helping with this (as they are with so many tasks in a classroom!). *But you must teach them how to make the tape loops.* This is a bit counter-intuitive, because it seems so easy to us. It is easy for little kids (even fourth or fifth graders!). Start by teaching just a few children at a time - perhaps a few "room helpers" that you invite up during lunch or before school or etc. Explain that you need a 2-inch piece of masking tape (model what this length looks like). Say: "Make an "O" with the piece of tape with the sticky-side out." There will be a lot of failed tape-loops before the group gets it right. But once they master this, you will save a lot of time changing classroom decorations and displays. And kids *love* to help you!

Toys

Most schools have a no-toy policy, but it is often not strong enough, or stressed adequately, to discourage kids from bringing toys into your classroom. This can cause a number of problems: one child may take another child's toy and a disagreement/fight breaks out; the toy gets lost (if it is an expensive one, the parent may get involved); children will play with the toys when they are supposed to be completing lessons, etc. Speak to veteran teachers to find out any school-wide policy and the extent to which it is enforced. Then decide what the policy will be in your class and explain it to the kids on the first day. My policy is that any toy I see will be confiscated. I will return it on the last day of school. If a child wants the toy returned earlier, then s/he must have a parent or guardian make an appointment to speak with me. Similarly, if the toy is an expensive one, and/or the parent is concerned, the parent can come see me to retrieve it prior to the end of the school-year. Note that the policy covers any toy that "I see"; this allows a child to have a toy in his/her backpack for an after-school activity, going to a friend's house, etc.

Zippers & Shoelaces

Teachers of the younger grades, and out-of-classroom teachers who work with younger grades, will be faced with untied shoelaces and unzipped zippers. If there are 32 children, that is a lot of shoelaces and zippers. Packing-up kids is hard enough without also fastening numerous overcoats and boots. My solution was to have children who had learned to zip/tie help the others. At the start of the year, I used a form of bribery: I gave stickers to the knowledgeable kids who helped others. For the first month or two of school, this meant that the two or three kids who knew how to tie shoelaces or zip zippers received a lot of stickers. But within a very short time, the rest of the class learned to tie and zip (the stickers may have contributed to this) and could take care of themselves. When a child learned to zip or tie, I rewarded him/her with a sticker. Within a few months of the start of the year, I did not have to give any more stickers.

10

Day 1
& Week 1

Chapter 10: Day 1 & Week 1

"What am I going to do the first day?"

This chapter attempts to answer that question. It reviews many of the topics covered in this book and sequences them in a play-by-play order to guide teachers through the important beginning of the school-year. While every school has a different schedule and teachers of different grades and subjects have different requirements, curricula, and schedules, the information in this chapter can be used as a template for the first few days and weeks.

<u>2-3 Days Before the First Day of School</u>
Before we look at the first day, let us look at some of the tasks a new teacher must complete in the days immediately preceding the arrival of students.

Different school districts require teachers to report to work at different times. Some teachers will report to school a full week before the students start and some will have only a day or two to prepare before the students arrive. If you are starting at a school whose teachers start just a few days before the students, it is a good idea to contact the administration ahead of time to inquire about earlier access to the school and the classroom. This will allow you to get a head-start on setting up the classroom. The tasks outlined below should be first on your to-do list when you report to your school:

- Find a friendly experienced teacher, preferably on your grade or sharing your subject-area, and ask him/her the questions in "Questions for Experienced Teachers." Take care to record this information for reference.
- Locate the teacher's manuals to the texts/curricula that your students will be using. Review the introductions, table of contents, and (at least) the first chapters.
- Introduce yourself to the custodian and the school secretaries.
- Find one second year teacher. This person went through what you are about to face just a year ago. Advice from someone who is "recently new" can be invaluable.

Much of the in-school time, prior to the students' arrival, will be spent attending orientation and training sessions and faculty meetings. Teachers generally do not have as much time as they wish to plan lessons and decorate the classroom in the days before the students arrive. Rather than worrying that everything is perfect (it won't be), focus on a few main things – the schedule and lessons for the first days and the door and the major classroom displays:

- Hang up colorful posters and/or subject-specific displays. There are great options in teacher supply stores – math posters, writing tips, etc.

- Create name-labels for the children's desks. These should not be affixed to the desks, as you may have students who do not show up, and you may also have last-minute additions to the class roster. With unexpected students, you will need to change some students' assigned seats, and it is easier if the name-labels can also move. I recommend making table "tents" from 5x9 index cards. Once folded lengthwise, you write the students' first names on one side. These table tents can stand on the table. Because they do not lie flat on the table, it is easier to read them from a distance (which is so important the first day, as you are trying to learn the students' names).

- Decorate the door. The single-most important way to prepare the room for students is to have their names on the door. This tells students that the teacher expects them. To decorate the door, you will need a class set of shapes. You may prepare these cut-outs yourself, but it is much easier and less time-consuming to buy pre-cut shapes for the classroom door (your first year in the classroom, you have got way too much to do spend time cutting and trimming 32 little yellow construction-paper buses!). Write the students' first names on the shapes. You will also need to cut colorful letters from construction paper or neon oak-tag, for the door to accompany the shapes. If you have purchased star-shapes, you would cut out, "Class 3-309 Reaches for the Stars" or "Class 3-309 is Off to a BRIGHT Start"; for apples, you would cut out, "Class 3-309 is a Great Bunch"; for school-buses, you could write, "Class 3-309 is Zooming to a Great Year." Make sure to have extra shapes on hand for unexpected students.

- Make bathroom/hall passes. Different teachers have different kinds of passes. I cut 4x4 squares from stiff bright-colored paper (oak-tag). I labeled each one "Hall Pass, Ms. McGown, Class 3-309." I laminated and made a hole in the corner of each one and passed a chain (30 inch) through. The students wear the hall pass when they are out of the classroom.

Chapter 10: Day 1 & Week 1

Teachers purchase many many things for their classrooms (see Shopping List). This will vary by school, the population, any school-mandated supplies, etc. Buying supplies is expensive, and teachers should work to limit their out-of-pocket expenses. At the same time, anything a teacher can do to ensure a smooth start to the year is important. A complete shopping list is in chapter two, but the following are the barest essentials:
1) Sharpened, yellow, #2 pencils (at least 80)
2) A class set of black marbled composition books (for the journal)
3) A large tin filled with crayon ends (or "nubs")
4) Loose-leaf paper
5) 5x9 index cards
6) Masking tape
7) Hall pass materials
8) Door decoration materials
9) Large black permanent marker
10) Classroom decoration materials
11) Throat lozenges

In the days leading up to the first day of school, teachers will spend a great deal of time finalizing lessons and picking up last-minute supplies. This won't change. At the same time, the more deliberate one is about saving and storing lesson plans and related documents, the less scrambling subsequent years and terms can be. No-one is writing lessons in long-hand any longer; unfortunately, not everyone organizes their computer files in a way that makes sense. If a teacher does not order his o her teaching materials in a sensible way, s/he will likely not re-visit them (for reflection, revision, etc). More disconcertingly, this teacher may re-create similar lesson plans each year, rather than working off existing documents. Organize your desk-top!

Lesson plans, especially for new teachers, and especially for the first few days of the year, should be very detailed. New teachers are nervous and this makes it easy to forget important steps and points. A new teacher wants his/her lessons to go as well as possible, and the greatest thing s/he can do to ensure this is to plan carefully. Most experienced teachers I know use detailed, nearly-scripted lessons for the first few days, because they still get nervous at the start of the year. Most of these teachers do not actually read from their "scripts," but the exercise of having prepared the detailed lessons, and reading through them in the days prior to the first day, ensure success. The more detailed your lessons are, the better the lessons and the first days are likely to go.

Chapter 10: Day 1 & Week 1

The Day Before the First Day of School

Prior to the eve of the start of school, teachers will have completed all the above – classroom and door decoration, lessons for the first few days, information gathering from senior teachers. It's now the day before the first day of school. New teachers must make sure to do the following:

- Review lessons for the first day. Rehearse them aloud (with the door closed, of course). Take this seriously, making sure to review all parts of the lessons. Make note of the pauses you will make, the specific questions you will ask, etc.
- Check in with a senior teacher for any last-minute "first day" tips.
- Place name cards on the desks.
- Do a final check before you leave: floors should be swept, desks or tables in neat rows or groups, the date written on the board; lesson plans, worksheets, etc on your desk.

The Night Before the First Day of School

Most teachers do not sleep well the night before the first day of school; new teachers do not sleep at all. Since you are likely to be groggy and excited and nervous in the morning of the first day, make sure to have everything ready the night before.

- Set the coffee pot to auto-brew.
- Stock good stuff for breakfast (you are not going to be hungry, but you will have to eat something).
- Put out clothes, including socks and a watch.
- Pack a (tasty) lunch since you will not have time to leave school to pick up something during the day.
- Have your schoolbag packed and by the door. Include a granola or sports bar, since you may be too nervous or rushed to eat a proper lunch.
- Set two alarm clocks.

The First Day

This is a sample first-day, with possible activities and lessons, and suggested times. All of these activities can be switched around, depending on the schedule at your school, preparation periods, mandated activities, etc.

6:30 Leaving Home

Leave home early enough so that you arrive to school at least an hour before the students.

Chapter 10: Day 1 & Week 1

7:00 Arrival to School

Check for notices or instructions in the office. Open your classroom and check that everything is in order. Review your lesson plans for the day. Make sure that all hand-outs and materials are ready and in the order of use. Finish your coffee and eat something. You will be nervous, so this may be difficult. At the same time, the day will be exhausting, and you will need the energy. A sports bar, a couple of fig cookies, etc. can make a big difference.

7:50 Morning Line-Up

(for a school-start of 8:00)
Most schools require that teachers pick up their students at a certain area the first days of school (and sometimes throughout the school-year). It may be the yard, the auditorium, the cafeteria, etc. Get to the designated arrival area at least ten minutes before the students. It will probably be chaotic on the first day of school. Expect this.

Some schools have rules about lining up children – one boys' line and one girls' line, putting the children in size-order, etc. You need to know if this is required at your school and whether it is enforced on the first day (rules of this kind are sometimes not enforced the first day, because the administration wants to get the children out of the arrival area and into the classrooms as quickly as possible).

You may have little control over the activities during morning line-up on the first day. Oftentimes, a school aide coordinates the coming and going of students and parents, and teachers are nearly ancillary. If this is the case, you will simply have to wait to be called; at that time, you will take your class out of the arrival area and proceed to the classroom.

8:05 Classroom Entry

Students will be entering your classroom for the first time; make sure it is a great first impression. Every aspect of this first meeting should be calm and orderly. You do not want to set the precedent of disorderliness or excessive noise in your classroom; you want to avoid having children associate any negative behavior or unnecessary noise with your classroom. From the first day, the children should experience your classroom as an inviting but calm and orderly place.

When you arrive to the classroom door, have the children make neat, straight lines in the hallway, following the rules you have decided to use (see Line-Up and Hall Passage). Do not allow children to enter the classroom until they are fully calm and quiet. Invite the students enter the classroom three or four at a time. Tell them to find the desk with their name on it. Students should place their jackets on the backs of the chairs and their backpacks on the floor next to the desks. They should then sit down quietly and wait for the other students to enter.

8:15 Name Game/Introduction
Play a name game as an engaging introduction. This will also help you begin to learn the students' names. There are countless options for this opening name activity; research the internet, and pick one that reflects the age of the students and your interests and personality.

8:35 Attendance & Supply Check
Take the attendance, and record it as required by your school/district (see Attendance and Student Jobs).

The students will have brought various schools supplies with them, some of which are acceptable and some of which are not. Go through the roster and check what each child brought. Where there are inappropriate items, tell the kids to put those things in the backpacks. Items that are appropriate should be placed in the students' desks. Tell the students that you will be discussing required supplies later in the day.

8:50 Un-Pack
Have the students in small groups hang up their jackets and put their book-bags away. Monitor carefully that there is no rushing, no pushing, etc.

9:00 Table Monitors
Explain to the students that each table will have a monitor (see Student Jobs). This student will be responsible for collecting work from the students at his/her table and distributing materials from the teacher. Tell the students that this job will change every two-three weeks. Assign the first table monitors (randomly). Have table monitors count how many students need pencils; the monitors will get pencils from the classroom supply and distribute them at the table.

9:05 Journal
Teachers must get a sense of the performance and ability levels of their students, and they must do this as early as possible. Assessing student ability and working level can be done informally, in a variety of ways. Many of the lessons or activities of the first few days can also serve as

informal assessments or diagnostics. Journal writing provides a super diagnostic of the students' writing ability. In addition, journal-writing is a great way to start the day (see Journal Writing). I emphasize journal-writing in my class throughout the year, and it is a great first-day activity.

I start journal-writing in a way that immediately interests the students. I write my own "journal" on the board. I follow the prompts and questions of the students. Start by saying: "You all are going to write a journal entry about yourselves in a little while. But first, I am going to write a journal entry about myself. If you were my teachers, what kinds of things would you like me to include in my journal? What kinds of things would you like to know about me?" I then encourage the students to ask me questions that I answer in my "journal" (the chalkboard). Throughout the years, the questions varied very little; the students ask about my first and middle names, my age, my parents, my pets, if I am married and have kids, the TV shows and music I like, what countries I have traveled to, etc. I have found that, for the most part, students ask only what is appropriate. I have rarely been asked an inappropriate question. When I am asked a question that I do not wish to answer, I simply say, "This is not an appropriate question," and I move on. No big reaction, and no special attention to the child who asked the impertinent or inappropriate question.

The class generally keeps me writing for 15-25 minutes. This is a long time, and though they are not active, they are enthralled. Teachers rarely share things about themselves with their students, and the kids respond enthusiastically to the attention and the honesty. I then hand out journals composition books (via the table monitors) and the students write their first journal entry. This rarely takes less than 15 minutes.

9:40 Line-Up and Hall Passage
Review rules and procedures for lining up (see Line-Up and Hall Passage). Discuss proper behavior for walking through the hall. Invite discussion and comments on the *rationale* for these rules.

9:50 Bathroom Trip
You will take a "trip" to the bathroom as a class. Review hall-passage rules again at the bathroom. Kids may get antsy while waiting for the others to finish in the bathroom. Monitor carefully by walking along the line and verbally rewarding good behavior (see Bathrooming).

Chapter 10: Day 1 & Week 1

10:05 Grammar Review/Diagnostic worksheet
Proper grammar is very important to me, and I stress it in my classroom.
I prepare a grammar activity that I will collect for review. We go over the
sheet and the instructions together, but the students work alone on the
activity. This gives me a sense of the students' ability in terms of formal
grammar, as well as their ability to attend to a task silently and on their
own.

10:20 School "Trip"
The purpose of this "trip" is primarily to reinforce the rules of passing
through the halls and to allow you to acknowledge and reward good
behavior. These trips, however, are also good breaks in the day. This is
especially important the first few days of the school-year, as the students
(and the teacher!) are not yet used to the rigid structure of school.
Another purpose of these class trips is to show the students points of
interest in the school – the main office, the library, the attendance office/
room, the computer lab, etc. If you are required to submit attendance
forms to a certain office, this is a good time to do it.

10:40 Preparation Period/Special
The preparation period for your first day could be anytime during the day
(see Types of Teaching Positions and Schedules & Periods). I precede my
prep period with the above "school trip." If the students go to the prep
teacher's classroom, we end our trip there. If the prep teacher comes to
our classroom, we end our trip in our room. In many cases, the classroom
teacher picks up the class after the prep period. Make sure to arrive at
least two minutes before the end of the period.

The best thing you can do during this time is to find a quiet place to sit
and relax for a few minutes.
   ➤ Make sure to go to the bathroom before you return to the class.

First and Last Period Preps: Many classroom teachers opt not to take
first-period or last-period preparation periods the first days of school.
This is because arrival and dismissal can be chaotic times, and the earlier
routines are established, the better for everyone. You should speak to a
senior teacher to determine what latitude teachers are given in regards to
taking and refusing prep periods at the start of the year.

Chapter 10: Day 1 & Week 1

11:25 Read Aloud & Comprehension Quiz
Reading is arguably the most important thing that students learn in elementary school. For this reason, it is absolutely essential to assess reading ability very early, and to begin designing and adjusting lessons.

For the first (or second) day, pick an enjoyable, short grade-level book or article to read aloud to the students. Read through it once, stopping to clarify points, ask questions, check for comprehension, etc. Tell the students that they will complete a short question sheet about the book. Tell them the questions will be about the events and characters in the book/article. Explain that you will read the book/article one more time; they should pay special attention so that they are able to answer the questions correctly. The second read-through, you will probably not stop (or not stop much as the initial read-thru).

Distribute a hand-out with questions related to the reading. There should be questions of differing types (multiple choice, true-false, and short answer) and of varying depth and difficulty. The students will work on these question forms alone. When the students have completed the reading worksheets, you will collect them for later review. After collecting the worksheets, spend a few minutes discussing the questions and the students' responses.

In certain settings – special needs children, ELL/ESL classes, bilingual classes, the teacher may opt to allow more flexibility with any diagnostic worksheets/assignments the first day(s) of school, as well as throughout the year. This is done primarily to reduce anxiety and to increase positive feeling and performance. In such settings, teachers may allow children to work together; or s/he may have the class share answers aloud, etc. Such practices will depend on the level and ability of the students.

For teachers who track behavior points, a good time to tally points is just before lunch (see Point Chart).

11:50 Line-Up & Hall Passage ·
Review the rules for traveling through the halls.

11:55 Lunch
(for a 12:05 lunch)
Allow ten minutes to travel to the lunchroom. Again, one of the main purposes of this trip is to reinforce the rules of passing through the halls

and to allow you to acknowledge and reward good behavior. Make sure to monitor diligently.

You: Return to the room, sit quietly (play some calming music), and breathe deeply. Eat something!

12:40 Pick Up Class from Lunch/Recess
(for a 12:45 end of lunch period)
Greet the students and have them line up properly. Once they are in order, proceed to the classroom.

12:50 Math Worksheet (Diagnostic)
Immediately after lunch, students are likely to be a little "looser." This will be the case throughout the school-year. For this reason, it is important to establish an after-lunch routine early in the year. I generally have a quick review worksheet or "quiz" immediately following lunch. The content of this sheet can vary – depending on the curriculum, special activities, upcoming tests, etc. Whatever the content, one aspect must be consistent: the assignment and instructions should be easy to understand. You want to get students into the habit of returning from lunch and getting right to work. This is easiest if the students can be self-directed, and this is possible *only if they know exactly what is expected of them* and if they can start on their own. The activity or worksheet should require little guidance from the teacher. For the first days of school, I found it helpful to review, before we went to lunch, exactly what we would be doing upon our return. I generally schedule math after lunch. Throughout the year, then, the students start the math lesson with a quick review worksheet. This sheet can be, and arguably should be, fun. Math, by its very nature, lends itself to games and puzzles. Such a quick review gets the students focused, and it calms them down after lunch (see After-Lunch Chaos).

The first math assignment serves as a diagnostic. I create a worksheet activity sheet of varying degrees of difficulty, with half just below the anticipated level of the students. The problems increase in difficulty, with the last few problems just above the anticipated level of the students. Students should be able to complete the bulk of the problems comfortably. We do look at the sheet together as a class, and I answer any questions (this is a practice that I stop after the first few days). I then allow the children to work alone to complete the worksheet. For K-1st, I allowed 3-7 minutes, 1st-2nd, 5-10 minutes, 3rd-up 10-15 minutes. Collect the completed hand-outs for review.

Chapter 10: Day 1 & Week 1

1:10 Social Studies/Neighborhood/Etc Lesson
Depending on the level of the students, it is a good idea to start the year with an introductory social studies or neighborhood/community lesson. Many elementary teachers like to begin their "social studies" with a community or class-building activity. There are many samples of great lessons in teacher publications, on the internet, etc. The textbooks used at the school will also be good sources for first day lessons and activities.

1:35 Welcome Letter & Supply List (Reading Activity)
I present my "Welcome Parents" and "Supply List" letters as reading activities (see Parents and Appendix II). Distribute the letters, one at a time, and have the students read them silently. Take questions and discuss. This activity accomplishes two things: (1) It is an informal assessment of the students' ability to understand text, and (2) It also helps ensure that the students can clarify any points their parents may have.

1:55 Homework
Distribute homework assignment sheets or have students copy homework (depending on the practice at the school and your preference). For the first day, I generally assign the following:
• "Home Information Sheet": parents must complete (child's full name, full name of all parents/guardians; name of all people living with child and relationship to child, mailing address, home, cell, and work numbers of parents/guardians, additional emergency contacts, etc)
• Reading/Literacy worksheet
• The children must have their parents sign the homework notebook or homework sheet.

2:10 Clean-Up & Pack-Up
Have students tidy their desks and the surrounding area. Table monitors will return "borrowed" pencils to you. Reverse of the morning un-pack. Make sure to reinforce proper behavior.

For teachers who track behavior points, they must tally any points at this time, and reward the students appropriately (see Point Chart).

2:20 Line-Up
Once the students are lined up, discuss any dismissal procedures with them. Remind them about maintaining order through the halls and in the dismissal area or yard.

Chapter 10: Day 1 & Week 1

2:30 Leave the Classroom
(for a 2:40 dismissal)
Dismissal may be fully coordinated by a school administrator or aide. If
that is the case, you simply need to help maintain calm. Parents are
likely to want to speak with you after school the first day; expect to spend
some extra time at dismissal the first week of school.

Back to the Classroom
You are going to have a giant list of things that you want to finish before
you see the students the next morning. This list is not reasonable; it is
also not going to get done. The best thing you can do is focus on a few top
priorities for this evening:
1) Read and comment in every child's journal
2) Grade/Mark and record each math worksheet.
3) Grade/Mark and record each grammar diagnostic.
4) Turn in any forms required by office/administration.
5) Tweak lessons for Day 2, based on experience today with students.
6) Go to sleep at a reasonable time.

Day 2
8:05 Journals & Homework Collection
In the beginning of the year, I give the students child-friendly prompts
for journal-writing (a question, a provocative scenario, etc). As a class, we
brainstorm ideas based on the prompt. I then allow 10-20 minutes for
students to write their entries (see Journal Writing).

I check homework while the students are working on their journals (see
Homework).

8:35 Attendance
Take the attendance, and record it as required by your school/district.
Pick a student to bring the attendance sheet to the proper place. Explain
that the "Attendance Monitor" is a job that you will rotate among
students (see Student Jobs).

8:45 Supply Check
Review the supply list and record which students have brought in which
of the required supplies. Have them store these items as you have decided
will work for your classroom. Remind the class of the deadline for having
brought in all supplies.

Chapter 10: Day 1 & Week 1

9:00 Reading/Literacy Lesson
Introduce the reading/literacy curriculum/materials for your grade/class. Do one of the first lessons recommended.

9:40 Hall Rules & Bathroom Trip
Review rules and procedures for lining up and for traveling through the halls. Bring the class to the bathroom.

10:00 Math Lesson (Start)
Introduce the math/problem solving curriculum/materials for your grade/class. Start one of the first lessons recommended.

Discuss the math "diagnostic" worksheet that the students completed yesterday.

10:30 Prep Period
(for a 10:40 prep period)
Allow five-ten minutes to travel to the prep teacher's classroom.

This prep period is a good time to review papers, read the morning journals, etc. Make sure to go to the bathroom before the preparation period ends.

11:25 Math Lesson (Finish)
Finish the math lesson(s) that you started before the prep period.

11:40 Map Skills/Geography "Game" (Diagnostic)
During the first few weeks, you will need to determine student levels in a variety of subjects. These assessments/diagnostics can often be presented as games. I like to start off the year with an activity about the map of the United States, our City, neighborhood, etc. The internet is a wonderful resource of games/activities on every subject imaginable.

11:55 Hall Rules & Lunch
(for a 12:05 lunch)
Review the rules of the lunchroom, as well as those for traveling through the halls. This is repetitive, and it may seem unnecessary to you. The fact is, however, that the routines and procedures a teacher sets up in the first few weeks of school help set the tone for the whole year. *Effectively setting up routines takes time and a lot of repetition.*

For teachers who track behavior points, this is a good time to tally points and to reward the students appropriately (see Point Chart).

Allow ten minutes to travel to the lunchroom. Again, one of the main purposes of this trip is to reinforce the rules of passing through the halls and to allow you to acknowledge and reward good behavior.

12:40 Pick Up Class from Lunch/Recess
(for a 12:45 end of lunch period)
Greet the students and have them line up properly. Once they are in order, proceed to the classroom.

12:50 Vocabulary Words
Introduce the spelling or vocabulary list (see Vocabulary/Spelling). Explain what the students will be required to do with the words in class and for homework and when the quiz/test will be. I generally prepare a word puzzle for this introductory lesson. There are great samples of word puzzles and games on the internet.

1:20 Current Events
Many elementary schools do not mandate the study of current events. I think it is important; in addition, the review and discussion of an article supports comprehension and literacy. For this activity, I find kid-friendly articles about some current topic (the internet is a good resource for these). I then create a lesson based on the article.

1:55 Read-Aloud
I am a huge fan of read-alouds, with bigger kids as well as younger ones. I try to fit in some read-aloud time most days. For the first read-aloud of the year, I pick a short book or story. For grades through 5th, I generally choose a favorite from Dr. Seuss' books or a chapter from one of the Mrs. Piggle-Wiggle books (see Read-Alouds).

2:20 Clean-Up & Pack-Up
Have students tidy their desks and the surrounding area. Table monitors will collect any items from students that go to you, and they will distribute to their groups any materials that must go home. Make sure to reinforce proper behavior.

For teachers who track behavior points, they should tally points at this time and reward the students appropriately (see Point Chart).

Chapter 10: Day 1 & Week 1

2:30 Line-Up
Once the students are lined up, discuss any dismissal procedures with them. Remind them about maintaining order through the halls and in the dismissal area or yard.

2:35 Leave the Classroom
(for a 2:40 dismissal)

Teacher's Homework Day 2
1) Read and comment in the journals.
2) Grade/Mark any papers and record.
3) Review Home Information Sheets and transfer to index cards (or to official files, depending on your preferences and any requirements at your school).
4) Turn in any forms required by the office/administration.
5) Extend lesson plans for the next few days, based on your experiences so far.
6) Go to bed at a reasonable time.

Week 1 Teacher To-Do List
The following should be completed or addressed within the first week of school:
• Home Information: Collect Home Information Sheets and transfer onto index cards (also copy to any required forms for the office). Follow up with children from whom you have not received the information.
• Study Habits: Review and practice good study habits (see Study Habits).
• Quizzes: Give at least three small quizzes – vocabulary/spelling, short-answer reading, and mathematics.
• Supplies: Collect supplies; follow up with parents who have not provided necessary items and/or those who have questions or problems about the supplies.
• Journals: students should write everyday the first few weeks. One afternoon, have kids decorate the first page of their journal. This should not be a free-for-all. Discuss with the class that students need to plan their drawing/decoration carefully and use the whole page. The drawing should represent an important part of their lives and be very colorful.
• Birthdays: Discuss how you will handle birthdays and birthday parties. At least one child will have a birthday in September, so this will be a big issue for him/her (se Birthdays and Parties)
• Punishments & Consequences: Within the first week of school, you need to have a discussion with the class about "big" infractions of school and

classroom policy. This may vary a great deal from school to school, and even grade to grade. Following this activity, I send a note to parents explaining the rules of the school and of the classroom, as well as any consequences. The parents have to sign this letter and return it to me (see Appendix II)

- Write brief thank-you notes to any staff or faculty member who was of special help or support in the first week or two of school (do this periodically throughout the school-year).

I

Questions for Senior Teachers

Appendix 1: Questions for Senior Teachers

Every school and district have differences in curriculum, practices, and policies. In addition, many schools and administrators, have idiosyncratic requirements or expectations that are not posted anywhere. There is a usually a school or district handbook that addresses many of these policies. Such handbooks, however, tend to be big and dry; they never seem to be something a new teacher can read through (and digest) during the stressful days before the start of the year. For this reason, a new teacher should reach out to more experienced staff members or administrators for information about district-specific and/or school-specific policies and procedures. This chapter sets forth questions that a new teacher should ask of his/her new colleagues.

The questions are grouped in three sections, depending on when in the year the information is most necessary or applicable:
- Part 1: Before the first day of school
- Part II: The first week or two of school
- Part III: The first month of school (before the first marking period)

Appendix 1: Questions for Senior Teachers

Part I: Before the First Day of School

Arrival Procedures
What time do the students arrive?
Do teachers pick up students from a common area?
If so, what time are teachers expected to be there?
Does each class have an assigned place? What's yours?
What is the contingency line-up area in case of inclement weather?
Do the children have to line-up in a certain way (size-order, boys' and girls' lines, etc)?
Who is the staff/faculty member in charge of Arrival/Morning Line-Up?

Attendance Procedures
How is attendance taken?
Is there more than one attendance form?
Where are these forms turned in?
Is there a time when these various forms are due?
Who is the staff/faculty member in charge of attendance forms?
Are students allowed to help with the attendance forms? (Some attendance forms are legal documents so there may be limitations on this)

Bathroom Policies - Students
Is there a required procedure for bathrooming students?
Are certain bathrooms designated for certain grades?
Is there a time when no student can leave the classroom to go to the bathroom?
Must students "sign out" when they are out of the classroom?

Bathroom Policies - Teachers
Where are the staff/faculty bathrooms?
Is a key required for the staff/faculty bathrooms?
Where do you get the key?

Classroom Decoration
What displays/charts are you required to post within your classroom?
Must your classroom door be decorated in a certain way?
Are there certain charts/graphs that are prescribed by curriculum? By the administration or a supervisor?
If so, do these items need to be displayed in certain areas?
How often do classroom displays to be changed?

Appendix 1: Questions for Senior Teachers

Are there any required first-day decorations?
Does the school supply any materials for classroom/door decoration?
Who is the staff/faculty member in charge of these materials?

Classroom Library
Are books in the classroom library supposed to be organized in a certain way?
Do books need to be "leveled"?
Is there a staff member who helps new teachers do this?
Is there a deadline for classroom libraries to be properly organized?

Custodian
Who are the custodians?
Is there one custodian responsible for your classroom/hall?
What supplies can s/he get you (e.g., paper towels, brooms)?
How do you arrange a ladder for use in your classroom?

Dismissal Procedures
When is dismissal?
Are students dismissed from their classes, or must they be brought to some common area?
If there is a dismissal area, when does your class need to be there?
If students are dismissed from a common area, where is your class assigned to stand?
To whom can you dismiss children? (parents only?)
What if someone unknown to you comes to pick up a child?
Can students leave from the common area un-escorted? Does this vary by grade?
What do you do with students whose guardian doesn't arrive?
How long do you have to remain with students who are not picked up?
Who is the person in charge of students who are not picked up on time?

Drills/Fire Drills
See First Week Section

Hallways & Stairwells
What policies are there for students walking in the halls?
Are students allowed to be in the halls/bathrooms alone (or must they always be in pairs)? Does this depend on the age/grade of the child?
Do teachers need to maintain "sign-out" logs for students to use when they are out of the classroom, or are hall-passes sufficient?
Are stairwells designated for "up" passage and others for "down"?

Appendix 1: Questions for Senior Teachers

Are certain stairwells off limits to certain classes (e.g., the "fourth grade stairs")?

Heading
Does the school require a certain heading on written assignments?
Must this be posted in your classroom?
Does this vary by grade?

Lesson Structure
Is there a required format for lesson plans at your school?
Must certain things be written on the board for lessons (e.g., objective, Do Now)?
Do supervisors collect lesson plans? How often?
What does your supervisor look for in lesson plans? (Most supervisors have a favorite lesson-plan part – a strong motivation or "hook," a strong closing, etc.)

Lunch – Students
Do classroom teachers have any lunchroom supervision responsibilities?
Where does your class sit in the lunchroom (assigned tables)?
Must the students sit in assigned seats in the lunchroom?
Can the students leave the lunchroom at any time? Who governs this?
Are students allowed to bring anything into the lunchroom to use when they're finished eating (e.g., books, toys, etc)?
Who is the faculty/staff member in charge of the lunchroom?

Lunch – Teachers
Where are the best (cheapest?) restaurants/sandwich shops in the area?
Do any offer discounts/specials to teachers?
Does the school (student) cafeteria provide lunch to teachers?If so, what is the cost?

Notebooks
Is there a specific kind of notebook required for the grade(s) that you teach?

Photocopies
What is the policy for making photocopies?
Can teachers use the copy machine(s) themselves?
Who is the faculty/staff member in charge of the copy machines?
Is there a limit on the number of photocopies teachers can make – either at a single time or for the year?

Appendix 1: Questions for Senior Teachers

Is there something teachers can do to make this better (e.g., supplying their own copy paper)?
How much in advance do teachers need to submit copy orders?
How long does it take for teachers to receive the copies?
Is there a shop in the area where teachers can make copies?

Plan-book
Is there a plan-book that all teachers in the school use?
If so, where do they get these plan-books?
Ask to look at another teacher's plan-book.

Preparation Periods
When are your designated prep periods each day of the week?
Who are the teachers who will be working with your students during these prep periods? What are their subjects?
Where are the prep teachers' classrooms?
Will the prep teachers pick up your students, or will you need to bring the class to another location?

Rewards/Prizes
Is there a policy about rewards or prizes for students?
Are some things allowed (stickers, etc) and others forbidden (candy or etc)?

Supply Room/Supply Person
Where is the supply room?
Who is the staff/faculty member responsible for the supply room?
What kinds of materials are available in the supply room?
Are there certain times when teachers can go to the supply room, or do teachers need to make appointments?
Note: many school supplies are in very limited quantity. It is often a case of "first come, first served." As soon as you find out about the supply closet, visit it.

Teacher Supply Stores
Where is the best teaching supply store in the area?
Are there shops in the area that extend discounts to teachers?
Is there a teacher or school ID card that you need to present to get a discount?

Appendix 1: Questions for Senior Teachers

Part II: The First Week of School

Absences/Lateness (Students)
What is considered excessive absence or lateness on the parts of
students?
When does the "office" want to be informed about excessive absences or
lateness?

Absences/Lateness (Yours)
Teachers should never be late.
Teachers should not be absent for at least the first full month of school.
What is considered excessive absence from teachers?
What is the call-in procedure when a teacher is going to be absent?
When are medical notes required from teachers for absences?
Are teachers required to prepare and maintain lesson plans and activities
for unexpected absences?
Where are such "absence plans" supposed to be kept?
Some schools have special policies regarding teachers' taking a sick or
personal day on Fridays and/or before or after a vacation; inquire
whether this is the case at your school.
See Coverages, in Part III

After-School
Does your school have after-school activities?
To what extent are you expected to, or strongly recommended to, work
after-school sessions?
Are you allowed to refuse to work after-school?
When in the year does the after-school program start?
If you are not teaching after-school, will you have access to your
classroom during the after-school program?
How late can you remain at school (there may be security and/or
insurance limitations on this)?

Birthdays
Does the school have a policy about celebrating student birthdays?
Are any practices forbidden?

Bulletin Boards (Common or Shared Areas)
Some schools have assigned common-area bulletin boards; is this the case
at your school?
If so, where is/are your common-area bulletin board(s)?

Appendix 1: Questions for Senior Teachers

Are there specific topics and/or types of student work that must be displayed on common-area?
When (How often) do the common-area bulletin boards need to be changed?

Drills/Fire Drills

There are many different kinds of safety drills that schools conduct. The fire drill is the most common, but there are also bomb drills, tornado/weather drills, intruder drills, and others. State and local laws dictate how often such drills take place, and schools often scramble to make sure that they schedule sufficient drills and that the students and faculty conduct themselves properly. New teachers should speak to veteran teachers to learn about the different drills that are held at that school and how often they are conducted.

What drills does the school conduct?
When is the first one usually scheduled?
Does faculty know about drills ahead of time? Do students?
What is the procedure for your class during a fire drill? (What stairwell? What door? Where to assemble outside of the building?)
What are you required to take with you (eg, official attendance folder)?
Are you forbidden from bringing anything with you (purse, phone, etc)?
If it is cold/rainy, may students get jackets? May you?
What is the procedure if your class is in a different part of the school (library, gym, etc)?
What is expected of you if you are on a preparation period or at lunch?
What if the students are at lunch?
What do you do if a child is out of the room (bathroom, counselor, etc)?

Grade-Keeping

Does your school have a required grade-book? If so, where do you get it?
Is there a certain way that grades must be recorded?
Are you required to record a minimum number of grades each week, each month, etc?
Does your school require that teachers send progress reports to parents?
If so, when do progress reports go out? Is there a required form or format?
At what point of a child's poor performance must the parent be notified (eg, notes must be sent to the parent if the child misses two homework assignments in a row, if s/he fails a quiz/test, etc)?

Homework

Does the school have specific requirements regarding homework?
Must homework be assigned every night?

Appendix 1: Questions for Senior Teachers

Are there specific requirements for homework for certain subjects (e.g., all students must have math homework every night)?
Does this vary by grade?

Home Information
What information about students/families/home must you collect from students?
Are there special forms you must complete with this information?
Where must this be turned in? When?

Payroll
Who is the secretary responsible for teachers' payroll?
Is this person receptive and/or knowledgeable?
If not, who should you speak to if you have questions about your checks, getting direct deposit, benefits, etc.?

Permanent Files (Students')
What specific items should you review on the students' permanent files?
What do you need to add to these files – and when?
Are there policies regarding how these files must be maintained, who may access them, etc? (Student files are generally considered legal documents, so there may be strict parameters on how they may be handled and who may view the contents)
Are the files checked periodically by supervisors?
If so, what are the supervisors looking for?

Special Education
Are there any designated Special Education children on your roster?
Where can you learn about the services they are supposed to receive?
Who is the faculty/staff member in charge of the coordination of services for special education students?
Who is the lead teacher(s) for the special education student(s) in your classroom?
Is there any support you can count on when "covering" a special education class (e.g., Are support staff required to be in the room? Do certain children have one-on-one aides?)

Spelling/Vocabulary Lists
Are spelling/vocabulary lists and quizzes required in your school? Are they forbidden or discouraged?
If spelling/vocabulary lists and quizzes are customary at your school, are the word-lists dictated to teachers?

Appendix 1: Questions for Senior Teachers

Can teachers make up their own lists?
Are there any limitations or recommendations?

<u>English Language Learners (ELL)</u>
ESL = English as a Second Language; TESOL = Teaching English as a Second Language
Are there children in your class for whom English is not their primary language?
Are these students mandated to receive any additional ESL/TESOL services?
What is the form of these ESL/TESOL services?
Who is the faculty/staff member in charge of the coordination of ESL/TESOL services/instruction?
Are any of your ELL students recent arrivals (new to the country)?
Are any of your ELL students new to "regular" (non-bilingual) classes?

<u>Teachers' Union</u>
Is there a representative from the Teachers' Union at your school?
Is this person considered receptive and/or knowledgeable?
If not, who are you supposed to speak to about union/contract questions?

<u>Testing</u>
When are the "big" standardized tests for your subject/grade?
More questions about testing are in the next section.

Appendix 1: Questions for Senior Teachers

Part III: The First Month of School

Book Reports
Are book reports required at your school?
Is there a required format for book reports?
Are students supposed to write a certain number of book reports each year? Does this depend on grade?
Can students choose any books for book reports or are there certain books (or genres of books) that they must read?
Is there a specific way that book report numbers need to be graded and/or tracked?

Child Abuse
Who is the social worker or the staff/faculty member in charge of family services at your school?
What exactly are you supposed do if you suspect a child is being abused?
What is the required action/paperwork?

Coverages
Note: A "coverage" is when a teacher is asked to cover another class, generally at the last minute, on his/her prep period or lunch period.
Are coverages common in your school?
Are teachers required to leave lesson plans, extra worksheets, etc. in case of an unexpected absence?
How are coverages rotated so that the same people don't always have to do them?
What is the compensation for a coverage?
What is the paperwork necessary for coverage compensation?
Are you allowed to refuse to do a coverage?

Gifts
Are teachers permitted to accept gifts from students/families? (ie, for birthdays, holidays, etc?)
Are teachers allowed to give gifts to students (birthdays, holidays, etc)

Grades/Progress Reports
Is there any midterm notification procedure, especially for parents whose children are doing poorly or who are in danger of failing?
Is there a school-mandated form for progress reports, in-danger-of-failing notices, etc?
What supervisory or administrative staff need to be notified?

Appendix 1: Questions for Senior Teachers

Parties
Are you allowed to have classroom parties?
Are there days and times during which parties are not permitted (e.g., some schools do not allow Halloween parties)?
What kinds of activities are permitted? Are certain activities permitted but discouraged?
Are there limitations on food in the classroom and/or at parties?
Are you allowed "healthy" food/snacks but prohibited from having candies or junk-food?

Report Cards
Are teachers required to submit report cards to a supervisor for review?
If so, when must report cards be submitted to the supervisor?
Who is your supervisor for report cards?
Does your supervisor want the report cards presented to him/her in a certain way (e.g., My AP wanted report cards to be turned into him stacked alphabetically, open, with a rubber-band down the middle)?
Are there limitations on what grades may be given (e.g., some schools do not permit A's the first marking period)?
How are report cards distributed?

Student Helpers
Are you allowed to have students help in the room with house-keeping tasks?
Are there certain times when this is permitted and/or prohibited?
Are there any tasks that the students are not allowed to do?
If you have students help you during lunch, after school or before school, do you need permission slips for this? Must an administrator be informed?

Taxes/Reimbursement
Are teachers compensated for teaching expenses (by the school, district, etc)?
If so, how are the receipts tracked and submitted?
Is there a due-date for the submission of receipts/forms for reimbursable expenses?
For teaching expenses that are not reimbursed by the school/district, how do you record them for taxes?
Can anyone recommend a tax preparer familiar with teachers and teaching expenses?

Appendix 1: Questions for Senior Teachers

<u>Testing</u>
When are the big (standardized) tests for your grade and/or subject?
Are there old copies of the test available for review?
Are the test-prep materials available to review?
Who is the staff/faculty member in charge of the coordination of testing
and of test preparation at your school – for your grade and/or subject?
When does the school start preparing children for the standardized tests?
Is this done formally (eg, all third graders practice for the math test
during fourth period for the month of February)?
Are there "official" practice test sessions for the different tests? When?
What rules exist around test-taking (seats separated, #2 pencils, etc)?
Does the school require that you enforce the same rules for non-
standardized test situations (teacher made tests or textbook unit tests)?

II

Forms
& Letters

Appendix II: Forms & Letters

Welcome Letter

August 30, 2007

Dear **Families of Class 3-309**;

Welcome to the new school year! I hope you are all as excited as I am. I expect to have a **wonderful** year!

This note is to give you some information about me, about my classroom, and about the third grade.

Third grade is an important and academically challenging year. Not only will students have weekly quizzes, monthly exams (mathematics, reading, essay-writing, science, and social studies), but they will also face a battery of four exams, each two hours long, in April and May. These are city and state exams.

I will work very hard to educate your child. I will usually come in early; and I will often stay late. I promise to communicate regularly with you. You can count on me to be fair, honest, and caring. I will treat your child as if s/he is my own. I encourage you to visit with me anytime you have a question or concern.

I must now ask for **your cooperation**. I will not succeed this year, and your child will not excel, without your help. You are responsible for the following:
1. The single most important aid to your child's learning is at-home reading. Children entering third grade should spend <u>at least</u> 15 minutes reading at home <u>every day</u>.
2. The supplies needed for third grade are different than those needed in the earlier grades. For this reason, I have included a list of the supplies that I require. Please note: ALL of these items are REQUIRED; and NOTHING ELSE will be allowed in class.
3. Your child will have homework <u>every night</u>. Please see that it is completed (or at least fairly attempted). An adult must sign the homework notebook every night.
4. Bedtime for your child should be no later than 9:00pm.
5. Your child must eat a substantial breakfast. The third grade lunch period is very late; and we do not have a morning snack.
6. Students should arrive to school by 8:35am.
7. Please have your child picked up on time, by 2:58pm.
8. Student absences should be kept to a minimum. Doctor's appointments and family vacations should be scheduled on weekends and during school holidays.

If we work together, I am confident that we will succeed.

Sincerely,

Carolyn McGown

Appendix II: Forms & Letters

School Supplies List Letter

August 30, 2007

SCHOOL SUPPLIES
for Class 3-309

The following is a list of the supplies your child will need for the new school year. I am very strict about what materials are allowed in class. Your child needs **ALL** of these things, and *NO OTHER MATERIALS WILL BE ACCEPTED*. I ask you to provide these items as soon as possible.

I realize that this is a long list, but it is the *only* time you will need to provide any supplies for the <u>entire</u> year.

10	composition books - MEAD, black, wide-rule, sewn binding
48	pencils - yellow, #2
1	pink rectangular eraser
1 box	crayons - CRAYOLA, 24 count
1 pair	scissors - FISKARS, pointed end
1 bottle	glue, white, 4 oz
1	duotang/portfolio folder without pockets
1	folder with pockets (any color/design)

Please note that these supplies are **for school use only**. Your child will need **additional supplies** - pencils, loose paper, and a pencil sharpener to be kept **AT HOME** for homework assignments.

I thank you in advance for your cooperation.

Carolyn McGown

Making Appointments Letter

September 4, 2007

Dear Parents of Class 3-309;

I know that many of you may want to speak with me – that you may have questions for me, about your child, my lessons, tests, homework, etc. I welcome your questions, and I would LOVE to meet with you to discuss your child.

Of course, we are all very busy, so we will have to <u>plan carefully</u> to arrange appointments. I am often available during the following times, but PLEASE make sure to give me **at least** two days' notice before coming to see me:
- Mondays: 10:15-10:55
- Tuesday: 8:00-8:30 and 1:35-2:15
- Thursdays: 11:05-11:45 and 3:00-3:30

The BEST way to contact me is to write a note in your child's **homework notebook**. In addition, this notebook is a *great* way to write me brief notes or ask quick questions.

I look forward to meeting with you!

Sincerely,

Carolyn McGown

Behavior Contract

Class 3-309 Behavior Contract

I _____, a student in Class 3-309, for the 2000/2001 school-year, do agree to adhere by the following rules:

> **I will not bring any TOYS to school. If I do bring toys to school, they will be taken away, and I won't get them back until June.**

> **I will not bring any GUM or CANDY to school. I will not chew any gum or eat any candy except with Ms. McGown's permission for special events or parties. I understand that any gum or candy I bring in will be thrown away.**

> **I will not bring any MONEY to school unless for school-related things. I understand that if I bring money to school, it will be taken away and returned to a parent.**

> **I will not be LATE. I understand that if I am late, I will not be able to participate in any special activities.**

I understand the above rules and consequences. I will not whine or complain if I get caught breaking any of these rules or if I suffer any of the consequences.

Student's Signature: _____

Date: _____

Class Rules & Behavior Contract Letter

September 6, 2007

Dear Parents of Class 3-309;

I am writing this letter to explain some of the rules for Class 3-309. I believe that behavior, attitude, and consistency are essential to success in school. For this reason, I am very *strict* about behavior.

I have discussed the rules with all the students in Class 3-309. Each student understands these rules, and the consequences, and has signed a "Behavior Contract," promising to follow all school and class rules.

If you have any questions, please contact me.
Carolyn McGown

Rules for Class 3-309

- **TOYS** and non-educational items are FORBIDDEN in school. All such items will be *CONFISCATED* and **returned in June**.
- **GUM, CANDY**, and snacks are *not permitted* in the classroom, except during special events or parties. Any gum or candy will be **thrown away**.
- **MONEY** should not be brought to school, except for school-related fees. If a child must bring money to school for another reason, the parent must send a note explaining this. Unauthorized money brought in will be *CONFISCATED* and **returned to a parent only**.
- **LATENESS** will not be tolerated. Students must arrive to school by 8:35am every day. Late students will not be permitted to participate in class parties, special events, or field trips.

I understand the above rules and the consequences, and I will do all that I can to ensure that my child follows them.

Signature of Parent: _____

Date: _____

Name of Student: _____

Sample Homework Notebook Page

	Oct 12, 2007	
	Homework Assignment	
1)	Write each vocabulary word three times, neatly, with	
	attention to spelling	
2)	Math workbook, p. 37, #1-5, #8-11	
3)	Second draft "Neighborhood" essay; edit and re-write,	
	double-spaced, on loose-leaf paper	
4)	Please sign: _____	

First Month Letter

October 1, 2007

Dear Parents of Class 3-309;

A month has passed since the school-year began! It's hard to believe; the time has FLOWN by! It has been a **fantastic** month!

I have enjoyed working with the students in Class 3-309. Each one is an interesting, bright, engaging child. They've all learned a tremendous amount, too! All the students in Class 3-309 now know their 2, 3, 4, 5, and 10 times tables. They've written great essays on pigs and chocolate factories. We've taken a neighborhood walk to the local library, where we heard some wonderful stories and every student checked out a book. They're reading these books and will be writing book reports in the next two weeks. In addition, EVERY child can spell "vichyssoise" (just ask!).

I look forward to many more accomplishments this year. I will share these with you regularly.

Please feel free to come to me with any questions or concerns you may have.

Sincerely,

Carolyn McGown

Good Kid Letter

October 15, 2007

Dear Ms. Marcelino;

Greetings from Class 3-309!

As you know, the school year began six weeks ago. This is a very difficult time of year for everyone, students and teachers alike. It is a period of adjustment and change. We all must learn countless new procedures, schedules, and routines. Additionally, third grade is an academically demanding year, because of the city's intense curriculum and the upcoming examinations in the spring.

Despite all this, I have some **very good news** to report.

I want you to know that your daughter, Massiel, has been a **joy** to have in my class. Your child has consistently been positive about school-work and helpful to classmates. She is also very cooperative with me. Massiel has displayed a tremendous level of maturity during this time.

You should be very PROUD of her!

Sincerely,

Carolyn McGown

Time-Out Essay

Name: _____   Date: _____

What have I done to receive a Time-Out Essay?

How does this behavior or action interfere with my learning or my classmates' learning?

Have I done this before? How many times? When was the last time?

What can I do to help stop this from happening in the future?

Index

Index

Index

Index

Index

Index

Thanks

Acknowledgements

About the Author

Thank You & Acknowledgments

The names mentioned in this book are the names of real teachers. They are individuals with whom I have had the pleasure of working, and from whom I learned, and continue to learn, a great deal. A number of other people contributed to this book as well in a variety of ways, many without realizing it. All of these individuals – those who have supported and advised me, championed this project, helped with edits and updates, assisted with rushed deadlines, catered to my computer fits and frustrations – have my warmest thanks: Kate Anderson, Kim Brockway, Jessica Brunner, Octavio De Alva, Christine Der Ananian (Bell), John Kendall, Wayne Reed, Ann Roer, Steve Rosen, and Jane Stone. For anyone I may have omitted, I offer my sincerest apologies. Please let me know, as I am already at work on the sixth edition!

This experiences that brought me to write this book would never have happened without the many children who passed through the doors of Class 3-309. My life has been forever changed for having known them. Though I was responsible for teaching them, I learned so much from each one. Their photographs are in my office, and I think of them all often and fondly: Randoll Abreu, Brian Acosta, Mabel Acosta, Georgecel Alicea, Rubianna Arce, Arlene Batista, Jennifer Batista, Irvin Bisono, Raymond Bisono, Alyssa Burgos, Olga Buzovetsky, Vanessa Calderon, Dioska Ceballos, Isamar Checo, Kimberly Collado, Cynthia Concepcion, Kelvin Cordero, Maria Cruz, Emmy De La Cruz, Erika De La Cruz, Emmily De Los Santos, Carlos De Moya, Jannedieth Decena, Darling Duran, Moises Espinal, Rodolis Estrella, Yeddifer Fermin, Steven Genao, Hussein Guerrero, Darlene Guillen, Marcus Harper, Silenys Henriquez, Cynthia Herbert, Elsa Heredia, Wilbin Heredia, Natasha Hernandez, Alexandra Hurtado, Evelina Infante, Jean Charles Isaac, Joel Jaquez, Richard Jiminian, Kevin Lagos, Rosercilis Lara, Chris Lopez, Steven Lozada, Massiel Marcelino, Noeralis Mata, Joshua Matias, Emmanuel Mejia, Giovanny Mejia, Roosevelt Mercado, Rodney Morales, Randy Morillo, Mariela Munoz, Humary Nunez, Marleny Nunez, Ricardo Ordehi, Pedro Ortiz, Arlene Peralta, Raymond Perez, Gabriel Pina, Roderick Rasuk, Alfred Rodriguez, Darlyn Rodriguez, Ivan Rodriguez, Ivelisse Rodriguez, Jose Rodriguez, Victoria Rodriguez, Christopher Roperto, Crist Rosales, Michelle Rosario, Christopher Ruiz, Yajaira Saavedra, Katherine Sanchez, Rafael Sanchez, Melissa Sosa, Emilio Tatis, Maoly Valdez, Jonathan Vasquez, Nicole Vazquez.

Finally, for all the encouragement, enthusiasm, and support, many thanks to Daddy.

Better with Nuts
Classroom Survival & Success for New & Developing Teachers

by Carolyn Olga McGown

Fifth Edition 2014
Fourth 2011
Third 2008

About the Author

Carolyn McGown taught in the New York City public schools, working across the grades, teaching science, elementary education, special education, and English as a Second Language. Her experience was primarily in under-resourced communities and Title 1 schools.

Upon leaving the K-12 classroom, Carolyn joined the training and support staff of the just-launching New York City Teaching Fellows program. She remained with the Teaching Fellows for five years, coordinating the pre-service training and on-going support for over 9,000 teachers. Carolyn then spent two years at Pace University working with Teach for America corps members and Teaching Fellows as a director within the Office of Alternative Certification. She then joined the faculty of Fordham University, where she was both a graduate instructor and the coordinator for graduate childhood and early childhood programs. She taught methods courses in mathematics, art, and social studies, along with graduate field practicum seminars.

For the past few years, Carolyn has worked as an independent educational consultant in New York City, working with public, private, and charter schools, and local colleges. She has taught in the CUNY Hunter Special Education program as a graduate instructor and field specialist. Her work has kept her in the field visiting teachers and schools regularly. Carolyn has also become an expert on teacher recruitment and hiring, offering workshops on navigating the job search. Her most recent project is a second book. It will be for teachers and parents of young children – strategies for supporting cognitive development for increased academic interest and success. As always, there will be an emphasis on urban education and under-resourced communities and populations. The book will be released in both English and Spanish. Carolyn is working towards an early 2015 completion.